Shepherding the Small Church

Shepherding the Small Church

A LEADERSHIP GUIDE FOR THE MAJORITY OF TODAY'S CHURCHES

Glenn Daman

Kregel
Academic & Professional

Shepherding the Small Church: A Leadership Guide for the Majority of Today's Churches

© 2002 by Glenn Daman

Published by Kregel Publications, a division of Kregel, Inc., P.O. Box 2607, Grand Rapids, MI 49501. For more information about Kregel Publications, visit our Web site: www.kregel.com.

Cover design: John M. Lucas

ISBN 0-8254-2449-6

Printed in the United States of America

1 2 3 4 5 / 06 05 04 03 02

To my wife, Becky, my best friend, wisest advisor, and a genuine co-worker in ministry. Her love is a constant evidence of God's grace. And to Nathan and Andrew, who continually remind me that my greatest title is Dad and my most important ministry is at home.

And to the thousands of pastors who minister in the small churches. Their faithfulness and work are often overlooked by men, but are not overlooked by God. Great will be their reward.

Contents

Appendices

Acknowledgments

*N*o book is written without the help of others—individuals who provide support, encouragement, and time to see the book to fruition. I especially thank the church families who have allowed me the privilege and joy of serving as their pastor. I thank the people of the First Baptist Church in Stevenson, Washington, and the congregation of the Cascade Locks Community Church in Cascade Locks, Oregon. Their love and support has far exceeded my worthiness. They are willing to accept my weaknesses and forgive my blunders. They are a true reflection of the bride of Christ.

I am grateful for Phyllis Landsem, Jerry Johnson, and Ruth Daman, who painstakingly proofread the manuscript. Their input and suggestions are greatly appreciated and were essential for the project.

Last, I express my appreciation for my parents, Wayne and Ruth Daman, who faithfully packed four kids into the car each Sunday to drive to a small country church in northern Idaho. Their love and commitment to Christ has been a genuine example of the wise parents reflected in Proverbs. Truly their children can "arise and call them blessed."

Introduction

Once upon a time there were two combines. They were vastly different from each other, as different as combines could be. One was big and one was little. The little combine wished it were big, but the maker of combines had made it small. Some looked down upon the little combine because it was small and because it did not have all the latest innovations, like the big combine did.

The big combine was the largest ever built. Everything about it spoke of newness, freshness, and bigness. It had all the latest tools and gadgets. When it decided to find a field to operate in, it conducted an assessment of the wheat to find the best place in the field so it could gather a maximum yield. It was a wheat-sensitive combine that met all the different needs that wheat might have. It had a special bin for small sprouts, segregating them from the mature wheat whenever the wheat was gathered. It was a purpose-driven combine that had a clear vision of making the combine manual relevant to modern strains of wheat, although some felt that in so doing the combine failed to fully study other portions of the manual.

This large combine required a number of full-time workers to operate the combine and make sure that everything ran smoothly and efficiently. The chief mechanic/operator was recognized throughout the country for his expertise in running combines. He wrote numerous books such as *Becoming Contagious Wheat* and *Rediscovering Combines: The Story and Vision of Willow River Community Combine*. Because the chief mechanic/operator was skilled at expounding the combine manual for others, he was asked to speak at Wheat Keepers and mechanic leadership conferences. He taught other mechanics and operators how to set up a wheat-sensitive combine and how to nurture the wheat. He even started a school to train and equip other mechanics and operators, offering degrees in combine-related subjects.

Because he was so busy writing books, speaking at seminars, and running the combine, he had little time to actually spend on the wheat. So, to take care of the specialized needs of the wheat, he hired other mechanics and operators—a wheat-development director who was responsible to assure that the wheat was properly nurtured for healthy growth and life; a young-wheat attendant to work with wheat that was going through the difficult transition to reach full maturity. There were even assistant mechanics, operators, and attendants to help the head mechanics and operators in their tasks. Thus, each part of the combine ran efficiently and smoothly.

The combine offered a support group for shriveled grains so that they would not feel inferior to fully developed grains. While the wheat enjoyed gathering in the bulk tank, smaller bins were needed so that the wheat could develop a sense of community. These small bins divided the grains according to age, type, and needs so that wheat could be with like wheat.

But for all the greatness of size, the large combine did have its problems. Over the course of the harvest, the operators noticed that they were getting a lot of wheat in the header, but they were also losing wheat out the back. This concerned them greatly. To become better at keeping wheat in the combine, they brought in a consultant to find out why grains were dropping back into the field. The consultant conducted seminars on gathering wheat and keeping it. But because the combine was so big, a lot of the wheat was overlooked. Furthermore, some grains remained in the combine but didn't feel like part of the crop—no one took notice of them because they got lost in the conveyor system between gathering, separating, and tending. Much of the wheat, however, found that in the large combine they could come and rest and feel good.

All in all the big combine was pleased with itself. Although problems occurred, as long as the combine gathered in more wheat than it lost out the back, it was happy. And so everything continued to run smoothly for this combine. When it ran, it sounded like the gentle breeze on a summer day. It sparkled in the sun as it stood tall, waiting for the harvest master to come for all the gathered wheat.

Unlike its large counterpart, the little combine clanked and rattled as it ran. Its paint was peeling and its metal was rusted. It was not the most efficient combine—many of its parts were old and some were slow to get things done. Because it was old, it had not adopted many of the newer innovations. It had worked for so many years that the mechanic/operator was reluctant to make changes lest they cause major problems with the combine.

There was only one mechanic/operator to make sure that the combine kept running. He did not have as much education or training as many other mechanics and operators, but he did his best, patching up the holes and oiling the squeaky bearings to keep things working. He did not write books and he did not conduct seminars, although he did attend several of the seminars taught by the mechanics and operators of the big combine. But they only made him sad. He realized that many of the ideas of the mechanics and operators for the big combine where good ideas and worked for big combines, but they would not work for his little combine. The little combine was just plain different, and it ran different from the large combines. He liked to read the combine manual, but found that he did not have a lot of time to read other books about running combines, because he was too busy spending time tending the wheat. Besides, all the other books were written by the same mechanics and operators who tended the large combines.

The little combine did not move very fast. Sometimes when it was gathering wheat, it would get plugged up, making it hard for new wheat to get in. When this happened the mechanic/operator stopped and made adjustments, and soon the little combine would be moving again. But for all its difficulties in getting wheat into the combine, very little of it went out the back. Instead, the wheat would come to full maturity. The little combine was not the fastest at gathering wheat, but it did an excellent job in caring for the wheat once it was in the combine.

Nor was the little combine a place of rest for the wheat. Instead, it put the wheat to work, helping to keep things going and helping it harvest more wheat. For in the little combine, even the wheat had to work if the combine was to keep going.

Sometimes the little combine would have problems and many thought that it would finally stop working. Some said that the little combine was not modern enough, that it was stuck in the past. Making needed changes and innovations was at times very difficult and took a great deal of work. But somehow, with the help of the mechanic/operator and some careful instructions from the maker of the combine, the little combine would chug along.

The little combine, though, had one thing going for it—the mechanic/operator was personally acquainted with each kernel of wheat. And because the little combine did not have a giant bin full of wheat, each kernel knew every other kernel and each one felt it was important to the combine. The wheat helped each other, and each kernel received special tending from the combine. When one of the kernels became shrived because of drought, the little combine would carefully nurse it back to health so that it became full and plump again. The little combine was more than just a combine; it was a community where wheat belonged, where each individual kernel was important and cared for. The wheat enjoyed being gathered together, mixing with wheat of all ages. The young wheat learned to value the wisdom of the old wheat, and the old enjoyed the enthusiasm of the young.

The little combine loved it when all the wheat was gathered together. Together, they celebrated the one who designed it and remembered the many generations of wheat that had been gathered together within this same little combine. In all this the little combine learned many things—that the harvest is not about the combine, but about the wheat; that effective operation is not just a matter of getting wheat into the combine, but it is taking proper care of the wheat so that it would yield even more wheat; that to be an effective mechanic/operator one must love not only the combine but must love the wheat and spend time with the wheat.

When the autumn winds began to blow, all the wheat waited for someone to gather it. The big combine began to gather wheat. With all its mechanics and operators and well-adjusted parts, it harvested wheat effectively and efficiently. But there were many places that the big combine, because of its size, could not go—little fields up narrow roads, distances too great and fields much too small. Even in the big fields, the large combine missed some areas. And it missed the wheat in the ditches and draws because the header could not get low enough to harvest those.

The little combine, on the other hand, went into these fields and gathered wheat. It went slowly and sometimes it would even stop to make repairs or fix problems. It clanked and clamored along, needing continual prodding from the mechanic/operator, who at times despaired of the little machine. It was not the most efficient and it did not always go smoothly, but still it gathered wheat. As the days grew cold and the wheat continued to ripen, the little combine plodded along, gathering wheat and nurturing it to maturity. The little combine went up the narrow rocky roads where the large combine could not go, and gathered the small fields of wheat. It went in the ditches and draws, where its small header could reach the shorter stocks of wheat. Although the fields were small and the stocks short, the wheat was of the highest quality, with nice big kernels. Because of the quality of the wheat in these little places, the maker of combines would use the seeds from these small fields to plant the next crop in the big fields.

And so the little combine learned that size and appearance are not what counts. What counts is participating in the gathering in, doing what the maker designed it to do. The little combine also learned that the size of the combine does not determine the quality of wheat. Even the smallest of combines can harvest some of the most hearty and productive wheat.

The little combine realized that the greatest work it could do was what the maker ordained for it, so that when people saw the combine, they saw the one who made it. The little combine, while not the biggest or even the best, did do one thing: it helped gather the wheat and thus it did what the maker designed it to do.

> "Do you not say, 'Four months more and then the harvest'? I tell you, open your eyes and look at the fields! They are ripe for harvest. The harvest is plentiful but the combines are few. Ask the Lord of the harvest, therefore, to send out combines into his harvest field." (John 4:35; Matt. 9:37– 38 paraphrased)

Being Effective in the Harvest

The vitality of a congregation is not found in its size or in its programs or budget. The vitality of a congregation is found in its fulfillment of God's purpose for the church. A church that has five thousand members and is growing may be just as unhealthy and ineffective as a church that has only fifty members and is declining. Conversely, a church with fifty members who are fulfilling God's mission can be as healthy and dynamic as a church with thousands of members. Churches do not close because they lack members and financial resources. Churches close when they are no longer being effective in fulfilling God's purposes for them.

Building an effective church begins with understanding the benchmarks for effectiveness. And the pastor and leadership must use these benchmarks to continually examine what the church is to be doing, how it is to do it, and why. Otherwise the congregation can easily become distracted by the pursuit of the insignificant.

Identifying What Effectiveness Is Not

To properly understand what an effective church *is*, one must first understand the common misconceptions regarding effectiveness. While each misconception may have some element of truth, when the misconceptions themselves become the *sole or primary factor* in evaluating the church the leadership will develop a distorted perspective.

First, *effectiveness is not determined by the number of members on the rolls.* Too often, numerical growth becomes a benchmark of effectiveness. The assumption is that a church, if it is effective, will be growing. An examination of Scripture, however, reveals that this is not necessarily the case. The growth of the church is not the responsibility of the congregation but, ultimately, of God. While the people are to be continually sharing the gospel, the redemptive work belongs to God (1 Cor. 3:5–9). Furthermore, God often calls his people to minister in areas where there will be few visible results (see Ezek. 2:3–8). Effectiveness, therefore, is not found in numbers but in accomplishing God's design for the congregation.

Second, *effectiveness is not determined by programs.* It is assumed that to be truly effective the church must have multiple programs. While necessary, programs are not the final measure of success. A church with a few programs may be far more effective than a church with multiple programs. When small churches try to duplicate larger churches that have a greater number of ministries, they may as a consequence become bogged down, trying to do too much with too few resources. In the end, people become discouraged and burned out when nothing gets accomplished.

Third, *effectiveness is not determined by outward behavior.* Small churches often exhibit a homogenous subculture that manifests certain characteristics and norms established by the people. Behavior patterns are established by the people's cultural values rather than biblical values. These values are then passed on from one generation to the next so that the church measures its effectiveness by how well it upholds the past traditions rather than what it is accomplishing for the kingdom of Christ. When this occurs, the church adopts an unbiblical view of success, which will distort its focus and undermine its divine calling.

Fourth, *effectiveness is not determined by a specific format.* Depending on the latest ministry fad, many churches seek success in ministry by implementing a format that another successful church has developed. In today's church environment, for example, it is assumed that successful churches use a seeker-sensitive model. Many rural churches, on the other hand, measure success by the traditional format of Sunday school, Sunday morning worship service, Sunday evening service, and midweek prayer meeting. For them, as long as the church maintains this model, it is effective. But Scripture does not identify nor follow one specific model. The way a church conducts its ministry will differ depending upon the community and people it wishes to reach.

Defining Effectiveness

Success cannot be defined by any external standards. Instead, effectiveness must be measured by the scriptural mandates assigned to the body of Christ. The effectiveness of ministry must withstand over time the scrutiny of the will of God as expressed in written revelation. While other standards may be suggestive, the final test of effectiveness is found in Scripture.

Effectiveness is defined by transformation (Eph. 4:12–13). The purpose of the ministry of the church is to transform the lives of people into the image and character of Christ. The spiritual maturity of the whole congregation will be a measure of the impact of the church. Paul writes that the ultimate intention of spiritual gifts is "that the body of Christ may be built up until we all reach unity in the faith and in the knowledge of the son of God and become mature, attaining to the whole measure of the fullness of Christ" (Eph. 4:12–13). Maturity occurs, then, when the whole measure of Christ is attained within us, that is, when Christ's life and character become manifest within us, by which we become complete. The goal of the church's ministry focuses upon the establishment of Christlikeness within each individual.

Effectiveness is defined by biblical and theological integrity (Eph. 4:14). Theology and doctrine stand at the heart of the true people of God. Thus, the church is a theological community designated by God to express and uphold biblical doctrines. The mark of maturity in a church is theological and biblical integrity, and steadfastness in biblical truth. The immature, on the other hand, having no theological and doctrinal roots that bring continuity to their lives, are easily swayed by various ideas and teachings. Thus Paul warns, "We will no longer be infants, tossed back and forth by the waves, and blown here and there by every wind of teaching and by the cunning and craftiness of men in their deceitful scheming" (Eph.

4:14). Doctrine and theology are not dead speculations that tickle the mind but leave the heart cold. True theology (which is the study of the person and activity of God) affects how we think, and makes radical demands upon our will, our attitudes, and our activities. When we truly understand the character of God we realize that we cannot be content to live life short of his demands. Without such an understanding, our belief and practice become man-centered rather than God-centered.

Effectiveness is defined by faith (Eph. 4:4–6). Faith is taking God at his word, not blindly but grounded in the belief that his Word reflects his character. The term *faith*, as used by Paul in Ephesians 4:5, reflects both objective faith (i.e., doctrine) as well as the subjective trust on the part of God's people. Indeed the two cannot be separated. True doctrine, when internalized through trust, must result in change, and godly trust stems from our awareness of who God is. As a church, our goal is to instruct people concerning the nature of God so that they might develop an unwavering trust in his promises and Word. Often, when Paul writes to a church, he praises them for their faith and trust in God (see Rom 1:8; Eph. 1:15; Col 1:4; 1 Thess. 1:8)—the measurements of the strength of the church. The church has impact when the congregation's trust and commitment to God become evident even to those around them. This faith finds expression in the worship and prayer life of the congregation as the church recognizes its dependency upon God. Faith finds expression in worship as it responds to the character, being, and activity of God. Prayer is an expression of faith in that people recognize not only their complete dependency upon God, but also their confidence that God will act according to his Word, his will, and our prayers.

Effectiveness is defined by relationship (Eph. 4:1–6). Effectiveness comes when the congregation moves from being an *assembly* of God's people to a genuine *community* of God's people, where love abounds, and where mutual care for one another becomes evident. In Ephesians 4:1–6 Paul focuses on the unity and love that is to characterize the church. Living worthy of our calling requires unity and harmony with the rest of God's people. The church, as a reflection of the person of God, ought to be marked by a strong corporate identity where love and patience are demonstrated to one another, where people strive to express the love and forgiveness that God himself manifests. The church grows when people become more loving, more accepting, more giving, more thoughtful, and more caring.

Effectiveness is defined by service (Eph. 4:16). Within a dynamic and vibrant church people become involved in the ministry. Members are more than pew-warmers who stumble in and out each week but fail to become involved in the work of the gospel. Not content to sit on the sidelines and pay a professional to do what they can and should be doing, each member does his or her part, exercising his or her spiritual gifts for the betterment of the whole community (Eph. 4:16). They want to be involved, not for power and recognition, but because they desire ownership of the ministry. They desire to be in the service of the King, bringing him honor and glory through their involvement.

Effectiveness is defined by relevancy (1 Cor. 9:19–23). The apostle Paul, when summarizing his own ministry, stated that he sought to be relevant to the people to whom he was called to serve (see 1 Cor. 9:19–23). Attaining relevancy does not mean compromising Scripture to fit cultural norms and beliefs; relevancy is making the gospel contemporary so that people understand the importance, validity, and truthfulness of the message. For relevancy to occur, the church must understand the secular community, and must understand the needs of people in order to minister to them. Effective churches focus upon heaven while their feet remain firmly planted in their community. Christ recognizes the importance of being relevant; he prayed that God would not take his people out of the world but protect them from sin's influence while they exist within their contemporary culture (John 17:15).

Building Toward Effectiveness

Following is an overview of the process for developing an effective church. Each step of the process builds upon the other. While each step is important, each is not of equal value. The most important steps are those that focus upon our *theology,* godly *character,* and biblical *mission*. The church can be hazy on its *vision* and still be relatively effective, but a church cannot afford to be shaky in its theology. *Theology* is the springboard for character, and character the springboard for the mission of the church. Without theology there is no basis for character and the mission of the church is reduced to social programs where people and their needs become the focus. Without character, the congregation can become abusive, legalistic, and damaging to the lives and spiritual growth of its church community. *Vision* is only as good as the church's understanding of its mission. Vision grows from an awareness of community and the biblical mandate given to the church.

Step One: Understand—Know the Culture

The ministry environment greatly influences what we do in ministry and how we are to go about doing it. Therefore, the first step in developing the church's ministry is to assess and comprehend the setting.

Community

To be effective we must first understand the people we are called to serve. Without such an understanding we will develop programs

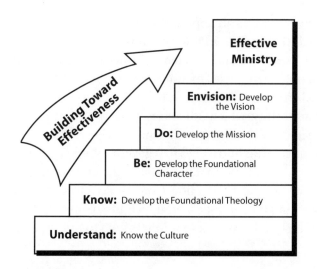

that fail to reach the people we have targeted to serve. Understanding community involves more than just being familiar with the names and faces of people. To penetrate the subculture of the community and to reach people requires in-depth understanding of the mindset and thinking of people. We need to know who people are and what they like. We need to understand their needs, their hurts, their struggles, their pressures, and their desires. Attempting to build an effective church without a knowledge of the community is like trying to build a boat without understanding the waters it will ply. A boat built for inland waterways will be far different from one made to sail the ocean. A ship designed for Arctic exploration will be constructed differently than a cruise ship. It is not enough to know how to build boats, we must know the intended purpose of the boat.

In order to be effective in ministry, we must discern whom we desire to reach so that we can tailor our ministry to specific people. People in rural areas are culturally different than people in suburban areas. The inner-city church requires unique ministries that are not found in rural or suburban areas. Each church is different because each community is different. Thus the starting place for developing a dynamic and vibrant church is an understanding of the community.

Church

Too often, pastors attempt to develop a direction and vision for the church that are not in touch with the people they serve. Every church is as unique and different as a person's fingerprints. Each congregation is comprised of individuals who are unique in personality, background, giftedness, and abilities. Every congregation has a different history, which influences its story and its perception of itself. Each church will react differently to circumstances, each will have unique norms and values that govern its policies. Each church has different traditions that direct the focus of its programs. All of these differences are part of how God has designed the body in order that it might be uniquely equipped to accomplish the specific task that he has designed it to fulfill. Failing to understand and realize these differences will result in frustration for the church, and will cause it to fail in accomplishing God's will and calling.

Step Two: Know—Develop the Foundational Theology

The second step to effectiveness is establishing the theological foundation of the church. A church will only be as effective as its theology, for its theology determines its ministries, governs its agenda, influences the transformation of people, and motivates people for action. The church is not a social organization, although it may conduct social ministries. The church is not a political institution, although it may be politically active. The church is not an educational academy, although it seeks to educate. The church is not a community service, although it will be involved in community affairs. The church is not a counseling center, although it heals the spirit. The church is ultimately a theological organism designed to correct, develop, and instruct biblical doctrines so that people are transformed in their motives, desires, activities, and attitudes in order to conform to the person of Christ. The ultimate task of the church is to bring people into communion with God. For this to happen we must know who God is, and coming to know God is what theology is all about. Therefore, to be successful, the church must instill within people biblical doctrines that confront and comfort the soul.

Step Three: Be—Develop the Foundational Character

The third step in developing the ministry of the church is to develop the character of the people who attend. Paul establishes the agenda of the church in Ephesians 4:12–13 when he states that the goal of the church is to transform people into the character and image of Christ. Thus, the most significant measure of what is happening in the church is not found by what is happening in the rolls but by what is happening in the pews. Are people being changed in their attitudes and actions so that they are in obedience to Christ? Christ states that obedience, not emotions or experience, measures the love people have for him (John 14:21). This obedience is summed up by two commands—love God and love others (Matt. 22:37–40).

Loving God involves more than worship. It includes a life of *obedience, worship* (both corporately and individually), *prayer,* the *study* of his Word, and a *life of faith.* To develop a commitment to and relationship with God people need to develop the spiritual disciplines that undergird their faith. The task of the church is to come along side of people and teach them how to have an in-depth relationship with God.

Loving others is a second aspect of inward character that deals with our horizontal relationships and the attitudes we maintain toward those relationships. Loving others involves the development of in-depth relationships with other believers that results in *mutual support, encouragement,* and *accountability.* Loving others, however, extends also to developing positive friendships with others outside the church.

Step Four: Do—Develop the Mission

Christ did not leave the church idle. He gave his people the three-fold responsibility of *proclaiming* the gospel of Christ, *transforming* others into faithful disciples, and *recruiting* those disciples for the service of the kingdom of God. This mission is continual in its scope ("end of the age," Matt. 28:20) and universal in its application ("all nations," Matt. 28:19). Every church in every location during every time period has this same responsibility. The church is to both be and do.

Reaching

Christ commanded the church in Acts 1:8, "But you will receive power when the Holy Spirit comes on you; and you will be my witnesses in Jerusalem, and in all Judea and Samaria, and to the ends of the earth." The responsibility rests upon the church to evangelize not only their local community, but the whole world as well. A church cannot be content merely to formulate ministries that serve its own congregation but must develop strategies to communicate effectively the message of Christ to those who dwell near the church. Effectiveness requires the church to penetrate its community by building relationships, which become avenues to share the redemptive message. Sharing the message requires the church to understand the people it is to reach so that it can communicate effectively. The apostle Paul recognized the importance of understanding the community: "Become all things to all men so that by all possible means I might save some" (1 Cor. 9:22). Paul never compromised the integrity of the message, but he recognized that different target groups required different method. The task of the church is to understand its community in order to constantly develop relevant methodology.

Teaching

The evangelistic efforts of the church feed the discipleship programs. Discipleship involves instilling within people the spiritual disciplines and biblical knowledge that will enable them to become mature, obedient disciples of Christ. The redemptive work of Christ in the lives of people finds its fruition when the church instructs people regarding biblical truth so that their characters becomes transformed into the image and character of Christ. The focus of the Great Commission is upon the development of disciples, that development being measured by obedience to Christ: "Therefore go and make disciples of all nations, baptizing them in the name of the Father and of the Son and of the Holy Spirit, and *teaching them to obey everything I commanded you.* And surely I am with you always, to the very end of the age" (Matt. 28:19–20, emphasis added). Too often people are taught the free salvation that Christ offers, but are not taught the practical responsibilities entailed by being a child of God. To be effective, the church needs to analyze how it will train people in the Christian faith.

Recruiting

A third responsibility assigned to the church is to recruit and train people into service of the King. The Christian life is not a life of solitude but a life lived in community. The community of God's people is not, however, a static organization. It is a dynamic organization that requires interdependency between its members. No one can live independent of others. Instead, everyone's personal growth requires the input and ministry of the other people. Nor can one individual regard himself or herself as unneeded by the rest (see 1 Corinthians 12). The role of the church in developing interdependency is to recruit and train people so that their spiritual gifts are utilized for the benefit of others. Paul emphasizes the responsibility of the church to recruit and train: "It was he who gave some to be apostles, some to be prophets, some to be evangelists, and some to be pastors and teachers, to prepare God's people for works of service, so that the body of Christ may be built up until we all reach unity in the faith and in the knowledge of the Son of God and become mature, attaining to the whole measure of the fullness of Christ" (Eph. 4:11–13). This preparation implies training and discipline so that the individual fulfills his or her own responsibility. The church should actively pursue people, involving them in the ministry of the church so that by their service the rest of the body benefits.

Step Five: Envision—Developing the Vision

Vision is the process of identifying the focus of the church and developing a strategy for accomplishing its biblical mission and purpose. Churches that prosper understand their communities and understand how they can accomplish the mission and purpose of the church within their setting (Rom. 12:1–2). They develop organizational structures and ministry programs that have clear objectives that relate to the vision, mission, and purpose of the church. They sustain clear communication so that people are well informed and trust is built within the congregation. People thus understand what they are to do, who is responsible for which assignment, and why that person is to perform it. The effective church constantly evaluates and analyzes its programs and the needs of people in order to increase its effectiveness. Within the small church the task of the leadership is to facilitate the process of identifying a unified vision by assisting the church in evaluating its ministries. Then leadership works to develop specific strategies for accomplishing that vision.

Implementing the Process

This book is not meant to be read and placed back upon the shelf. Rather, the purpose of this material is to provide a framework for discussion between the pastor, board, and leadership to evaluate and formulate an effective ministry within the small church. The ministry development worksheets in appendix A (p. 255) are designed to be completed with the board and leadership in order to implement and maintain a healthy church—one that is accomplishing God's mission within the local congregation. When the small church is accomplishing God's will and purpose, then it is a critical worker in the harvest.

Further Reading

Crandall, Ron. *Turn Around Strategies for the Small Church*. Nashville: Abingdon, 1995.

Hughes, Kent, and Barbara Hughes. *Liberating Ministry from the Success Syndrome*. Wheaton, Ill.: Tyndale, 1988.

Klassen, Ron, and John Koessler. *No Little Places*. Grand Rapids: Baker, 1996.

Spader, Dann, and Gary Mayes. *Growing a Healthy Church*. Chicago: Moody, 1991.

ONE

Understanding the Community

Understanding the will of God cannot be divorced from the ministry of the church. But to be effective, the church needs to know its environment. While our biblical theology and understanding of Scripture must govern the ministry, dictate the parameters, and evaluate every methodology, the culture greatly influences our approach to ministry and program development. Thus, to develop the ministry of the church and the methodology for determining that ministry, it is important that the church and its leadership have a thorough understanding of the church's setting. The setting entails both the culture of the community, as well as the culture of the small church.

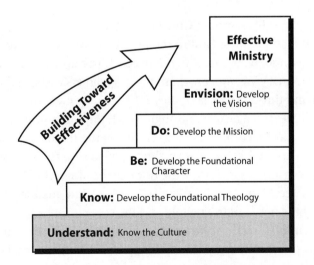

We begin, therefore, by examining our culture and community, not because it is the most important but because it influences how we go about implementing each of the various stages of effectiveness.

Knowing Our Rome

Ministry is not performed in a cultural vacuum. Instead, we are to perform our ministry in the streets, marketplaces, and communities that surround us. The church is called to proclaim Christ not just in the sanctuary but to the world in which we live. We are not to be isolated from our world; we are to live within it, changing it through the redemptive message of Christ. The church—no matter where its location—exits on the mission field. Thus, to be effective, we must understand our communities and develop ministries that reach those not only inside the church but outside the church. Understanding necessitates assessing our community in order to effectively communicate the gospel. Assessing the community begins by understanding our ministry environment. The ministry environment is the cultural, social, and economic setting of the community at large in which the church finds itself ministering.

Learn the Needs of People

Throughout his ministry, Christ sought to communicate the message of the kingdom of God to the people of his day. Whenever he sought to do so, he began with the needs, hurts, and interests of the people (John 4). We, too, proclaim the gospel message both through actions and through words (James 2:14–18). By meeting the needs of people we gain a hearing through which the redemptive message of Christ may be communicated. Christ, being the master evangelist, often spent a great deal of time ministering to the needs of people even as he was sharing the hope of the kingdom of God (for example, see Matt. 15:30; Luke 6:17–18). In like manner, understanding the needs of the people and the community enables us to develop ministries that address those needs, at the same time affording opportunities to share the hope of Christ. Outreach is especially critical in rural areas where people are judged by their work ethic and their willingness to help other people. The people respect and respond to a pastor who is involved in the community.

Adapt Ministry to the People

The passage of *time* affects the mentality, worldview, and attitudes of people. An area that was once a logging community may now be a bedroom community to a larger city. An area that was once ultra-conservative may be more politically moderate as new people move in and bring new ideas that challenge the older established attitudes. As a result, the ministry of the church changes. What worked forty years ago in the church will no longer work because the people are vastly different.

Something similar may be said of *location*. Every community is different even from the other communities that surround it. The farm community in Montana differs considerably from its counterpart in Nevada or Alabama. The suburb on the east side of the city will demonstrate different characteristics and outlooks than one on the west side. Just as individuals differ, so individual communities manifest distinct features and qualities.

It is not surprising, then, that a program or a philosophy of ministry that experiences success in one area flops miserably in another. To be effective, the church needs to develop a philosophy and approach to ministry unique to its particular setting. In 1 Chronicles we read of the men of Issachar, "who understood the times and knew what Israel should do" (1 Chron. 12:32). Because these men were sensitive to the situation confronting Israel, they were able to make a proper choice for political action in establishing David as the king of Israel. So also the church today, to determine the direction in which it needs to go, must understand and adapt its ministry to it, environment.

Effectively Communicate the Gospel (Acts 17:22–31)

While the gospel message never changes, the vehicle by which we communicate the message changes depending upon the people to whom we are speaking. The apostle Paul was an effective communicator of the gospel because of his remarkable ability to declare the message in a way that the people could understand. When he spoke with the Jews who where entrenched in the Old Testament, Paul proclaimed the message of Christ by starting with the Old Testament history (Acts 13:13–41). When addressing the pagan philosophers in Athens, however, he couched his message in their philosophy and religious viewpoint (Acts 17:22–31). Paul's approach to evangelism was to start where his listeners stood spiritually and then seek to move them where they needed to be. He could do this because he had a thorough understanding of the people he was addressing. When we recognize and appreciate the type of people we are serving then we can present the message in a way that they comprehend. When we attempt to communicate without this appreciation, we often speak in a cultural language that our listeners do not identify with or grasp. Some people respond to a direct confrontation with the gospel; others will respond through a demonstration of love and compassion. Some respond through the denunciation of sin, others respond through the proclamation of the love and forgiveness of Christ. To develop the right strategy we need in-depth knowledge of our listeners' cultures.

Find Acceptance (1 Cor. 9:19–23)

To be accepted by a community, a person or group must be willing to conform to the cultural outlook of the people of that community. Failure to do so results in the messenger being viewed as an outsider. If we do not understand the pressures and problems confronting the African-American community, we will never be effective in ministering to them. To gain acceptance into a rural community necessitates sensitivity to the pressures and problems plaguing the agricultural economy. While we can never compromise our message in order to be accepted, we can adapt our behavior and culture in order to be accepted, thus creating avenues to communicate the gospel. Paul well understood this: "Though I am free and belong to no man, I make myself a slave to everyone, to win as many as possible. To the Jews I became like a Jew, to win the Jews. To those under the law I became like one under the law (through I myself am not under the law), so as to win those under the law. To those not having the law I became like one not having the law (though I am not free from God's law but am under Christ's law), so as to win those not having the law. To the weak I became weak, to win the weak. I have become all things to all men so that by all possible means I might save some. I do all this for the sake of the gospel, that I may share in its blessings" (1 Cor. 9:19–23). No one could accuse Paul of compromising the integrity of the gospel just to be accepted by others. Yet he realized to gain a hearing with people he must adapt himself to their culture. Therefore he had Timothy circumcised in order to gain acceptance by the Jews, even though circumcision was biblically unnecessary (Acts 16:3). Every community and church places behavioral and social expectations upon those who are accepted into the group. To be influential in the community the pastor must understand and minister within these expectations. Only when those expectations violate the teaching of Scripture should a pastor resist them.

Identify the Target Group

In most cases, especially in ethnically and culturally diverse areas, no one church will effectively reach all people. Reaching people involves understanding both the personality and spiritual giftedness of the congregation as well as the people in the community. With this knowledge the church can identify those people that God has equipped and called it to reach. A church that ministers in, for example, areas where there are many migrant workers must determine whom it will best reach—the Spanish speaking migrant workers, or the English speaking people who employ them. A suburban church needs to identify if it will be more effective in reaching white-collar executives or blue-collar workers.

Study the Cultural Context

Culture involves how people formulate their understanding of life, how they view their world, what motivates them to action. Culture also encompasses values, spiritual beliefs, demographics, and social patterns.

The Spiritual Climate

Each community has a different spiritual climate. Some communities are receptive and open to the presentation of the gospel and the ministry of the church. Others are tolerant of the church, but uninterested in the message of Christ. Still others are antagonistic and openly hostile. In examining the spiritual climate Rick Warren suggests asking five questions:[1]

1. What do people consider to be the greatest need in the area? Asking people in the area this question serves to get the people talking and sharing their thoughts about the community and gives insight into the needs of people within the community.
2. Where do people attend church? The purpose is not to steal sheep from other evangelical churches but to gain an understanding of the spiritual receptivity of the people. Those who attend other Christian churches should be encouraged to keep doing so.
3. For those who do not attend church, why do they think people today do not attend church? Asking people why they do not attend a church will only put them on the defensive. Asking why *others* do not attend keeps defenses down and will more likely result in respondents sharing why they personally do not attend.
4. What things would respondents look for in a church if they were to attend? This question enables the church to gain an understanding of the kinds of programs that would interest people. To effectively reach people, the church needs to have ministries relevant to those people.
5. What advice would respondents give to a church that desires to better serve the community? Again this question provides invaluable feedback for the church from those who do not attend. The call of the church is to minister to the people surrounding them, therefore the church needs to know how it can better serve those people. This data can be used by the church to evaluate its evangelistic programs.

The Demographics

In smaller communities, developing a demographic assessment of the community can be done by asking people to describe their neighbors and friends and then compiling the information. In larger communities, an assessment can be attained through government agencies or demographic research organizations. Other information can be obtained by accessing the Internet. The following information should be identified:

- Age: What is the median age of the people in the community and how many people fall into in each age bracket?
- Family status: How many children are in each family and what are their ages? What is the marital status of the people? What percent are divorced, remarried, widowed, or living together?
- Employment and economic base: What are the primary industries and job opportunities within the community? Is there a predominant industry undergirding the economy of the community?
- Income level and social status: What is the average income of the community and the average social status? Do people have a high or low standard of living?
- Education level: How much education does the average person have? How much education is required for employment opportunities within the community?
- Nationality and ethnic background: Is there a dominant ethnic background within the community? Does the ethnic heritage of the community have any affect upon the religious base within the community?
- Religious background: Has a particular religious tradition influenced the community in the past or the present?
- Geographic boundaries: What is the geographic extent of the church's ministry? Is the influence of the church limited to a part of a city or town, the town itself, or the surrounding areas?

The Culture

Culture consists of the ideas, norms, formal, and informal structures that typify a specific group of people. To understand a community, one needs to discern why the community acts the way it does, and examine why it upholds certain values and performs certain practices. Such an appraisal affords the church a clearer perception of cultural influences, which not only affect people within the church, but also the programming of the church. Cultural understanding requires, too, that the church be sensitive to the present setting and the ongoing changes in the area. Culture is, after all, not static but continually changes and evolves as society changes and evolves.

Regarding mindset and lifestyle, which of the following characteristics predominate in your community:

- Active versus sedentary: Are people's lifestyles filled with activities, or do they spend their leisure time quietly?
- Family versus career focused: Do people form life goals based upon their careers, or upon their family relationships?
- Individualism versus community: Is there a strong sense of community and are people measured by their contribution to the community, or is there a strong sense of individualism apart from community relationships?
- Politically conservative versus politically liberal: How a community votes provides insight into its values and beliefs. Does the community vote primarily liberal, or does it vote primarily conservative?
- Environmentalists versus land-use proponents: Do people view the environment and land as something to be preserved in its "natural" state, or something to be used by humanity for personal livelihood?
- Traditional versus progressive: Does the community evaluate issues by past traditions and resist change, or does it place little value in traditions and have a more innovative outlook that welcomes change?

- Religious versus secular: Does the community have a strong religious heritage, or are people uninvolved in religious activities and secular in their mindset?
- Stable population versus mobile population: Does the population of the community exhibit a high turnover rate, or is the population in general stable? What are the factors contributing to the turnover rate?
- Homogeneous versus multicultural: Is the community predominately influenced by one cultural expression, or are there multiple subcultures and ethnic backgrounds within the community?
- Relational versus accomplishment: Are people evaluated by their ability to relate with others, or by what they can accomplish and achieve?
- Blue collar versus white collar: In regard to the economic base, does the community consist predominately of professionals, or is it constituted primarily by the working class?
- Federalism versus libertarianism: Does the community hold to a strong centralized government, or does the community prefer a decentralized government and view the federal government with suspicion?
- Cosmopolitan versus provincial: Is the community strongly cosmopolitan and have a strong interest in world events, or is it more provincial and concerned only with the events happening locally?
- Academic/education versus nonacademic view: Are people educated and analytical, or uneducated and more pragmatic in their outlook?
- Futurism versus here and now: Are people anticipating the future and future events, or are they predominantly concerned only with the present?
- Hi-tech versus low-tech: Are people in the community influenced by the technology movement, or is the community as a whole not yet "plugged in"?

The Social Centers

Identify where people congregate, what social events are supported, and where people go to be with their neighbors and friends. Lyle Schaller mentions the "third place" of people:

> For generations most Americans lived at home (the first place in their world), journeyed to work (the second place, although for some workaholics this became their first place), and found a third place where they could relax and be identified for who they are as individuals. In the first place, we are identified by kinship roles, in the second place by our job, skill, position, or title. In that wonderful third place, our identity is in who we are as a person.[2]

Previously, in many rural communities, this third place was the church. Now many other social clubs (Lions, Kiwanis, etc.), service organizations (volunteer fire department, ambulance service, etc.), or recreational groups (softball league, basketball or volleyball group) have replaced the church as the social center. In many cases the church still mistakenly views itself as the social center, when in reality that is no longer the case. Thus the church must identify what the community social centers are and seek to reach people by becoming active in them rather than expect people to come to the social functions of the church.

The Customs

Customs are the long established practices that become an integral part of the community's infrastructure—types of clothing worn, activities attended and supported, mannerisms, and habits. To gain acceptance into the community one must adhere to these customs otherwise he or she will always remain an outsider. Thus the church needs to examine what customs mark the particular community it serves.

The Community History

Every community has a different story. Whether the story is verbalized or not, it serves to undergird the fabric of the community. New people eventually learn and become part of the story, or they remain outsiders. For the church to understand the community, it needs to have a clear understanding of its history.

The Cultural Indicators

There are many other cultural indicators that can be surveyed to gain greater insight into the cultural background of the community.

Music: What type of music is popular within the community? What are the most popular radio stations? At community sponsored musical events (such as the community fair), what type of music is most often played and what groups are brought in?

Reading material: What magazines are the most popular within the community? Talk with the librarian and with the local businesses that sell magazines. What type of books are most often read or purchased?

Local newspaper: The local newspaper is more than just a recording of local news; it is a record of local culture. The articles written describe the culture, and by reading the local newspaper, the church leader can gain insight into the interests of the people.

Community organizations: Community organizations play a vital role in the social and cultural structure of a community. The organizations that are the most popular likely express key values that mark the area.

Assess Community Needs

The goal of examining the community is to understand the concerns of people. Doing so affords the church an opportunity to minister to their needs, which in turn affords the church an opportunity to bring them to a redemptive knowledge of Christ. While the church is to proclaim the gospel, it is also called upon to minister to the needs of people (Matt. 15:31–45). The critical questions for the church to ask are: What are the social, emotional, physical, or financial worries of people? Does the church have the means to minister to these? While the church cannot meet all the problems of people, it can and should seek to minister to some of their needs. Effective evangelism begins with meeting needs so that the redemptive purposes of the church may be realized.

Personalize the Target

After the assessment is done, then the church can personalize the target community by creating a composite profile of a type of person within the area (see appendix E on p. 278 for example composite). By doing so the church can clearly articulate whom it is to reach. This composite can serve as a guide for the church as it seeks to develop the direction for its ministries.

Integrate the Assessment

The final step is integration. The community assessment is of no value if it does not influence the ministries of the church. The church should ask several key questions:

How are we going to reach this person with the gospel of Christ?

What programs would interest and minister to the need of the community?

As these individuals join our church, do they carry attitudes and behaviors that need to be corrected? People who enter the church often carry with them emotional and cultural baggage that can be a detriment to their spiritual growth. These matters need to be corrected through biblical instruction so that people are being conformed to the image of Christ.

By answering these questions, the church can formulate goals and strategies relevant to the community. When the gospel becomes real to the people, then they will be reached for Christ. Making the gospel real happens when the church understands its community and integrates that knowledge into the ministries it conducts.

Evaluation and Implementation

1. Read through the book of Acts. Identify the manner in which Peter and Paul adapted their methodology to fit the culture

of the people whom they were serving. How does their example serve as a model for the church today?

2. With the board and members of the church, interview twenty people in the community who do not normally attend church, asking them the five questions posed by Rick Warren. Condense their responses in a one page summary.

3. Write a two-page (double-spaced) summary of the typical person in the community (see appendix E on p. 278 for example composite) by using the six steps outlined in the course material. For demographic information visit the web site http://govinfo.kerr.orst.edu/govdoc/govinfo.htm.

4. Complete worksheets 1–6 of the Ministry Development Worksheets in appendix A.

Further Reading

Flora, Cornelia Butler, et al. *Rural Communities, Legacy and Change.* San Francisco: Westview, 1992.

Jung, L. Shannon , and Mary A. Agria. *Rural Congregational Studies.* Nashville: Abingdon, 1997.

Vidich, Arthur J., and Joseph Bensman. *Small Town in Mass Society.* Princeton, N.J.: Princeton University Press, 1968.

TWO

Understanding the Church

E very sociological group has a distinct set of cultural norms and expectations that set it apart from other groups. The church is no different. People associate with one another because they have certain similarities and bonds that connect them with shared expectations, ideals, norms, values, and behavior patterns. When a group lacks these common threads, conflict and disunity result causing people to separate themselves from one another. To be accepted as a leader of the group, a person must understand, share, and affirm these cultural norms, otherwise the person will be viewed as an outsider.

Consequently, it is important for the pastor and church leaders to be able to identify and minister within the context of the specific church's cultural setting. Ultimately the only persons who can truly understand a specific church are those who minister within it. Just as no two people are exactly alike in their values, beliefs, and cultural expectations, so no two churches are exactly alike. However, there are general characteristics that mark the small church which provide a framework for the leader to gain a better understanding of the congregation.

Characteristics of the Small Church

The small church is different from its larger counterpart. It worships differently, it views leadership differently, it views ministry differently. Often, leaders mistakenly assume that the principles of leadership and ministry operate the same, regardless of a church's size. The result is that the leader becomes frustrated that the people are not following, and the people become discouraged because the leader is taking them in a direction they do not want to go. Leadership is not only the ability to know what needs to be done, but also knowing how to motivate and influence people. We need to understand the characteristics and distinctives that mark the small church. While no church will manifest all fifteen of these characteristics, in most cases there will be several that predominate.

Characteristic 1: The small church is relationally driven.

Perhaps the single most important distinctive of the small church is that it is relationally rather than program driven. There exists within the congregation a family atmosphere where individuals are considered part of a bigger family, where relationships become more important than performance and organization. The small church has a place for everyone and shows concern for everyone. Relationships are emphasized rather than programs and ministries. Rather than the life of the church revolving around the worship service or the programs, it centers on the relational bonds of the congregation.

This relational factor has enormous impact on how the small church functions and organizes its ministry. Within the small church, it is not the position that gives power and authority to the individual but the relationships the person has with the other members. Consequently, the pastor is often not the primary leader of the congregation. That role is often given to an individual or individuals who, by their personal interaction with others, influence the rest of the church.

Because the church is relationally driven, the programs and organization of the church are determined and monitored by the effect they will have upon relationships. Opposition arises against anything that becomes a threat to unity. Since people are more important than performance, small churches often overlook poor performance rather than confront the individual and risk the relationship.

Characteristic 2: The small church works through informal channels.

Because of the close relational bonds, decisions are often made over coffee rather than formal meetings. When there are formal meetings, it is more of a social event rather than a business event. Goals are verbalized rather than written. Policies are based upon the effect the situation will have on individual relationships rather than on the organization as a whole.

As leaders, the challenge is to develop and maintain the organizational structure in a way that does not threaten but enhances the fellowship of the congregation. While policies and procedures for conducting church business are important and should be implemented, they should be communicated informally and in relational terms, rather than through formalized channels.

Characteristic 3: The small church works as a whole.

When the church acts, it acts as a whole rather than as individual parts. The whole congregation makes decisions rather than a representative few. People desire to know what is going on in every program and ministry even though they are not directly involved. The small church functions as a participatory democracy where everyone wants a voice and wants to be involved in the decision process. Even when the vote is perfunctory, people still demand the right to vote. The ultimate decision making authority resides with the congregation rather than with the board or pastor.

This is especially true regarding the vision and direction of the church. Whereas in the large church, the senior pastor sets the direction of the church, in the small congregation the vision must arise from the people themselves. Rather than the pastor being the vision setter, he becomes the vision facilitator, one who helps and coaches the congregation as they set the agenda for the future.

Characteristic 4: Power and authority reside in the laity rather than the pastor.

The small church is owned and operated by the laity rather than the pastor. Because of this, the pastor is less important to the operation and health of the small church than the larger counterpart. While the pastor may retain the title, the power of the church belongs to the people who have built and operated the church for generations. If the pastor comes into conflict with that authority, then the pastor will often be asked to leave.

The pastor, to be influential, needs to focus upon being a shepherd, friend, and an advisor, rather than attempting to be the administrator and chief executive officer. To be effective, the leader needs to be sensitive to when it is necessary to exert leadership and authority and when it is necessary to allow the people to take the initiative. It is true that the pastor and board members are ultimately accountable to God regarding the spiritual oversight of the congregation, and that often times requires making difficult and sometimes costly decisions. Although we should never compromise biblical truth to avoid confrontation, we should not authoritatively demand that people follow blindly. Leadership is servant leadership, where we sacrifice our own personal agenda and pride for the well being of the whole.

Characteristic 5: The small church relates as a family.

The small church operates as a family. In order to become part of the family, a person must be grafted in. This depth of relationship takes time to develop, thus making it difficult for first timers to be included. If you ask any small church what their community strength is, they probably will say it is their friendliness. Yet, if you ask people who attend for the first time what they disliked about their visit, they may respond that the church lacked personal warmth. This standoffishness is not intentional, but a result of the close-knit community, where people already have their social needs met. They do not feel any need to reach out. While they may greet newcomers after church, or even invite them to lunch, they are unmotivated to spend the time and energy to cultivate an in-depth relationship. New relationships might weaken existing bonds. Consequently, leading the small church involves helping people realize the importance of reaching out to visitors to develop close relationships with them.

While this close unity makes evangelism difficult, once a person is accepted and made a part of the congregation, it is even more difficult to get out. When a person is absent, someone will call and inquire if they are sick. They will be missed and the church will not let go of them without a fight. While it may be hard to get in the front door of the church, it is even harder to slip out the back.

Characteristic 6: Communication occurs through the grapevine.

Everyone knows what is going on because everyone talks about it. The rule of thumb regarding the grapevine is that the smaller the church and more close knit the people, the more the grapevine will be an asset. In such cases, there are no secrets within the church. What is communicated privately will be publicized openly. But that may not be so good when people find out about issues under discussion and form entrenched opinions before the leaders are ready to have the information disseminated. Therefore, open communication is often the best procedure.

On the other hand, the larger the church and the more socially separate, the more likely the grapevine will carry misinformation, requiring clearer and more formal communication on the part of the leadership. If the grapevine becomes a liability to the church, then the leadership needs to develop formalized ways of communication to inform the congregation of issues before they are broadcast on the grapevine.

Characteristic 7: Traditions and heritage undergird the structure, ministry, and culture.

Within the small church, traditions are more than ruts; they are the stories and bonds that tie the present congregation to past generations. Because the small church values both past and current members, traditions play an important role in the life and expression of the church. The people tend to be slow to change, for change breaks apart what was constructed by past members. Each church has a story and each story has a human hero. New people need to learn the stories so they also can highly value the people behind them. Each church has sacred cows that are untouchable. They may be major issues, such as a particular program, or they may be as minor as the time of a service or the place of the pulpit. The reason they are sacred is because they connect to previous generations. The pulpit is sacred because it was built by Fred's great grandfather, one of the founders of the church. To replace the pulpit would be tantamount to forsaking the heritage of the church. The leaders need to identify these sacred cows, discern the reasons they are important, and address needs for change sensitively.

Characteristic 8: The church functions and worships intergenerationally.

Because the congregation is a family, to divide them by age is to split the family. People in the small church not only enjoy being with other family members, they often resent any segregation (other than during the Christian education period). While they may have a separate service for the children, they still want the children present during part of the worship period, not only because they think it is important for the children to sit during the service, but because they enjoy seeing the children sing and participate when the church family gathers to worship God and celebrate the familihood of God's people.

In contrast to secular society, where generations tend to segregate and compete, in the small church each generation looks out for the interest of others. The older generation values the younger people for their new ideas, whereas the younger people value the wisdom and even traditions of those who are older.

Characteristic 9: The focus is upon people rather than performance.

In business management, people are measured by performance. If individuals fail to live up to expectations, their job is given to another. In the small church, the focus shifts to the individual instead of performance. Thus, a person is kept in a particular position even if others are more qualified and would do a better job. If the person fails to be responsible, others quietly do the job and nothing is said. People do not want to hurt the person's feelings by being critical. Even though they may complain about the person's performance, ultimately they continue to overlook it because they value the person.

Because the small church stresses people over performance, the congregation is not goal or task oriented. Those who try to manage by objectives are met with indifference and apathy. People do not belong to the church or come to meetings to be organized and accomplish lofty objectives. They come to be present in the company of their friends and family who share their faith in God. Consequently, the effective leader must focus upon management by relationships. Instead of developing goals to accomplish tasks, the pastor needs to develop people who will minister to others. Instead of finding the most qualified person to fill a particular role, the pastor needs to informally train the people in those positions.

Characteristic 10: There is a place for everyone.

The small church has a place for everyone. Whether it be the mentally slow person who runs the sound system or the retired grandmother who teaches the adult Sunday morning class, everyone is given the opportunity to be involved. Most large churches would gladly have the percentage of participation that often is exhibited in the small church.

One reason so many people are involved is that the small church acts on the premise that involving people is a way of including people. In the larger church, people need to earn the right to be involved by their faithful attendance. In the small church, people are involved in hopes of getting them to faithfully attend.

A second reason is that there is an intense desire to have everyone involved. When filling roles and responsibilities, the church often does not ask who is the best qualified, but who is not involved in any ministry within the church. The idea is that the load needs to be spread around. Like a family where everyone is given a chore around the house, so also the small church seeks to give everyone a task. After all, it is their family responsibility.

Characteristic 11: The small church values relatives.

Because of its size, the small church usually has a higher percentage of people related to other members of the church. This interrelatedness has tremendous impact in the life of the congregation. Key leadership positions are often filled according to bloodlines. Individuals whose family has a long history within the church are often chosen for leadership roles at a younger age than those who do not have such a history. When one individual steps down from the board after serving for many years, that position is given to his son, because the position has traditionally been assigned to his family. Only when there is no younger member, or the younger family member is spiritually carnal, is the position given to another.

Often a person or family dominates because of their blood ties. We will look more at this when we compare church types (see p. 51). Leadership involves working with these individuals in making decisions and setting direction.

Characteristic 12: The small church values generalists.

In an age of specialization, the small church values and utilizes generalists who can do a number of different jobs and responsibilities. Because there are few workers to perform the multiple tasks within the small church, greater value is placed upon leaders who can do a number of things satisfactorily rather than an individual who can do one thing extremely well. The larger the church, the greater the need for specialists. The smaller the church, the more the need for generalists. This not only involves developing competence in a number of areas; it means being willing to do several kinds of tasks. Beyond being a preacher, the pastor also may need to be a Christian education teacher, a youth director, a song leader, and a property caretaker. The people will not value their pastor so much for his expertise in one particular field, as for his willingness and ability to perform a number of different responsibilities. Quality is not measured by how well one performs in one area, but how one performs in a number of areas.

Characteristic 13: There is a place for everyone and everyone has a place.

Place is extremely important in the small church. Like a family that sits in the same place for every meal, so also each person sits in the same place Sunday after Sunday. When someone is absent, everyone notices that their place is empty, and they are missed. Even after their death, their place remains. People will remember the place where Grandma Jones sat. Place is more than a worn spot on a pew; it is a symbol of belonging in the church family, security in a world that is insecure. It becomes part of the memory and story of the congregation.

Place is not only a seating arrangement, but also a place in the ministry of the church. People are never excluded, but are readily accepted into the church. If jobs are not available, jobs will be created. This is not just because there is more than enough work to do, but because the small church operates under the belief that part of belonging is serving. Place is a spot on the pew and a position in the ministry.

Characteristic 14: The small church has its own calendar and timetable.

Every small church functions according to a calendar. This calendar is often seasonal and tied to the employment base for the community. For an agricultural community, summer months are often extremely busy for the farmers. They will avoid commitment to any program, especially from Monday through Saturday. During the winter months they have more time to commit to the ministry. In such a community, programs and ministries that run from October through April will be more successful and effective. Similarly, in ranching communities, the church needs to guard against planning special events during calving season, when ranchers must stay at home to keep an eye on their livestock. Community events such as the county fair may also have a significant influence upon the church calendar.

Characteristic 15: In the small church, people give.

People in the small church have a strong sense of ownership of the church. As a result they are willing to give their time and money to the church. However, they may view giving differently. Instead of a set amount, they may give based upon current needs. When the church struggles financially, they rise to the occasion, giving far more than ten percent. The budget, when it is made, is suggestive rather than determinative. When a need arises, it is met, regardless of whether it fits in the budget. Because of this, the church never is fully solvent. There is always just enough. Yet in the end those in small congregations outgive those in many larger churches. The difference is that they need to be able to see and understand the need. When a missionary comes, they give generously because they immediately identify with the work and understand its problems. When they are asked to give to a program with which they have no personal ownership, the money trickles in.

Understanding Church Types

To understand the small church we must understand its organization. Two factors significantly influence how the church functions. The first relates to its growth patterns, which affects how it views itself. Each church grows differently and the manner in which it grows affects the congregation. The second relates to the organizational model under which it operates.

Growth Types

Small churches are not a downsized version of large churches just as local mom and pop grocery stores are not a downsized version of national supermarkets. But in addition to understanding how the small church differs from its larger counterpart, we must also understand how small churches differ from one another. A problem with classifying churches is failing to consider the uniqueness of each church. Examining the different types enables the leader to better understand his or her own church in order to adapt his or her leadership to the particular setting.

The Enduring Church

Enduring churches will not and cannot experience any significant numerical growth within the congregation. Through no fault of their own, they will always remain small. Yet, even though the church remains small, it endures through the ups and downs and ebbs and flows of ministry. While always on the brink of extinction, it somehow continues to remain open, proclaiming the gospel in the pulpit and through its various, but few, ministries.

There are a number of reasons why a church will not grow, but two exert the most influence:

Population base—If the population of the whole community is nominal and static, opportunities for the church to experience any substantial numerical growth are reduced. This is especially true in rural areas. Although the recent trend to move back to rural areas has brought new life to some churches, many still struggle with the challenge of serving a dying community.

Cultural barriers—A church that serves one particular cultural group in a larger cultural setting may find it difficult to reach people. A Protestant church in a community strongly dominated by Catholicism will find growth difficult not only because of the religious differences but also because of the cultural differences that characterize the forms of worship and styles of organization.

The Growing Church

The growing small church shows moderate to rapid growth (both through conversion and transfers) and is changing from a small church to a medium or large church. In most cases, these churches will be either newly established, located in growing communities, or situated in areas that have a sufficient population base to support a medium to large church. As a rule, the growth will occur shortly after the church is established. In rare cases, a growing church will be located in a rural area.

The Specialized Church

Specialized small churches are those that have the potential for numerical growth but choose to limit growth in order to maintain a specialized focus. They may, for example, be ethnic churches in a community that is largely composed of a specific racial background. While the ethnic church could change and minister to the larger community, doing so would alienate the people they are seeking to serve. Likewise, specialized churches that deliberately seek to minister to those who are drawn to the small church would lose the essential quality to which people are attracted.

> **Important Questions for the Specialized Church**
>
> How will a change in the size of the church affect the people we are serving and the type of people we are reaching?
>
> How will the church maintain its evangelistic efforts while remaining small?
>
> How will the church retain the qualities of a small church should growth occur?

The Stagnant Church

Stagnant churches are churches that have become lethargic and ineffective in ministry. Not only are they not growing, they are no longer striving to minister to the community in which they live. They are marked by an inward, self-absorbed focus of ministry, demonstrating a lack of concern for the spiritual, physical, and emotional needs of others outside the church. They no longer have

---

Indications of a Stagnant Church

There is a lack of passion for evangelism.

Ministry focuses inward, so that resources are devoted to the needs of the congregation, rather than those of the wider community.

Traditions are more important than people.

New people encounter resistance assimilating into ministry and leadership.

There is a lack of obedience to Scripture.

---

any vision or sense of urgency in fulfilling the Great Commission. They are adept at developing and running programs, but inept in producing spirituality in people.

Churches that have reached a plateau or are declining, however, are not necessarily stagnant churches. Nor does numerical growth necessarily reflect a spiritually healthy church. Even a growing church may be failing to achieve the spiritual transformation in the lives of people, which is the core of its ministry and purpose. The final test of a church is not size or numerical growth but the degree to which the congregation is being obedient to the whole teaching of Scripture (Ezek. 2:3–8).

Renewing the stagnant church requires leadership that exemplifies spiritual vibrancy in the leader's own faith. Leaders need to prayerfully consider what the causes of the stagnation are and address them. Bringing healing to an unhealthy church requires time, gentle and loving confrontation, and an unwavering commitment to see the church through the process. Too often pastors who desire to lead healthy churches are not willing to go to the troubled church and bring health to it.

The Declining Church

The declining small church is one that used to be larger but has now declined in membership. Perhaps the single most important factor affecting transitional churches is the changes occurring within the community. A church that was once homogeneous may not be able to cope with the needs of new residents within a community, and as a result they are not able to integrate new people into the church. Decline may occur because of loss of population within the community itself. While stagnant churches may be losing members because of a spiritual problem, the decline may have come for different reasons. It is important for leaders to recognize the difference and minister in an appropriate manner. A danger in the declining church is that people will live in the past rather than seek to remain relevant and committed to the work of the gospel today.

Organizational Types

The organization of a small church deals with how the church functions, its approach toward leadership, its perspective of ministry, and its decision-making. The overarching model is that of a family. Just as a family shares its joys and struggles with mutual concern, so also the congregation joins together with a bond extending beyond age or social boundaries. And just as there are different types of families, so also there are different types of church families.

The Traditional Family

In the traditional family model the husband, wife, and children follow traditional roles handed down by the previous generation. A patriarch or matriarch greatly

---

Working with the Tribal Chief

Recognize the importance of their role and take advantage of their wisdom and knowledge.

Seek their support for programs and proposed changes before they are implemented.

Communicate with them, so that they can help represent needs, issues, and vision to the entire group.

Minister to them by developing their spiritual and leadership abilities.

Make certain that they give others an opportunity to voice their own ideas and opinions. While they are influential, they must not be allowed to intimidate.

The Small Church Family Models

	Traditional Family	Blended Family	Cosmopolitan Family	Ethnic Family
Pastor	instructor, shepherd	guide, assistant in goal setting, shepherd	visionary, spiritual and organizational leader	teacher, someone adaptable to ethnicity
Leaders	determined by family, history	determined by current involvement	determined by vision, ability to set goals	determined by ethnic background
Plans and direction	set by tribal chiefs and congregation	set by pastor and congregation	Set by pastor and board	set by ethnic agenda
Focus of people	traditions that tie this generation with past	traditions and current situation	future-oriented assessment of trends	ethnic heritage
Worship style	traditional	mix, but nothing that pushes limits	contemporary	home culture oriented
Programs	inward focus on the congregation	inward focus with some outward emphasis	outward focus	outward focus within home culture
Evangelism	family and friends	family, friends, near neighbors	unknown masses	within ethnic group
Membership	exclusive— hard to get into, out of	restrictive	inclusive	inclusive within ethnic group
Decisions	made before meetings	made by congregation	made by few; ratified by all	determined by custom
Location	rural	exurban	suburban	
Church life	close-knit	somewhat open	open with few bonds	centered in customs

influences the decisions. The extended family remains important because of bloodline.

Similarly, in a traditional family model for the church, people look to the pastor to provide biblical instruction and pastoral care, but the direction is set by the congregation. Instead of people looking to the pastor to provide key leadership, they look to a tribal chief. This individual (or individuals) is often a matriarch or patriarch who is looked up to by the whole congregation for his or her wisdom, spiritual insight, and character. Often this person has considerable influence, not only because of his or her position within the church but because of his or her position within the dominant family. If this person opposes any idea, it is quickly rejected by the whole congregation.

With this paradigm, tradition plays an important role because it ties the present congregation to the past family members who have built the church. Worship and music follow traditional forms, the church being reluctant to adapt the use of drums and guitars.

Because of close family ties, the church is often hard to get into. To become a part of the family, a new person needs to be "adopted," taking time to build up trust and personal relationships. Until that point, new people may feel on the outside. On the other hand, once a person is "adopted" it is hard for him or her to leave the church since people aggressively act to keep that person in the fellowship. If he or she misses several Sundays, that person will be missed and other members will call to find out why he or she has not attended.

Those in leadership will find it difficult to implement change, even when crucial to effectiveness within the programs. To bring about effective change, the leadership will need to work carefully and strategically to introduce new ideas without threatening past traditions.

The Blended Family

Because the blended family model includes different people from different backgrounds who come together to form a new family, it does not demonstrate the same characteristics as the traditional family. Step-siblings do not share the same values and traits because the backgrounds are different, resulting in tension as the two groups interact.

In much the same way, the blended church setting is one not dominated by one particular individual or family. Instead, people from different backgrounds and traditions are brought together to form the congregation. While culturally homogeneous, they are not as strongly driven by traditions. While some customs remain crucial within the church, these traditions are less pronounced. The blended church is more open to change, but not anything that pushes the edges of acceptability. Programs remain established, although new forms and ideas may be introduced and accepted. The worship service will be somewhat traditional, although contemporary forms may be added as long as they do not replace the older styles. While people will be open for change, they will still be reluctant to change as they still have some ties to the past.

The pastor of the church will have more influence in setting the direction of the church, although the church still will be governed by congregational vote. The pastor will be looked upon to be an instructor and advisor of the various ministries and will be expected to provide some oversight. Those in positions of leadership are chosen because of their past involvement within the church and the length of attendance. While new people may gain leadership positions, it will only be after they have proven themselves over time. Decisions will be made by the whole congregation at the various meetings.

The church will be more open to new members but there are still some restrictions on how quickly people will be placed in positions of leadership. Because the church is not dominated by bloodlines, the pastor and board will have more influence and authority, especially after the pastor has remained in the church for a number of years and built up trust.

The Cosmopolitan Family

The cosmopolitan family model stands at the opposite end of the ministry spectrum from the traditional family church. While the traditional family church remains steadfastly bound to past traditions, the cosmopolitan church is always seeking to push the edges. This church is often located in suburban or urban areas that have a high percentage of baby boomers. It often will be a new church with a higher turnover rate within the congregation, thus lacking any ties to previous generations and their traditions.

The pastor is called upon to be the visionary and program developer with the board. Positions of leadership are assigned to those who have new ideas and the ability to carry them out, so that the congregation is focused on the future rather than the past. Decisions, even when they require ratification by the whole congregation, are made by a representative few. The worship style will be more contemporary with the inclusion of guitars, drums, and upbeat music. Where these instruments are not available, tapes and CDs will be incorporated. The church will be open for new people and will readily accept them as members and elevate them to positions of leadership. Within the programs, more stress will be set upon quality of service than relationships.

The danger confronting the cosmopolitan church is they can become so oriented toward activities, they lose sight of their calling to develop character. The church having a number of programs can be mistaken for demonstrating marks of true spirituality. The task of the leadership is to assure that the congregation maintains their biblical focus and priorities even as they conduct their ministries.

The Ethnic Family

The ethnic family model, in contrast to the other three styles of church organization, is not so influenced by location as by the ethnic background of the congregation and community. This may be a hispanic church in a migrant area or a Polish church in a North Dakota community that was settled by immigrants. How the church chooses its leaders and does its ministry is defined by the ethnic background of the people. The pastor may not have the same ethnic background, but a successful leader will respect and support the ethnic traditions of the people. Those accepted into membership and placed in positions of leadership must often first demonstrate their adherence to the customs of the community. The ethnic church will reach out to people of the same ethnic background.

Ministering within the small church means understanding factors influencing the perspective of the people. Each organizational model has its strengths and weaknesses, and ultimately each church will possess characteristics that are as distinct as a person's fingerprints. By deciphering these broad models, the pastor and leadership can cultivate and challenge the people to move beyond their paradigms to build a biblical perspective that governs all it does.

Understanding the Trends

Ministry is not static, but dynamic. It is not conducted in a sterile test tube, isolated from the winds of culture. Instead, the culture in which we live intertwines with the programs we conduct. As a result, the trends that blow across the cultural landscape infiltrate the cracks of the church and affect the ministry and flow of the congregation. Some of these trends are positive, resulting in new opportunities to reach people for Christ. Others undermine the foundation of the church and, if not confronted, assault the stability of the ministry. Still others are neutral, having in themselves no moral or spiritual implications but radically affecting the manner in which the church conducts its ministry.

While the number of trends and cultural influences confronting the church rapidly and continually changes, six play an important role in defining and influencing the manner in which the church serves its people and its community.

Mobility

People are constantly on the move. Where farmers once tilled only the land in close proximity to their home, now it is common for them to travel thirty to forty miles to reach segments of their farm. In order to benefit from various climates, ranchers have summer and winter ranges in different states. People in small towns will drive to larger cities for their shopping, socializing, and church activities. People in the city will by-pass a number of solid, evangelical churches of varying sizes and denomination to attend the church of their choice. The effect of this movement means that the church, even in rural areas, cannot assume that people will attend just because their doors are open. The church needs to carefully examine whom it desires to reach, what it is doing to attract people, and how it will keep them once they start coming.

Multiple Social Centers

In small towns, the church used to be the social center within both congregation and community. People would pack the church to hear a gospel-singing group or traveling evangelists because it was the only social and entertaining activity around. So many social activities are available now that many feel overwhelmed. For adults there are social clubs such as the Lions; the local volunteer fire department; softball, bowling, and golf leagues. For the children there are swimming meets, little league, junior soccer, Boy Scouts, and Camp Fire Girls. Increased opportunities for social activities, coupled with a decline in leisure time by as much as one-third since the early 1970s, has resulted in the modern family feeling pulled in a number of different directions with little time for church activities.[1] No longer is the church a social center for the community, and now churches struggle to get even their own members to attend special events. Getting the unchurched to attend seems impossible. Consequently, the church has to rethink how it will conduct its evangelistic programs in order to attract new people.

Poverty

Poverty is not just an inner-city problem. The percent of families below the poverty line is approximately the same in rural and non-metropolitan areas as it is in the central city. Between rural and urban areas, however, there is a marked difference in the percentage of poor families who receive welfare. Fifty percent of inner-city families below the poverty line receive assistance compared to only thirty percent of people residing in rural areas.[2] As a result, in smaller communities more emphasis is placed upon community assistance than federal programs. The church needs to be sensitive to the economic needs of people and be willing to assist people as a way of gaining an audience for sharing the gospel of Christ. Social action is not just for the inner-city church; it is for the rural church as well. Food baskets during the holidays, special offerings for needy families, providing presents for children, having clothing exchanges where out-grown clothing can be made available for others, deacon's funds, etc., are all ways that the smaller church can demonstrate the love of Christ and reach people in the surrounding area.

Economic Shifts

Many smaller communities have had a significant change in their economic base. Agriculture and timber no longer supply jobs and industry to support and attract new people. Tourism, industry, and a host of other business opportunities have brought new people and new economic forces to the community. Small towns that were once isolated from larger cities have become bedroom communities, causing a major shift in the mentality and cultural mind-set of the population. Where the populace was once homogeneous, they now find themselves culturally eclectic. The result has been new people with new ideas coming into the church and challenging the established patterns set by the "old timers." The whole congregation needs to demonstrate cooperation as everyone sorts through a menagerie of different ideas concerning music, Bible versions, behavior patterns, and expectations. Everyone needs to focus upon the unity we have in Christ and the importance of being sensitive to the other person's expression of personal faith. The leadership needs to hone their conflict resolution skills as different traditions collide within the programs, worship styles, and ideas.

Population Shifts

In the past one hundred years significant population shifts have changed the way in which the small church conducts ministry. While the percentage of people living on the farm has declined from 39 percent in 1900 to only 1.9 percent in 1991, the number of people living in rural areas has risen from 45 million in 1900 to 68 million in 1990. In the last ten years, the percentage of the population who live in rural areas has risen from 26.3 percent to 27.3 percent, resulting in new evangelistic opportunities for the church.[3] The challenge is to be attractive to people moving into the community and to include them in the life of a congregation that has been dominated by blood lines and tradition. People moving into an area will be more influenced by popular culture than are those who have lived their whole lives in the community. They will have different views about political and social issues, often finding a church unattractive, not because of the theology or programs, but because of the political and social values of members.

The Church Growth Movement

Whether we realize it or not the church growth movement has drastically influenced (both positively and negatively) the landscape of the small church. Positively, it has raised the awareness and importance of outreach and evangelism. It has shown the church the value and necessity of understanding their communities and the thought process of the unsaved. It has assisted the congregation by providing helpful ideas for reaching people with the gospel. Negatively, it has redefined success in ministry so that success, and even spirituality, is measured by the numerical growth rather than the heart and character of people.

As a result of this emphasis on numbers, pastors have become discouraged by the lack of apparent results. People's and the pastor's expectations have changed, so that if numerical growth does not occur, people blame the pastor and the pastor blames the people. While we should recognize the contribution the church growth movement has made, we should guard against its negative influences. We need to be more evangelistic, but we also must see that salvation is ultimately the product of divine initiative, rather than personal efforts. It comes from the convicting work of the Holy Spirit, not excellent programs (1 Cor. 3:3–9). Thus, the focus must shift from the results of evangelism (the responsibility of which is God's) to the process of faithful proclamation (which is the responsibility of people). The critical question is not whether the church is adding to its numbers, but whether people are sharing their faith with their neighbors, friends, and coworkers.

Evaluation and Implementation

1. Complete Worksheet 7 of the Ministry Development Worksheets (appendix A).
2. Draft a three page description of your church, focusing upon the type of church it is, the characteristics and distinctives that mark it, and the way if affects your leadership.
3. Write a short summary answering each of the following questions:

   What factors within your community and church affect the growth potential of the church?

   How is your present church similar to and different from the other churches you have served? From other churches in your area?

   What trends in society, in evangelicalism, and in your community have most affected the church? Why?

Further Reading

McCarty, Doran. *Leading the Small Church*. Nashville: Broadman, 1991.

Pappas, Anthony G. *Entering the World of the Small Church*. Bethesda, Md.: Alban Institute, 1988.

Ray, David. *The Big Small Church Book*. Cleveland: Pilgrim, 1992

Schaller, Lyle E. *The Small Church is Different*. Nashville: Abingdon, 1982.

———. *The Small Membership Church*. Nashville: Abingdon, 1994.

THREE

Developing the Theology of the Church

*B*uilding a healthy ministry is much like building a house. The most crucial step is not knowing how to finish; it is knowing where to begin. Where and how the carpenter begins will dictate the outcome, stability, and beauty of the structure. Without a proper foundation, the house will not be a home, but a death trap, ready to collapse upon the family that sought refuge there.

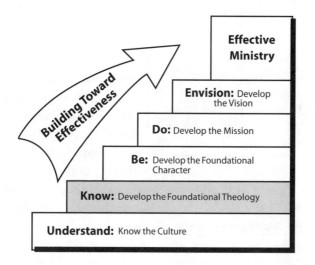

The same is true for the church. Without the right foundation, no matter how right the programs, how dynamic the leadership, or how many principles of church growth are followed, the church is doomed from the outset. Therefore, the most important consideration is the starting point and foundation for the ministry. The question of foundation is equal to that asked by Solomon concerning the foundation for life. Solomon, in the book of Ecclesiastes, focuses upon the struggles of how one builds his or her life. After a life-long search dealing with all the incongruities of life, he concludes that the starting point is to "fear God and keep his commandments" (Eccles. 12:13). The fear of the Lord involves understanding the nature of God and his activity within the affairs of humanity. Without this understanding, life becomes empty, with no meaning, no direction, and no foundation.

The Forgotten Jewel

Much of what is written today concerning ministry development focuses upon the mission, vision, and programs of the church. To be effective, we are told, the pastor must have a clear vision from God for what the church is to become. Usually this vision is couched in the context of numerical growth and program development. The assumption is that to be an effective church, one must have a dynamic seeker-sensitive service, multiple programs and ministries that are directed to the felt needs of people, and a highly visible building. More often

> The theology of a church will have a greater impact upon the future health of the church than will all of the church's programs and strategies.

than not, there is little said regarding the theology and teaching of the church. Nevertheless, the church, without a solid theological and biblical base, no longer has a basis for ministry. A church can survive and be reasonably successful spiritually without a clear understanding of its vision, but it cannot survive shoddy or incorrect theology. Without a biblical theology as a basis, the church is reduced to a social organization that operates programs rather than supports a ministry that challenges the hearts and minds of people with biblical truth. In order to transform people into the image and character of Christ, the church must know something about his image and character.

Defining Theology

In the modern church, theology has been maligned because of misconceptions regarding its nature and purpose. Tragically for many, the word theology conjures up notions of dead speculations and arguments that have nothing to do with either the Bible or daily living. To them, theology is divisive, boring, impractical, and irrelevant to daily life. But correctly understood and applied, theology forms the fabric of consistent Christian living. The term itself comes from the Greek words *theos,* meaning "God" and *logos,* which refers to "discourse, language, or study." Thus, theology is the language of God. It is the discussion that we have regarding him. Theology, in regard to a biblical understanding, includes the study of religion or of man's view of God and the supernatural. More important, however, biblical theology is the study of the God of Scripture as he has revealed himself in both natural and written revelation. Properly studied, biblical theology is unifying and foundational for practical living.

Biblical theology encompasses all four aspects of traditional theology: exegetical, historical, systematic, and practical. To separate one from the other is to undermine the very nature of true theology. While each of these four disciplines may be studied independently for the purpose of academia, one should never be studied in complete isolation from the others. To study systematic theology unrelated to practical living is dead orthodoxy. Practical theology without systematic, exegetical, or historical theology is pop psychology.

The Study of God

Theology is the contemplation of the being, nature, and activity of God and creation's (including humanity's) response to him. Because the church is a spiritual institution, it must think spiritually. Because it is a theological institution, existing in relationship to God, it needs to think theologically. The ultimate task of the church is not to teach people to think rightly about themselves; it is to teach people to think rightly about God.

Since the focal point of the church is the study of God, theology is what unites all churches in a common purpose and ministry. To the degree that a church provides people with a greater understanding of God and our relationship to him is the standard by which the ministry of that church will be judged a success or failure. If the church fails to do so, the church has blundered no matter how apparently successful its programs and rapid its growth.

As the study of God, theology encompasses four critical dimensions of his person:

First, theology is the study of the nature of God. The person and work of God is to be the constant focus of the hearts and minds of people. To think rightly about God, and ultimately about ourselves since we are made in his image, we must have a thorough understanding of the character and being of God. Because knowledge proceeds action, we need to know about God in order to live properly before him.

The lack of understanding of the nature of God has led to trivializing God within the church. God is reduced to manageable deity that is determined by our experience rather than his self-revelation within Scripture. He becomes a cosmic helper to go to in time of need rather than one to whom we must submit our whole life, will, dreams, actions, and desires. The modern man no longer is concerned about who God is. The focus has shifted to who man is; God is someone who serves us rather than someone to whom we render service. Donald W. McCullough warns,

> Any god I use to support my latest cause, or who fits comfortably within my understanding or experience, will be a god no larger than I and thus not able to save me from my sin or inspire my worship or empower my service. Any god who fits the contours of *me* will never really transcend me, never really be God. Any god who doesn't kick the bars out

of the prison of my perceptions will be nothing but a trivial god.[1]

To be accepted by God we need to approach him on his terms, which requires that we understand him. Otherwise we are in danger of reducing God to someone we can manage. To think rightly of ourselves, we must first think rightly of God. Charles Spurgeon showed the depth of his understanding of theology and spirituality when he preached, "The highest science, the loftiest speculation, the highest philosophy, which can ever engage the attention of the child of God, is the name, the nature, the person, the work, the doings, and the existence of the great God whom he calls his Father."[2]

All Christians who desire to mature in Christ must become students of the nature and character of God. The greatest threat to evangelicalism is not the liberalism and secularization of our society; it is the abandonment of the study of the nature of God.

Second, theology is the study of the work of God. God's nature is revealed in his activity. Like a master artist who expresses himself in the paintings he develops, so God reveals his character within the actions he performs. Paul points out that creation is more than a scientific work of God; it is a revelation into the very nature of God so that anyone who looks upon creation discovers enough of God's character to understand his or her need for him (see Rom. 1:20). The actions of God revealed in Scripture are not mere Sunday school stories told to make us feel good. They are the self-revelation of God. Thus, theology encompasses both the character of God and the activity of God. Theology requires that we understand the redemptive work of Christ, for without the understanding of redemption we are stunted in our comprehension of God.

Third, theology is the study of the relationship between God and creation. God is a relational God who is intimately involved within his creation. He has not abandoned the world he formed to run itself; rather he is in constant relationship to it. Because theology is concerned with the totality of the being of God, it cannot bypass the interaction between God and creation. Theology thus explores the purpose of creation in respect to God, the way creation reveals God. It seeks to examine how God made the universe, why he did so, the purpose of its continual existence, and the future that it has.

Fourth, theology is the study of the relationship between God and humanity. We were created in the image of God in order to glorify and serve him (Isa. 43:7). At the core of our existence is the need to love God and be loved by him. When this need is unmet, humanity is driven by despair and hopelessness. To have this need met is to discover the key to genuine peace and joy even in the midst of chaotic and tragic circumstances. The question theology seeks to answer is why this relationship is critical, how to establish and maintain it, and the goal and purpose of it. It is this knowledge that enables the individual and the church to become competent for life and ministry.

A Creed

Necessary for a theological foundation is the establishment of doctrines, creeds, and concrete statements that describe the nature of God and our relationship to him. What has traditionally been called systematic theology involves the orderly arrangement of a coherent statement of belief. While this has increasingly come under criticism in the modern church, it nevertheless has played an important role in the maturation and ministry of the church. From its inception, the church formulated creeds and statements of faith that reflected its understanding of God. The New Testament writers used several different terms to refer to these creeds.

Didaskalia. The term refers to both the act of teaching and the content of what is being taught. Paul uses *didaskalia* to warn Timothy that the time will come when people will not "put up with sound doctrine [*didaskalia*]. Instead, to suit their own desires, they will gather around them a great number of teachers to say what their itching ears want to hear" (2 Tim. 4:3). In other words, people will forsake biblical doctrines with their practical demands and pursue a theology that enables them to live as they choose. Instead of giving in to these individuals, the church needs to uphold the teaching and doctrine of the Scriptures (1 Tim. 4:6; 2 Tim. 4:2). The basis for Paul's conviction was that the doctrines of the church were not the work of men but the outgrowth of divine revelation (2 Tim. 3:16). Consequently, these doctrines needed to be carefully guarded (1 Tim. 4:16) and to serve as the basis for examining one's conduct (1 Tim. 1:10).

Pistis. This word was commonly word used by the New Testament writers to refer to "active trust." *Pistis* was also used to refer to that which is believed, thus the body of faith or doctrine. This usage is reflected in such passages as Romans 1:5; Jude 3; 1 Timothy 1:2–3; Titus 3:15. These creeds are not mere academic statements of the early church; they are the framework from which one builds a coherent worldview. They are not merely doctrines confessed but beliefs that form the foundation of one's values and ethical and spiritual structures. Thomas C. Oden points to the nature of doctrines and creeds:

> Christians who first said *credo* did not do so lightly, but at the risk of their lives under severe persecution. We listen carefully to those who are prepared to sacrifice their lives for their belief. To say *credo* (I believe) genuinely is to speak of oneself from the heart, to reveal who one is by confessing one's essential belief, the faith that makes life worth living. One who says *credo* without willingness to suffer, and if necessary die, for the faith has not genuinely said *credo*.[3]

With the present dearth of theological thinking within the church, one wonders if there is little to live for, much less die for. The biblical doctrines, creeds, and faith of the church must form the core teachings that govern the church and for which the church must be (and was) willing to die.

A Way of Life

Theology has another side. Not only is theology a statement of the church's creeds and beliefs, it is to be the basis of the lifestyle of the individual and the church. Thus, theology is confessions about the person of God as well as the daily outworking of those beliefs in common life. Theology is not theology until it is lived theology, for it is in the daily living of our beliefs that we begin to understand its true meaning. It is in the practice that we begin to discover the joy of who God is and what he has done for us in Christ.

Theology is reflected in obedience. The apostle Paul, in writing to the Romans, states that obedience comes from one's beliefs: "Through him and for his name's sake, we receive grace and apostleship to call people from among all the Gentiles to the obedience that comes from faith" (Rom. 1:5). What we believe about God will determine how we act before God.

The importance of lived theology is further highlighted by the teaching of Scripture concerning the "wise" individual. Wisdom is what enables the individual to live life successfully—success defined not by the world's definition, but God's. Wisdom involves the ability to know how to act and react within the context of the "fear of the LORD" (Prov. 1:7; 9:10; 15:33). Hence, the understanding of God's integrity and justice results in honesty (Prov. 20:23), justice (Prov. 17:15), and truthfulness (Prov. 12:22) on the part of man. The true sage is one who understands the character of God and lives in harmony with that character as it has been revealed in the order of creation and biblical revelation.

Theology is the basis for spirituality. Much of what is written today divorces spirituality from theological content so that spirituality becomes experiential and subjective. While many elements of spirituality result in subjective and experiential expressions of faith (but not necessarily always), it is nonetheless crucial to realize that spirituality must be based upon biblical and theological truth. The ultimate goal is not to have emotional experiences that enthrall the soul but to "take hold of that for which Christ Jesus took hold of me" (Phil. 3:12). It is to "know Christ and the power of his resurrection and the fellowship of sharing in his sufferings, becoming like him in his death, and so, somehow, to attain to the resurrection from the dead" (Phil. 3:10–11). We find God, not by looking at the depth of our experiences but by the study and application of biblical truth and theology.

Donald McCullough's warning is well heeded: "We do not find God by looking deep within ourselves or by following our best instincts or by heeding our consciences or by listening to a 'still small voice.' Navel-gazing—even spiritual navel-gazing reveals nothing but navels."[4] To act Christianly we must think Christianly.

If spirituality involves maintaining an intimate relationship with God so that we are being transformed into the character of Christ, then theology becomes the basis by which we understand who God is. Spirituality is lived theology. Thus, the church is to be a place where people are not only taught to *think* Christianly, but also to *live* Christianly.

Theology is the basis for the purpose of the church. In Matthew 22:37–40, Christ outlines the purpose of the church by describing the heart and character of his people. The church, to fully attain what God has called it to be, should be marked by genuine love for God and love for people. All that is to characterize the church is summarized in these two commandments: Love God, love your neighbor.

To fulfill its purpose to love God requires that the church maintain authentic worship. Worship is much more than experiential entertainment. Worship is reflection and exalting the nature and activity of God (Ps. 138). By praising God and worshiping him, people gain a greater perspective and understanding of life and its apparent incongruities (Ps. 73:15–17). But without sound theology, the church has no foundation for praise. Rather, worship is reduced to empty emotionalism. On the other hand, true theological reflection should always result in praise as the individual becomes captivated by the God revealed in Scripture.

The basis for fulfilling the church's purpose to love your neighbor is not found in sociological or cultural agreements; it is found in the nature of God and our relationship to him. Our union with Christ brings the spiritual demand for unity with the believers (1 John 1:3–4). The motivation and foundation for this harmony is the fellowship within the triune God (John 17:21).

The Necessity of Theology

Theology, as the source of true wisdom, becomes the foundation from which ministry is built. It is theology, not ministry philosophy, that ultimately provides the backbone of the Christian community. Thus, theology holds importance for many reasons.

First, theology is essential for faith. The heart of fruitfulness is not the formation of the right program, but the establishment of a living and dynamic theology. While theology as the foundation has been much maligned, it nevertheless stands as the cornerstone for the church. Without proper theological undergirding, the church loses the basis for developing a ministry that has eternal significance. A proper theological mind-set is central to maintaining the essence of faith (1 Peter 1:13). Carl F. H. Henry warns that without theology the church no longer has any basis nor content for its faith:

> The loss of that Biblical heritage means the loss of one's soul, the loss of a stable society, and the loss of an intelligible universe as well. The intellectual suppression of God in His revelation has precipitated the bankruptcy of a civilization that turned its back on heaven only to make its bed in hell.[5]

Second, theology is necessary for divine fellowship. In the mind of Paul, fellowship with God is not just an emotional experience whereby one makes a redemptive confession of Christ. Genuine fellowship is the intimate, personal knowledge of God (Philippians 3:8–11). This knowledge is the personal response to the self-revelation of God in Christ and surpasses all worldly achievements Paul had attained. To forsake the pursuit of the knowledge of God, which is the essence of theology, is to lose close fellowship with him. To maintain our spirituality and spiritual conduct, we need to maintain a clear focus upon the person, nature, and activity of God, which stands at the heart of Christian theology.

Third, theology is essential for godly living. Without a proper theology we fall prey to our corrupt nature. The fool in Proverbs is not one who lacks intellect or even common sense, but one who acts and reacts to the affairs of life without any awareness or consideration of God and his order within creation. The fool is the one who says there is no God (Ps. 14:1), going about his or her life governed by his or her own conscience (Prov. 12:15; 28:26) rather than being governed by the reflection of God's nature and demands upon humanity. The fool "is one that hath lost wisdom, and right notion of God and divine things which were communicated to man by creation; one dead in sin, yet one not so much void of rational faculties as of grace in those faculties, not one that wants reason, but abuses his reason."[6]

To forsake theological reflection is to allow the corrupt human nature to regain control over one's life and conduct—to become, in the writings of Proverbs, a fool. This same theme of godliness based on theology continues in the New Testament, where the writers continually base Christian living on the theological understanding of salvation (see Col. 3:1–17).

Fourth, theology is essential for guidance. When the church sacrifices theological reflection for therapeutic, man-centered contemplation, we lose the foundation for determining our conduct and practice. True spirituality is found in an understanding of who God is and how we are to respond to him individually and corporately. Anything less becomes humanism in sheep's clothing. Without a biblical theology, the church no longer has a teacher for how to conduct itself individually and corporately (2 Tim. 3:16–17). Techniques, programs, and simplistic answers then replace a spirituality based upon the

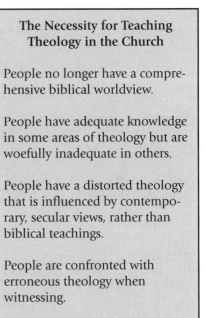

The Necessity for Teaching Theology in the Church

People no longer have a comprehensive biblical worldview.

People have adequate knowledge in some areas of theology but are woefully inadequate in others.

People have a distorted theology that is influenced by contemporary, secular views, rather than biblical teachings.

People are confronted with erroneous theology when witnessing.

People become confused by the claims of conflicting theologies.

knowledge of God. David Wells is prophetic when he calls the church to regain a Christian practice built upon the pillars of confession (i.e., what has been crystallized into doctrine):

> Theology involves the cultivation of those virtues that constitute a wisdom for life, the kind of wisdom in which Christian practice is built on the pillars of confession and surrounded by the scaffolding of reflection. And yet this formation is too simple, for what I have in mind is a kind of spirituality that is now exceedingly rare—the kind of spirituality that is centrally moral in its nature because God is centrally holy in his being, that sees Christian practice not primarily as a matter of technique but as a matter of truth, and that refuses to disjoin practice from thought or thought from practice.[7]

He goes on to warn,

> As the nostrums of the therapeutic age supplant confession, and as preaching is psychologized, the meaning of Christian faith becomes privatized. At a single stroke, confession is eviscerated and reflection reduced mainly to thought about one's self. That being the case, the responsibility of seeking to be a Christian in the modern world is then transformed into a search for what Farly calls a "technology of practice," for techniques with which to expand the church and master the self that borrow mainly from business management and psychology.[8]

Without the guidance of theology, sin becomes a "paradigm" needing to be shifted and evangelism becomes a "marketing strategy." Practice (individual and corporate) is no longer grounded in and guided by the nature and character of God. No longer does the church have a footing on which to grapple with and answer the complex social problems and issues that confront modern society.

Fifth, theology is necessary for a proper worldview. Secularization is the divorce of faith from everyday life. What people do on Sunday has little to do with how they live through the rest of the week. The reason for encroaching secularization is that people no longer have a consistent worldview governed by biblical truth. Instead, their lives are compartmentalized. Faith in God has no impact on secular actions and attitudes. The church needs to teach people how to act and think Christianly, not just in regard to their church involvement but also in all aspects of life. The Christian faith is to have an impact on how we perform duties at work (Eph. 6:5–9). Theology should mark relationships with our neighbors (Col. 4:5; 1 Thess. 4:12), spouses (Eph. 5:22–33), children (Eph. 6:1–4), and fellow members of the body of Christ (1 Cor. 12). It should salt our speech (James 3:1–12), and our attitudes (James 1:2).

Assessing Theological and Spiritual Health

Theology is more than just a byword of seminary students; theology is central to the health and well-being of the congregation. Therefore, it is necessary for leadership to evaluate the theological basis of their churches. The task of leadership is not to allow theology "to just happen," but to deliberately formulate and guide the church in the development of biblical theology that governs both congregational and individual life. Doing so requires the leadership to continually have their finger upon the theological pulse of the church.

Misconceptions

In determining a church's theological and spiritual health, however, it is a common mistake to judge the congregation by external marks that focus on outward actions rather than the inward heart. While it is true that the inner character of people will be manifested by the outward acts (James 2:14–17), it is not true that the outward acts always reveal the inward reality. The difficulty in assessing a church's corporate spirituality and theological integrity is that these two dimensions, properly understood, deal with the internal attitudes and motives of the individuals who make up the community.

Instead of measuring the spirituality of the church by an external standard of behaviors, leadership and community must measure the spirituality of the congregation by examining the inward qualities of godliness. Are the people within the church moving toward the person of Christ, manifesting his qualities in thought and action? If a church becomes stagnant or begins to move away from the reality of God's presence, then the church is no longer spiritual or theological, no matter how doctrinally correct it may be or how faithfully it adheres to a "biblical" code of outward conduct.

Nor are theology and spirituality related to numerical growth. The assumption often has been made that churches growing numerically are the more spiritually fit, and that churches that are not growing or are declining have lost touch with genuine spirituality. Paul, however, makes it clear in 1 Corinthians 3 that the growth of ministry is the sovereign work of a gracious God, not a reward for being "more spiritual."

Another misconception is that spirituality can be measured by doctrinal correctness. The church in Ephesus, according to John in Revelation 2:1–7, was marked by doctrinal purity, yet they still were in danger of being judged severely by God for they had lost their first love (i.e., genuine spirituality). While doctrinal purity and correct biblical theology are important they do not affect the spirituality of the church until they dictate practice.

Marks of a Theological and Spiritual Church

The measure of theological correctness is ultimately determined by the character of the congregation. Spirituality is the inward state of the people, demonstrated through outward behavior. Thus, in surveying the spirituality and theology of the church, one begins by examining the values that distinguish the congregation. Values are the behaviors and attitudes that people desire to or are expected to manifest, the inward qualities that determine how the congregation acts as a whole and as individuals. Values may be expressed or unexpressed; they may be biblical or unbiblical, based upon the culture of the community or the subculture of the church itself. The task of the leadership is to examine the actions of the community and prayerfully analyze the core values that these actions reveal. The leadership must then determine which are the core values that need to mark the church and seek to ingrain these values so that they replace unbiblical ones.

When examining the spirituality of the congregation, the leadership needs to be sensitive, too, to the people's awareness of God's presence and guidance, manifested in the corporate prayer life. Genuine prayer is not seeking God's rubber stamp of approval upon our ministries; rather it is seeking divine strength, empowerment, and wisdom to accomplish God's ministry. It is the recognition of God's sovereignty, of his sufficiency, of his availability. It is a reflection of our understanding of both his transcendent and immanent nature. To build the ministry and spirituality of the church, the leadership needs to manifest and build within the church a solidarity of prayer and a unification that is centered on individual and corporate prayer.

The spirituality of the church is also demonstrated in genuine and authentic worship of God within the life of the congregation. Worship is the essence and expression of faith; for worship is a reflection of our understanding of the person of God and what he has done for us. The greater the awareness of God's presence within the congregation, the greater becomes the display of worship. Thus leadership needs to facilitate and lead the community in worship. Spiritual ministry will point people to the person, nature, and being of God. One way to assess the effectiveness of any ministry is to ask whether or not it is drawing people's focus, in submission and praise, toward the person of God.

A church that is spiritual and theological will have a solid scriptural and doctrinal understanding that undergirds its faith and practice. Therefore all the various ministries should provide solid biblical teaching that seeks to support and reinforce the Scriptures as the sole authority for life and godliness. To facilitate people's spirituality, the church aids people in cultivating a view of the Bible reflected in Psalm 119. As a result, people will see the Word of God as the foundation for avoiding sin (vv. 9–16), dealing with discouragement and adversity (vv. 25–32), guidance in life (v. 105), and as a basis for fellowship with God (v. 176).

Authentic spirituality involves loving relationships. An examination of Scripture reveals that interpersonal relationships are not just an anthropological pursuit but a theological concern as well. The book of 1 John reflects upon the theological implications of our redemption as it relates to interpersonal relationships. Because God demonstrates his love in Christ's sacrifice, we are under obligation to love others sacrificially (1 John 3:16). The nature of God's love defines our understanding of relationships. Consequently, the failure to love others is a theological problem concerning our understanding of the nature and person of God and what he has done for us.

While additional indicators of the spiritual and theological condition of a church could be cited, the point for the church leadership is that they must assess and build the theology and spirituality of the church if the church is to be effective in ministry. There are no shortcuts in these significant areas. One may compromise in organizational structuring; a church may be weak in developing objectives, goals, and planning; a church may be unclear of its vision and still be effective. But a church cannot afford to be spiritually and theologically anemic. No amount of organizational structuring can overcome the lack of genuine and in-depth godliness within the congregation. The church leadership is responsible for keep their fingers on this pulse of theology and spirituality (see Heb. 13:17) and to evaluate the church based upon an understanding of the importance of these dimensions. When we lose sight of their importance, then the church is doomed no matter how great the programs.

Developing the Theology of the Church

Establishing a biblical theology involves a four step process in which the congregation is taught the elements of doctrine. As in the case of all discipleship, the instruction should be intentional, systematic, and focused upon the practical implementation of the truths communicated.

Step one: Develop theological thinking in the leadership of the church.

Formulating the theological foundation for the church begins with the leadership. Leadership should be based upon correct theology and the role it plays within the congregational life. Training for leadership should focus upon both the spiritual qualifications of the leader as well as foundational doctrinal truths. This is not to say that all leaders need to have formal training, but they should have enough understanding to be able to evaluate and develop ministries consistent with sound doctrine.

Step two: Develop teaching strategies for the four-fold nature of theology.

Instruction, to be complete, needs to provide the elements of exegetical, biblical, systematic, and practical theology. Failure to teach all four ultimately results in a distorted perspective.

Exegetical Theology

Instructing the congregation involves not only teaching them from Scripture, but also teaching them how to study and interpret the Bible. It is often assumed that people know how to properly interpret the Word of God. More often than not, people approach Scripture with the perspective of "spiritual quips" rather than a coherent, developed message. The goal of teaching the congregation exegetical theology is to train them to see the message of the Bible in its cultural, historical, and grammatical context. The church needs to teach people how to read a portion of Scripture in its immediate context, in the context of the book in which it is found, and ultimately within the context of the whole Bible. Readers need instruction in doing both word studies and topical studies.

Biblical Theology

Developing the context of the whole Bible involves an understanding of its total teaching. Although biblical theology is a branch of exegetical theology, it cannot be adequately covered in a series on hermeneutics. Therefore, teaching should be provided with the goal of giving an overview of the continuity found within Scripture. This teaching should deal with the relationship between the Old and New Testaments, and the relationship between the people of Israel, and the covenants, and the church. Biblical theology includes understanding the major themes of Scripture, identifying the correlation between the covenants, etc., all of which are included in a well-rounded study of biblical theology.

Systematic Theology

This branch of theology deals with the formation of a logical, consistent understanding of the teachings of Scripture related to the various studies found within systematic theology. The goal of a developed systematic theology is not to provide academic and philosophical arguments and conclusions. Rather the goal is to provide people with a coherent understanding of God and his creation so that they can develop a consistent worldview that governs their thoughts and actions. To provide this view, the church should offer introductory classes as well as continually teach on more complex issues related to systematic theology. Furthermore, issues related to systematic theology can be taught to children so that they might build a consistent, biblical worldview that provides a foundation for developing an understanding of the world in which they live. Teaching systematic theology should include a study of major areas of theological study such as theology proper, soteriology, eschatology, ecclesiology, anthropology, christology, and pneumatology.

Practical Theology

All doctrinal teaching should be done in conjunction with practical theology. Rather than seeing practical theology as a totally separate division of study (i.e., what is now often covered in discipleship classes), it should be joined with the other disciplines, that is, each branch of theology should be taught with practical application. Nevertheless, the church can teach special courses dealing with the practical disciplines of the Christian life necessary for growing in maturity. Practical theology focuses upon areas such as spirituality and spiritual disciplines. It includes, too, the identification and development of spiritual gifts, understanding and implementing leadership skills, and developing a biblical perspective of marriage, family, work, political action, leisure, and relationships.

Step three: Preach theologically.

By this we mean that every sermon and every principle drawn and applied should be theologically based. That is, practice should be an outgrowth of the biblical teaching and understanding of God. It is tragic that theological preaching does not always take place. One study of two hundred evangelical sermons revealed that only 20 percent of the sermons were grounded in or related to the nature, character, and will of God. The responsibility of the preacher is to continually communicate the theological basis for the principle he or she is teaching. If a principle is not rooted in the character and activity of God, then the preacher needs to either rethink the principle or reevaluate how it is being communicated.

Step four: Provide people opportunities to express their theology.

The theology of the church is reflected in its prayer life, worship, and service. Prayer is not just a reflection of our need; it is a reflection of our theology. To foster the prayer life of the church, there should be times when prayer is the focal point, such as concerts of prayer and a twenty-four hour day of prayer.

Every worship service should be evaluated by its effectiveness in pointing people to the person and activity of God. While the worship service may entertain, it should not be merely entertainment. While it demands human participation and may address human needs, it should not draw attention to humanity. Instead, it should always draw attention to God.

A theology of service is built upon the expression of one's understanding of God and his redemptive work in the lives of people.

People need to be taught that service is not merely a duty but an expression of worship. As such, it is a reflection of the church's theological understanding of who God is. While the task of the church is to teach sound theology, it should also develop opportunities for people to serve in order for them to respond to their theology.

Evaluation and Implementation

1. Complete Worksheet 8 with the board (see appendix A).
2. Identify one or two key theological issues that need to be addressed within the church and develop a strategy for training in this area.
3. Outline a strategy for teaching theology within the church.
4. How has secularism affected our worldview and how can the church correct this impact and develop a Christian worldview that is grounded in sound theology?
5. How does theology form the basis for daily living? How can theology be taught to encourage Christian living?

Further Reading

Armstrong, John H. *The Coming Evangelical Crisis.* Chicago: Moody, 1996.

Guinness, Os, and John Seel. *No God but God.* Chicago: Moody, 1992.

McDermott, Gerald R. *See God: Twelve Reliable Signs of True Spirituality.* Downers Grove, Ill.: InterVarsity, 1995.

Moreland, J. P. *Love Your God with All Your Mind.* Colorado Springs, Colo.: NavPress, 1997.

Wells, David. *No Place for Truth.* Grand Rapids: Eerdmans, 1993.

FOUR

$\mathcal{D}$eveloping the $\mathcal{C}$haracter
of the $\mathcal{C}$hurch: $\mathcal{L}$oving $\mathcal{G}$od

$\mathcal{T}$he ministry of the church stands or falls, not by the programs, but by the character of the church. When assessing the church, often the focus is placed upon the number, variety, and nature of the programs. Numbers, bucks, and ministries are counted. If the spirituality of the church becomes weak, however, then the ministry will be greatly hindered, with little or no eternal accomplishments achieved.

When discipling new converts, the focus belongs on developing character. The process of discipleship involves teaching the individual to be like Christ in mind and heart. The ultimate test of the Christian faith is not what one does but what one becomes. Without the inward reality, the Christian life is reduced to external legalism that destroys genuine faith and the intimate relationship with God that stands at the heart of the gospel message.

Becoming a Character-Driven Church

A church without godly character is an empty shell of the gospel, void of the true meaning of the biblical message of Christ's redemptive work in the lives of people. Throughout Scripture, the community of God's people is likened to a living body. The essence of the body is not its outward appearance, but its inward life. A spirit can survive without a body, but a body cannot survive without a spirit. So, too, the spiritual nature of the church can endure without programs, strategies, and marketing but the church, with its plans, ministries, and duties, cannot live without the spiritual life that comes through an intimate relationship with God. A church without character becomes a social institution—not the living organism that God intends. The sage warns, "Above all else, guard your heart, for it is the wellspring of life" (Prov. 4:23). The heart of the church is the wellspring for the vitality of the congregation. The true Christ-centered church is a character-driven church.

When Martha and Mary sat at the feet of Jesus, they each had different ideas about what was to engage their lives and mark their relationship with the Savior. For Martha, the focus was upon activities and duties. She set about filling her life with tasks and responsibilities, resenting Mary because she was little concerned about external goals. Instead, Mary sought to remain at Jesus' feet and absorb his teachings. For Mary, being taught by Christ and being changed inwardly was far more important. When Martha's agitation grew to the point where she could no longer stand it, she demanded that Christ rebuke Mary for her lack of activity. Jesus' response must have surprised and, perhaps, confused Martha: "Martha, Martha," the Lord answered, "you are worried and upset about many things, but only one thing is needed. Mary has chosen what is better, and it will not be taken away from her" (Luke 10:41–42). This gentle rebuke was not a condemnation of her desire to make a meal but was a refutation of her idea that activities were more important than inward devotion. The term translated "distraction" (NIV) in verse 40 means "to be pulled or dragged away," the implication being that Martha, perhaps herself wanting to sit and listen to Christ, felt the pressures of providing hospitality so that she was dragged away from what was important in order to pursue the insignificant. Christ, therefore, reminded her that the most important priority was not the preparation of food, but the preparation of the heart.

If the church is not careful, it can easily fall prey to the same temptation and snare. We can become so involved in doing the business and ministry of the church that we neglect the importance of developing godly character, which springs forth from intimacy with God. We can easily become distracted by the insignificant. To avoid this we must reaffirm the priority of character development.

Character Determines Priorities

Israel was on the threshold of the promised land. In the days that would follow, they faced a significant and disruptive transition in leadership. Moses, who had led them for over forty years, was stepping down and Joshua was to assume leadership. Additionally facing them was a major change in entering the land. Not only would they have the responsibility of driving out the people before them, but also they had to establish new cities, new forms of government, industries, social activities, homes, places of worship, and a host of other tasks confronting a people settling into a new region as a new nation. The priority list of Israel would have filled many clay tablets. In Deuteronomy 10:12–13, under the inspiration and guidance of God, Moses outlined for them the priorities they were to maintain while settling in the land: "And now, O Israel, what does the LORD your God ask of you but to fear the LORD your God, to walk in all his ways, to love him, to serve the LORD your God with all your heart, and with all your soul, and to observe the LORD's commands and decrees that I am giving you today for your own good."

Israel, then, was to focus upon character development rather than building a nation. The responsibility of developing a new nation was secondary to the importance of becoming a people who manifested genuine love for God.

Character development remains the focus of the church because our character influences how we use our time, resources, energies, and finances. What the church believes, the values it upholds, the character it manifests will significantly determine what the church does. Without genuine godliness within, there exists a great gulf between what the church says it believes and what the church actually does in its practices and actions.

Paul warns of the dangers of trying to develop programs, ministries, and plans without the foundation of character. After his extensive treatment of the various gifts within the church and the interdependency that is to exist between each member of the congregation, he points out that all these are of no value without love (see 1 Corinthians 13). He concludes, "And now these three remain: faith, hope and love. But the greatest of these is love" (v. 13). Without the foundation of character all our activities can become misguided and our priorities distorted.

Character Is the Church's Concern

The ultimate responsibility of the church is not to develop programs and ministries but to transform the inward character of people so that they manifest the character of Christ. The mandate of the church is to "make disciples" (Matt. 28:19). Disciples are people who exhibit the marks of Christ in their lives. The programs of the church are to be designed to impart godliness in order to change people's character. While programs are necessary, it should never be forgotten that programs are the means to the end, not the end itself. Paul writes to those in Corinth that he desires to present them before God with purity and godliness: "I am jealous for you with a godly jealousy. I promised you to one husband, to Christ, so that I might present you as a pure virgin to him" (2 Cor. 11:2). For Paul, ministry was not just about getting converts but bringing people to Christ so they might be transformed inwardly before

Christ. The message of Christ focuses upon character transformation: "For the grace of God that brings salvation has appeared to all men. It teaches us to say 'No' to ungodliness and worldly passions, and to live self-controlled, upright and godly lives in this present age, while we wait for the blessed hope—the glorious appearing of our great God and Savior, Jesus Christ, who gave himself for us to redeem us from all wickedness and to purify for himself a people that are his very own, eager to do what is good" (Titus 2:11–14). When we experience the salvation of God, we escape the clutches of Satan and the tragedy of hell. But just as important, we become changed inwardly through a personal relationship with Christ in order to be holy and blameless before him (Eph. 1:4; Col. 1:22). The purpose of the church is to actively and intentionally seek to change people.

Character Determines God's Blessings

In Psalm 24:3–5, David, a man of in-depth character, sings, "Who may ascend the hill of the LORD? Who may stand in his holy place? He who has clean hands and a pure heart, who does not lift up his soul to an idol or swear by what is false. He will receive blessing from the LORD and vindication from God his Savior." God pours out his blessing upon those who possess godly character. Within the Old Testament the people mistakenly thought that God's blessings were contingent upon sacrifices and religious rituals. Through the prophets God reminded Israel that it was not the external forms but the inward reality that formed the basis for God's favor. Even today, we can mistakenly think our activities within the church will bring about God's favor and blessing upon the church. It is often assumed that if we only develop the right program then we will experience numerical growth and spiritual renewal. Programs without character, however, are like sacrifices without obedience. They mean little and accomplish nothing. To enjoy the benefits of God's favor, the church needs to manifest the character of Christ within the whole congregation and the individual ministries within the church. John condemns the church in Sardis because they, like many today, had a great reputation for activities but no heart (Rev. 3:1–6). Christ's evaluation of the church is that "I have not found your deeds complete in the sight of my God." Ministries require character to be approved and blessed by God.

Character Supports Effective Leadership

Much has been written about leadership, but it is unfortunate that most of the focus has been upon the performance and duties of leadership rather than the heart and character of those who aspire to lead. Today the emphasis is upon credentials and accomplishments rather than character and godliness. People are enamored with the number of degrees, the volumes of books, the name-recognition of the individual, and a host of other accomplishments. But Paul, in assessing the foundation for leadership within the church, points to individual character (1 Tim. 3:1–13; Titus 1:6–8). Joseph Stowell summarizes the importance of character:

> But focusing on credentials and ignoring the process will ultimately, though perhaps unwittingly, erode the platform of respect by leading us to compromise our character. As leaders it's easy to compromise the effectiveness of our ministry by making choices in ministry based on whether or not our own standing in regard to praise, profile, or prosperity will be elevated. Shepherds, however, who resist the temptation to violate the process of character for the gain of credentials, strengthen the platform from which they minister.[1]

Character is what validates leadership within the church. When leaders lack godly character, they will ultimately misuse authority and position to the detriment of the congregation.

Character Motivates Service

When character drives our ministry, then our service to the church is no longer a duty but a privilege, no longer a drudgery but a joy. The apostle Paul was well acquainted with the pains, struggles, triumphs, sorrows, joys, and problems of ministry. He knew what it was like to be rejected, misjudged, criticized, and mistreated. Yet in all this, Paul remained driven to ministry so that quitting was unthinkable. What motivated him were not the rewards, the recognition, or the approval of men; rather it was his love for Christ. Paul writes in 2 Corinthians 5:14, "For Christ's love compels us, because we are convinced that one died for all, and therefore all died."

While it is unclear whether the love mentioned is love for Christ or Christ's love for us (or perhaps both), it was clear that the inward character of Paul drove him to preach the gospel. Everyone in ministry, whether pastor or layperson, will encounter difficulties and problems. While both lay and professional ministry has incredible joys and triumphs, it also has overwhelming discouragement. What sustains a congregation through the ups and downs will be the inward qualities of each person. When people are not driven by godly character and by God's power working through them, then they will not have the resources to sustain them. They will quickly burn out, rapidly becoming discouraged when outward success and achievements are not attained. When God's people are motivated by godly character we realize the joy is in serving, not in the accomplishments of great and mighty things. When God accomplishes great things through a church's ministries, the entire congregation can be thankful for what he has done. When things are difficult and ministry hard, we can all still rejoice because we have the privilege of serving. When God called Ezekiel to serve the rebellious people of Israel, God makes it clear that Ezekiel had to be sustained in his ministry through godly character, which comes from obedience to God's Word (Ezek. 2:3–3:15). Because it was character rather than accomplishments that motivated Ezekiel in ministry, God would make him "as unyielding and hardened as they are. I will make your forehead like the hardest stone, harder than flint. Do not be afraid of them or terrified by them, though they are a rebellious house" (Ezek. 3:8–9). The motivation of the church to perform the mission and vision of the church will be directly related to the character manifested by each member of the congregation.

The Meaning of Character

The writer of Hebrews states that one of the responsibilities of leadership of the church is to keep watch over the congregation "as men who must give an account" (Heb. 13:17). In other words, God will hold the elders of the church responsible for the spiritual health and vitality of the congregation. To accomplish this health and vitality, leaders need to properly understand what spirituality is. Spirituality involves a personal relationship with God based upon an understanding of whom God is, how he acts, and how we are to respond to him (i.e., true theology) as revealed in our character. To evaluate the heart of the congregation we need to understand what character is.

Character is the distinctive nature of the individual that serves to govern his or her activities and attitudes. Character involves our moral ethos, our personality, values, and behaviors. Character involves the inward condition of one's soul and spirit. Character is formed by one's understanding of God and the appropriate response to him. It is the correlation between spirituality and inward being and nature. When we speak of spirituality we are referring to a relationship with God as it is revealed in character and actions. The writer of Scripture expressed character as being transformed into the nature and character of Christ. Godliness comes when Christ is dwelling within (Eph. 3:17) so that a person develops the same attitude and mind-set exhibited by Christ (Phil. 2:5). Paul writes that the purpose of God's redemptive work is to transform us into the nature and image of Christ: "For those God foreknew he also predestined to be conformed to the likeness of his Son" (Rom. 8:29). This process of character transformation is not accomplished instantaneously at the moment of salvation. The transformation involves a lifelong process in which the Holy Spirit continues to work within our lives. Paul writes, "Not that I have already obtained all this, or have already been made perfect, but I press on to take hold of that for which Christ Jesus took hold of me" (Phil. 3:12).

The task of the church is to take part in the process. While God is the ultimate cause of all character transformation (Phil. 1:6), he utilizes the church to accomplish the task and he holds the leadership of the church accountable for evaluating and assessing the progress the people are making. When a church no longer manifests the character of Christ in all its attitudes, actions, and plans, then it no longer remains vital to the kingdom of God and is in danger of being removed by God (Rev. 2:4–5).

The Nature of Character

The key question in evaluating the church is, "What qualities are we to look for in order to assess the congregation?" Christ himself has given us the key to assessing the heart of the church: "'Love the Lord our God with all your heart and with all your soul and with all your mind.' This is the first and greatest commandment. And the second is like it: 'Love your neighbor as yourself.' All the Law and the Prophets hang on these two commandments" (Matt. 22:37–40). In the evaluation of Christ, love forms the moral backbone for all character and action. From these two commands all the laws of God find their source and meaning. This love is not the emotional giddiness or experiential feelings that often characterize our view of relationships and spirituality today. Instead, this love is the determination of the will that dictates and transforms all our actions and attitudes. Without this commitment, all expressions of spirituality, morality, and personal action become plagued with self-centered motivations. The task of the church is to instill this horizontal and vertical expression of love. Evaluating the church's character involves the evaluation of its love for God and its love for people. All that is to mark the church and govern its ministries are summarized in these two commandments: Love God, love your neighbor.

The Essence of Character

Character begins with our relationship with God. Theology addresses not just the mind; it should penetrate and transform the will. Love in the Old Testament was more than just an emotional response to God; it was to enter into a covenantal relationship with him. It was the response that one was to give God as the suzerain, acknowledging his holiness and supremacy over the affairs of humanity. The measure of love, then, was found in the obedience of the will to the law of God that is revealed in Scripture. The essence of this love is measured by people's loyalty to God through exclusive worship (Deut. 6:13–15; John 4:24), complete dependency (Ps. 32:6; 1 Thess.

5:17), and uncompromising obedience to his law (Deut. 15:5; John 14:15).

Loving God Through Worship

The church that loves God is a church that worships him. Christ emphasized the importance of worship as an integral part of our relationship with him: "A time is coming and has now come when the true worshiper will worship the Father in spirit and truth, for they are the kind of worshipers the Father seeks. God is spirit, and his worshipers must worship in spirit and in truth" (John 4:23–24). In worship, the people of God respond, both individually and corporately, to the nature and being of God.

The contemporary literature stresses that the church, to be effective, must have a dynamic worship service with a worship team, praise choruses sung off overhead projectors, with a contemporary style of music. Yet for many small churches, such worship is impractical (it is hard to sing choruses with a guitar when no knows how to play, and the pianist has the ability to only play in one tempo: slow), and it can be destructive if it forces people to worship in a manner they may resist. Although the small church has limited resources, it can demonstrate authentic and powerful worship. By developing a style that is sensitive to the people and community, guided by the vision and purpose of the church, the congregation can have a service that glorifies God and draws people into fellowship with him.

Worship begins with the leader's and congregation's understanding of the nature and purpose of worship.

Worship exalts the person of God. Worship is centering the individual and congregation upon the nature and being of God (Luke 4:8; John 4:23–24; Rev. 14:7). As such, the intent of worship is not to entertain or to provide people with an emotional experience. To make worship merely an emotional experience through moving entertainment shifts the focus from God to man. The paramount concern is not what man experiences, but what God expects and desires. Is he pleased? Is he exalted? Is he glorified? Is he served? Worship and praise are a sacrifice offered to God (Heb. 13:15).

Worship is personal. No one can worship God on behalf of another. Worship is the inward response of the individual to the God he or she has been called to serve. In the book of Psalms, the psalmist continually expresses his desire to personally praise God in the community of God's people. It is not enough for the psalmist that others honor God; he himself must express praise and adoration (Pss. 27:4; 35:18; 42:4). Worship involves both the public declaration of praise as well as the private exaltation of God (Ps. 34:1–2; 2 Cor. 12:3–4). For the congregation to be captured by the praise of God, people must first individually learn to stand in awe of him. Corporate worship is an outgrowth of individual worship.

Worship is corporate. Worship is what the congregation is to do when it gathers together. Just as every individual was created to glorify God (Isa. 42:7), so also the church exists for the purpose of exalting God (1 Cor. 10:31; Rev. 1:6). All the activities the church performs—whether its worship services, programs, or extracurricular activities—are to be performed in such a way that God is exalted. If not, the church has failed to fulfill its mission.

Worship requires excellence. The sacrificial system reveals that God does not accept second best. He desires only what is perfect and without blemish. As the people approached God they were to approach him with only the best of the flock. This is true for us as well. Excellence and quality are not determined, however, by how well people perform but the degree to which they utilize their abilities, talents, and resources. When people do their best then their worship is acceptable and pleasing to God, no matter how inept it might appear to outsiders. The responsibility of the small church is not to emulate the large church in its perfection regarding music and worship, but to utilize its abilities to the fullest. If the piano player pounds out the tune with two fingers but he or she is the best musician that a small church can offer, then the quality and excellence pleases and exalts God.

A Theology of Worship

Formulating a philosophy of worship requires the congregation to build upon a proper theology of worship.

Worship is the celebration of God's character. The character of God was for the psalmist the foundation for his confidence in God's redemptive acts on his behalf. Because God is loving and good, the psalmist could call upon God with assurance that he would answer (Ps. 86:5–7). At the heart of the psalmist's praise and worship was the awareness of God's infinite character. Worship, then, involves the affirmation and response to the nature and being of God. It is a jubilee, a joyous recounting of the being of God.

Worship is the celebration of God's activity. The God of the Bible is a God who acts. He does not passively watch the affairs of humans but becomes actively involved, bringing salvation and deliverance to all who call upon him. His redemptive works are so all-surpassing that there is nothing humanity can give back to repay the debt of love owed. The only appropriate response is the public declaration of God's works. To be the beneficiary of God's work is to place oneself under the obligation to praise him publicly, so that his works done in secret are proclaimed openly to his people (Ps. 35:18).

Worship requires personal faith. Worship, first and foremost, can only be truly performed by a genuine child of God (John 4:23–24). There cannot be genuine reverence without submission and there cannot be submission without repentance. The term worship itself means to bow down in subjection. Worship, without genuine faith, becomes mere entertainment, moving the emotions but not capturing the soul. Praise, while at times emotionally moving, should never be equated with mere feelings. It is not merely an emotional response to God, but a response of faith whereby one affirms one's belief in God and his redemptive work. The idea that one should have a "worship service" for the unsaved is a myth. For worship can only be done by the true people of God. One can only truly worship God through the acceptance of Christ. Consequently, the focus of the worship is upon the saved rather than the unsaved.

Worship relates to quality of the heart. Quality is not defined by outward performance but by the inward condition of the heart—the attitudes and motives by which one approaches God. While one can perform a task well, it may be unacceptable to God because it does not stem from the heart (Isa. 29:13–16; Ezek. 33:31; Matt. 15:3–9).

Instead of accepting such worship, God condemns it as unauthentic and hypocritical. The reason the small church can have a great worship service is because it does not require a worship team, a musically talented song leader, a dynamic preacher, or a gifted pianist. All that is required is a sincere and pure heart before God. All too often the focus is upon the form rather than the heart. God's concern is for the heart of the worshiper, not the form by which he or she worships (John 4:24).

Worship is not related to size. Size does not make worship more effective. A huge choir and a large auditorium does not provide a higher quality atmosphere for genuine praise. The five thousand in Acts did not manifest more genuine worship than did the handful of people who met in a house church in Ephesus (see 2 John). In most cases, the small church does a reasonably good job of worship for, in an unpretentious way, it celebrates the person of God and his activities in the lives of everyone attending. A crowd is not required to fulfill the elements of genuine worship—praise, confession of sin, communion with God, and the response of submission to him. All that is required is a genuine heart of obedience before him.

Characteristics of Small Church Worship

The small church does not (nor can it or should it) try to duplicate the worship form of the larger church. Small churches worship God differently than their larger counterparts. Leading the congregation in worship requires an understanding and utilization of these differences.

The small church worships relationally rather than emotionally. The larger church conducts worship in the context of celebration and emotional experience. Within the small church, worship is orchestrated in terms of relationships and mutual interaction. Whereas the larger church worships through the power and majesty of a pipe organ, resounding choir, and unison singing of hundreds of voices, the small church worships through the solidarity, familiarity, and love of a close-knit community. People are lead in worship by Aunt Betty not because she can sing well (she can't), but because they know her love for God and have witnessed her daily life of heartfelt wonder of God. They worship with her because they celebrate the unity they have in Christ and the fact that God accepts them for who they are, not because they posses exceptional talents.

The small church worships through participation rather than presentation. Worship happens when everyone becomes involved. When the small church gathers, they celebrate together, albeit unprofessionally and unpolished, with simplicity and self-acceptance, knowing that God does not just call the great, the powerful, the polished, the talented, or the skilled. He also calls the ordinary, the mundane, the average (and below average), the unskilled, the untalented, the uncouth, and the clumsy to enter into a relationship with him and worship him in the sincerity of their faith. In the small church, everyone can have a place and find avenues to participate in worship. The children are permitted to take the offering, the untalented are given opportunity to sing, the uneducated can teach, the developmentally disabled are placed in charge of the sound system, and the social misfit can serve as a greeter. To deny them these opportunities removes the heart from worship.

Place is more important than location. Within the small church, the atmosphere that facilitates worship is not the beauty of the building or the aesthetics of the location, but the fact that each person has a place. People sit in the same pew Sunday after Sunday, not because it is assigned to them but because in a chaotic and transitory world they desire to have a place where they are secure, where they belong, where they are accepted, and where they are reminded of God's abiding presence with them. Coming to church each week and sitting in the same place serves as a reminder that they are secure in God and that he is present with them in the common affairs of life. They worship God because they belong and are a part of the community of God's people. They worship there because a crucial part of their own life stories is written within the walls of the church. They have been married, dedicated their children, and grieved the loss of their dead within the walls of the building. The church is more than a building; it is a history book, reminding them of God's activity in their lives and of their place with the people of God.

Singing comes from the heart. Music is not an artistic performance but the song of the people in response to God. The congregation may not sing well, but they sing with a worshipful attitude. In the small church, one learns to measure the music by the spirit with which people sing. The danger for any church (big or small) is that the music can be reduced to a performance, or time filler, rather than a response to God. The purpose of the musical expressions is not to move the person emotionally. The object of the service is not to provide an enjoyable service (although it may be the by-product). The focus involves leading people into a dynamic and life-changing response to God. This happens when people stop listening to how their neighbors sound and begin to focus completely upon the person of God, so that people sing with their hearts (Ps. 40:3).

Worship in the small church can be authentic. The small church does not need to focus upon worship that is grand, but it must strive to worship authentically. Authenticity can easily be spotted within the small church, for it is achieved when one's life matches one's worship. Because of the smallness, there can be greater accountability, which challenges each to be honest and open before God rather than to put on a facade of superficial spirituality.

Planning Worship in the Small Church

Developing a dynamic worship service involves the interplay between spiritual sensitivity, biblical instruction, congregational understanding, and planning. Following the prompting and guidance of the Holy Spirit enables the worship leader to move the congregation into the presence of God. Planning for a dynamic service is not, however, divorced from biblical truth (John 4:23). A theology of worship and a biblical understanding of the character of God are crucial lest the worship director lead the congregation to a misguided and misdirected experience.

Developing a service that guides the people and the congregation to experience the reality of the being of God does not happen haphazardly; it involves careful planning and creative coordination. Yet such planning is often difficult to achieve in the small church. Often the planning for the worship service falls upon either the pastor or a layperson, both of whom are already strapped for time because of their many other commitments within the church. The result is that the planning of the service often becomes a mirror of the previous week, the only difference being the new hymn numbers inserted in the bulletin.

Nevertheless, by following basic worship principles, the church can maintain a vibrant and exciting worship service that incites people to worship and draws others into the church as well. Planning begins with an understanding of the elements that constitute a worship service. Scripture reveals a minimum of four critical ingredients that should mark the assembled body of Christ.

The first ingredient is *praise and adoration*. David realized that when the people of God gathered together, each individual was to recount what God had done for him or her (Pss. 42:4; 43:4). One of the purposes of the gathering together of God's people is that they might testify to one another of the redemptive and gracious acts of God. Within the small church such declarations occur naturally. Because the small church revolves around relationships, people are more open and free to share. In the worship service, opportunities should be given for people to publicly praise God, either through personal testimony or through hymns and choruses of praise.

The second ingredient is *declaration of the Word*. At the core of the New Testament church's worship was the preaching and teaching of the Scriptures. Scripture was more than incidental in the worship service; everything they did revolved around the public proclamation of the revealed Word of God, making it the centerpiece in the early church's worship (Acts 2:42; 1 Tim. 4:13; 2 Tim. 4:2). Today, with so much of the focus upon the singing and emotional experience, the church is in danger of abandoning what is to be the very core of its worship. So crucial is the Bible to worship that in reality everything else either leads up to the proclamation of it or responds to it.

A third ingredient of the worship service is *confession*. The realization of the being of God always elicits awareness of one's sinfulness, one's need for confession, and for prayer for mercy and grace (see Isa. 6:1–9). When the church assembles, they come together to confess corporately their sins and pray for forgiveness (Neh. 9:3; James 5:16). Songs and hymns that acknowledge our dependency upon God and our need for the outpouring of his grace serve to bring us to the point where we open our wills to the reception of God's Word.

A fourth ingredient is *communion*. Worship is what the congregation does in relationship with God. The goal of worship is to draw the people into communion with God, where God speaks and challenges the individual through the ministry of his Word, and people respond to him in prayer and petition. Communing with God involves speaking and listening to God. Speaking with God comes through prayer and petition so that when the church gathers, it comes together to pray with and for one another (Acts 2:14). The congregation listens to God as it responds to and interacts with the proclamation of the Bible (1 Tim. 4:13; Col. 4:15; Acts 20:7).

The fifth ingredient is *response*. The time of response enables each individual to respond to the worship experience through commitment and submission to the will of God. This includes the closing period after the sermon, the giving of tithes and offerings, and the celebration of communion. Worship without a response is merely a diversion from daily life rather than a directive for everyday living. Therefore, the leader of the service needs to determine when people should offer a response as well as the type of response desired.

Eight Principles for Planning a Worship Service

In commenting on how the body of Christ is to gather together, Paul writes that it is to be done orderly so that all might benefit and be strengthened (1 Cor. 14:26–33). This necessitates careful planning. Eight principles will help to facilitate that planning.

First, make the focus the exposition of Scripture. Reading, exposition, and application of Scripture makes a worship service dynamic. Because Scripture is the focus, a church of any size can worship biblically. Worship that pleases God is worship conducted "in spirit and in truth" (John 4:23). Identify and correctly interpret a selected portion of Scripture and then think through how the passage relates to the circumstances facing people within the congregation.

Second, worship should be appropriate for the size of the church. Considering what the small church does well rather than focusing upon its weaknesses enables the church to develop a worship service that honors and exalts God and leads people into a focus upon him. Because of its size, the small church can enjoy more interaction and participation than its larger counterpart. Spontaneous testimonies, the involvement of children, and interaction within the sermon can strengthen and highlight the benefits of being small and lead to a more dynamic and meaningful worship.

Third, make the focus the character and activity of God. The ultimate test of all worship services is whether or not people's awareness of God is heightened. Before planning begins, the leader should ask, "What do we desire to communicate about God in this service?" While each individual part may not directly point to God, ultimately the whole service should draw attention to specific attributes or activities of God.

Fourth, worship in a form people are comfortable with. Worship leaders blunder when they develop a form or style that is foreign to the congregation and community. To be an effective leader, he or she needs to listen well. How do people want to worship and what are the taboos? This is not to say that people cannot be taught new forms or styles. They can and should. Paul, in Ephesians 5:19 and Colossians 3:16, implies that worship can be conducted in a number of different styles. People who enjoy hymns can broaden their worship experience by learning to enjoy choruses. But they should not be forced to sacrifice their manner of worship in the process.

Fifth, plan around a unified theme. Every part of the service should have a purpose and a reason. By being intentional in planning, the leader can avoid disruptions. When the parts are not supportive of the whole, the service becomes like a basketball game that suddenly changes into a football game. The rules change and no one is sure what is going on or what the objective is.

Sixth, seek participation rather than just observation. The strength of the small church worship service is that everyone can actively participate rather than merely observe others perform. The worship leader is not the player; rather he or she is the coach who orchestrates the movement of the congregation in the worship experience. Involving the congregation occurs when the leader plans how the people will participate in the service. Participation is especially important with children. Since the small church worships as a family, the service should be sensitive and involve all members of the family. Planning for a children's sermon, singing choruses the children are familiar with, and having children sing special songs are some of the ways to enable children to feel a part of the church family.

Seventh, don't overlook the details. Every element of the service—from the announcements to the sermon—should be viewed in the context of worship. Worship does not just naturally happen within the congregation—it requires continuity of all the parts. Planned spontaneity and formalized informality can be an effective means of facilitating an atmosphere of praise. For example, structuring opportunities within the service for people to share praises dealing with a specific topic that is the focal point of the whole service enables people to become participants rather than just spectators.

Eighth, alter the minors but maintain the major. Some variety is helpful in worship, but too much can become a distraction at best and a source of division and conflict at worst. Before making major changes in the form, prepare the people and obtain their approval. Surprises will usually cause a negative reaction within the congregation.

Planning the Service

While planning is essential for effective worship, there is not one right way to formulate the program. Since each church is governed by different sociological frameworks, cultural norms, and theological nuances, each church will approach the service differently. What works in one church will be ineffective in another. A few guidelines can, however, help the worship leader navigate the process.

First, determine the overall purpose. The purpose of a service refers to its objective in the lives of the worshipers. Purpose determines the focus and flow of the program. Some services are celebrative while others are solemn and reflective. Some focus upon praise while others draw the individual into repentance and self-abasement before God. The book of Psalms reveals a variety of moods, focal points, and objectives that characterized the worship of Israel. Purpose gives the worship program continuity, coherence, and harmony. It answers the question, "What should the worshiper experience and realize about God in this service and how should it affect our lives?"

Second, develop the outline. Once the purpose is identified, the next step is to determine what will happen in the service. While the small church often follows an established pattern, some elements can be altered to enhance the service. Any significant change should be discussed by the board and congregation before it occurs. Developing an outline helps determine what will occur and when. For example, how many songs will be sung? When will the special music be played? When will the offering be taken? What will be the focal point of the congregational prayer?

Third, use available resources. Often the small church has more resources at its disposal than it realizes. It may not have a choir, but it can have children sing. It may not have an orchestra or a worship team, but it can utilize cassette tapes. Having just the men sing on Mother's Day can replace a choral number. Meeting outdoors on a hot summer day can be more comfortable and can also add another dimension that enhances the awareness of God's creation or the church's obligation to reach beyond the walls of the building.

Fourth, identify the specifics. Once the purpose is identified and the outline is developed, then the worship leader is ready to fill in the details. A number of areas need to be addressed in the details of the service. Answering some of the following questions may be helpful:

- What choruses and hymns are to be sung and in what order?
- What is the sermon topic?
- What topic will be addressed by the children's sermon?
- How will the offering be introduced?
- What Scripture will be read and when?
- What will be the focus of prayer? Will the pastor lead in prayer or will the congregation pray?

- What sins need to be confessed or behaviors need to be challenged? When will people have opportunity to address these issues?
- How are people being asked to respond to the message and what opportunity is given them to respond, whether it is in a hymn of affirmation, a time of confession, or a physical response of dedication?

The most critical question in addressing the service is not who will do what and when but why they are doing it and how does it reflect scriptural truth and biblical theology. Only planning and discernment can answer these questions.

Prayer: Loving God Through Dependency

A church that prays is a church that loves God. The key to maintaining closeness and intimacy in any relationship is communication. To build closeness we need to share with one another the joys and sorrows, the triumphs and tragedies, the dreams and disappointments, and the struggles and temptations. Without in-depth and honest communication the relationship withers on the vine. So it is in our relationship with Christ. Through prayer we communicate with God to maintain a vital link with him.

But prayer is more than communication; it is also the recognition of our complete and total dependency upon God. When we pray we are acknowledging that we need God's direct intervention in our lives for we are powerless apart from him (Mark 9:28–29). Prayerlessness reveals independence and an attitude that we can handle life and ministry on our own. Such an attitude undermines the strength of the church and leaves the congregation open to the subtle defeat and temptations of the Adversary (Eph. 6:12). Prayer becomes the means by which God works through the church.

The Importance of Prayer

Prayer remains one of the most difficult tasks of the church, for prayer has traditionally been assigned to the mid-week prayer service, which has been forsaken even in the most traditional church.

To recapture the importance of prayer the church needs to recognize the place prayer holds in the spiritual life and in the vitality of the congregation.

Prayer is the expression of a dependent heart. Effective ministry can only be accomplished when we become completely and entirely dependent upon God's empowerment and strength. Only when we yield our own pride and self-sufficiency to Christ, humbly recognizing that apart from him we can do nothing, can we truly be effective in ministry. Paul writes in Philippians 4:6, "Do not be anxious about anything, but in everything, by prayer and petition, with thanksgiving, present your requests to God." Everything the church does should be undergirded by prayer because it recognizes our complete dependency upon him. A spiritually healthy church is one that prays before it acts.

Prayer aligns our desires with the will of God. While God uses our prayers to accomplish great things, perhaps the greatest work of prayer is that he changes our will and desires as we pray. Often our prayers are misguided, plagued by distorted motives (James 4:2–3). As we pray and acknowledge our dependency upon God, he works within our will and our desires so that we conform to his divine plan (Rom. 8:26–27). For the church to know and follow God's will, it needs to be immersing everything it does in prayer. A reason churches experience conflict over programs and ministries stems from their failure to pray corporately for the decisions confronting the church.

Prayer is the basis for God's blessing. Every congregation desires to realize the rich joy of having God's blessing poured out upon them and their ministries. Yet we often miss this blessing because of our lack of prayer. Christ challenges our lack of prayer in Matthew 7:7–8: "Ask and it will be given to you; seek and you will find; knock and the door will be opened to you. For everyone who asks receives; he who seeks finds; and to him who knocks, the door will be opened." When we pray, God answers.

Prayer is the basis for forgiveness. John writes that the remedy for sin is confession (1 John 1:9). Confession can only occur in the context of prayer. Just as individuals need prayer for forgiveness so also the corporate community must acknowledge its failures and seek the cleansing power of Christ's forgiveness (Josh. 7; Neh. 1:6-7).

Prayer is the basis for divine assistance. Because of our insufficiency and weaknesses we are in constant need of God's help. Within the ministry of the church we encounter all kinds of difficulties that exceed our abilities to overcome, whether it be a counseling situation, a conflict over programs, or a troubled child in a Sunday school class. These kinds of problems demonstrate our constant need for God and his help and strength (Heb. 4:15–16; Ps. 145:18).

Prayer is made in conjunction with planning. Prayer does not violate or replace wise planning and sound preparation; rather it is offered in conjunction with these (Neh. 4:9). As we pray we are to set goals, establish procedures, and make preparations.

Prayer is to be the hallmark of the church. Isaiah challenges the people of Israel to be all that God intended for them to be. They had mistaken God's blessing for favoritism, becoming snobbish and exclusive to the surrounding nations. To correct this, the prophet reminds them that they were a means to reach foreigners. In the midst of this missionary challenge, God states, "These I will bring to my holy mountain and give them joy in my house of prayer. Their burnt offerings and sacrifices will be accepted on my altar; for my house will be called a house of prayer for all nations" (Isa. 56:7). The fame of the congregation of God's people is not the dynamic services, or the great social programs, or the unique and entertaining ministries; it is to be their prayer life. Too often the lack of prayer speaks more of a church than does its dedication to prayer.

Prayer: The Responsibility of Leadership

Effective leadership does not begin with developing a vision, outlining goals, and building strategies and programs. It begins with prayer. Without prayer, headship loses it validity, vitality, and influence. Prayer is the means by which God works through the individual to challenge and affect people. Samuel recognized the importance of prayer when he confessed to the people, "As for me, far be it from me that I should sin against the LORD by failing to pray for you" (1 Sam. 12:23). So important was prayer to the apostles that they did not allow administrative duties and needs to distract them from their time devoted to prayer (Acts 6:4). For them prayer was not a duty or a luxury or something they did when they had an open slot on their day-timer. Prayer was their business. A call to leadership within the church was a call to be devoted to prayer. It is most unfortunate that much of what is written about leadership today focuses upon administrative duties and not the prayer responsibilities of the leader. The church should never be content with prayerless leaders. The church should demand it, holding their leaders accountable to pray, guarding their time that they can be devoted to prayer, setting prayer as one of the highest priorities and responsibilities of its pastor and lay leadership. A benefit of a small church is that the leadership knows each family personally and can pray specifically for each individual within the church. Each member of the board can be assigned a segment of the church for whom they can pray. The Sunday school superintendent can pray for the teachers and for each child.

Scripture reveals a number of areas in which leaders are to pray for their people:

- Leaders are responsible to pray for people's spiritual growth: "I keep asking that the God of our Lord Jesus Christ, the glorious Father, may give you the Spirit of wisdom and revelation, so that you may know him better" (Eph. 1:17).
- Leaders are to pray that people will have a right perspective: "I pray also that the eyes of your heart may be enlightened in order that you may know the hope to which he has called you" (Eph. 1:18).
- Leaders are to pray continually for people: "I thank my God every time I remember you. In all my prayers for all of you, I always pray with joy" (Phil. 1:3–4).
- Leaders are to pray for the love and unity of the church: "And this is my prayer: that your love may abound more and more in knowledge and depth of insight" (Phil. 1:9).
- Leaders are to pray for the church's spiritual discernment: "so that you may be able to discern what is best" (Phil. 1:10).

- Leaders are to pray that people might be pure and blameless: ". . . and may be pure and blameless until the day of Christ" (Phil. 1:9).
- Leaders are to pray that people will know the will of God: "We have not stopped praying for you and asking God to fill you with the knowledge of his will through all spiritual wisdom and understanding" (Col. 1:9).
- Leaders are to pray that people's conduct might be pleasing to God: "And we pray this in order that you may live a life worthy of the Lord and may please him in every way" (Col. 1:10).
- Leaders are to pray that people will fulfill God's purpose: "We constantly pray . . . that by his power he may fulfill every good purpose of yours and every act prompted by your faith" (2 Thess. 1:11).
- Leaders are to pray for the physical and emotional needs of people: "I pray that you may enjoy good health and that all may go well with you" (3 John 2); "Is any one of you sick? He should call the elders of the church to pray over him and anoint him with oil in the name of the Lord" (James 5:14).

Prayer: The Responsibility of the Congregation

A strong measurement of the health of the church is the amount of time that it spends praying corporately. Having an impact in the community begins with prayer. Too often the congregation merely goes through the motions, without really becoming a church committed to prayer. Prayer becomes general, superficial, and impersonal. When a church is marked by prayer, members are open to praying for personal and specific physical and spiritual needs. Keeping a church devoted to prayer requires constant work and planning. The congregation must be taught continually. They must be reminded that they are to pray and what they should ask of God.

They are to pray for the leaders of the church. The pastor is only as effective as the people praying for him or her. As the pastor serves the church, he or she should enlist a handful of people who will partner together with him or her to be devoted to prayer on his or her behalf. Paul recognized the importance of people praying for him. A common theme in his books was the request that people pray for him and his ministry (Rom. 15:30–31; 2 Cor. 1:11; Eph. 6:19–20; Phil. 1:19; Col. 4:3–4; 1 Thess. 5:25; 2 Thess. 3:1–3). As the pastor develops partners in prayer he or she can keep them abreast of specific requests.

They are to pray for one another. In Acts 2, the church experienced incredible growth and prosperity. People were being added daily by God to the congregation. Scripture does not tell us about their programs (although Acts 6 indicates that the church operated different ministries and programs) nor does it tell us about their methodology. Rather, it attributes the success of the early church to their devotion "to the apostles' teaching and to the fellowship, to the breaking of bread and to prayer" (Acts 2:42). Whenever anyone in the community of believers encountered problems, the church community went before God on their behalf (4:24). When people were assigned new ministries, the church community first prayed for them (6:6). A church praying for one another will be unified, demonstrating mutual care for one another.

They are to pray for the programs and ministries. When Nehemiah determined to rebuild the walls of Jerusalem, the first thing he did was to pray for the wisdom of God and the success of the program (Neh. 1:4). Whenever he encountered a major decision within the project, he first prayed (2:4) then acted. When he encountered opposition, which caused the people to become discouraged, he prayed (4:9). Programs and ministries will be successful only when prayer undergirds the plans, strategies, and people's involvement. As important and beneficial as management skills are, they can never compensate for a neglect of prayer.

They are to pray for the unsaved. When writing to Timothy regarding the responsibilities that he was to exemplify and teach to the congregation, Paul states, "I urge, then, first of all, that requests, prayers, intercession and thanksgiving be made for everyone" (1 Tim. 2:1). The church is to pray for the lost, that they might be receptive to the gospel and understand its message. We are to pray that God will work within the unsaved, bringing conviction. We are to pray that we will have opportunity to share the gospel of Christ.

They are to pray for people to be involved in ministry. The church is a work vessel not a luxury cruise. Involvement within the ministry of the kingdom of God rests upon every individual within the body of Christ. Therefore we are to pray that God will send people to work in the church for the advancement of Christ's kingdom (Matt. 9:38).

Building the Prayer Base of the Church

A number of different ways can be followed for building the prayer base of the congregation. But the process is not nearly as important as the goal—developing a congregation that undergirds in prayer its community life and ministry. The method by which this is accomplished will be dependent upon each individual, but seven steps will assist leadership in facilitating the process.

Step one: Evaluate the prayer base of the church. The key to developing a "house of prayer" is to be intentional. Begin by examining all aspects of the ministry and life of the congregation and assessing the prayer support that each receives. Are people praying for the people they serve? Are the leaders meeting together in order to pray for the congregation? Are ministry groups praying together for their ministries? Do people pray before decisions are made? Does the pastor have adequate time to pray? Does the pastor have prayer partners who are praying specifically for him or her? Are people open and honest about prayer needs? Do people have a strong sense of dependency upon God and an awareness that nothing can be accomplished except through his strength?

Step two: Identify areas where prayer support remains insufficient. After the evaluation, identify two or three areas in which there can be a greater focus upon prayer. Meet with the leaders and people involved in these areas and identify ways to bolster the prayer base of the ministry. Develop strategies for building the base so that God will begin to work.

Step three: Preach and teach the congregation on the importance and principles of prayer. Often people do not pray effectively because they have never been taught. We mistakenly assume they know how to pray and understand the importance of prayer. To teach them, the pastor can preach a sermon series covering the biblical principles regarding prayer. The Sunday school classes can be used to teach people of all ages.

Step four: As leaders, set the example. Paul encouraged Timothy to make visible his faith so that people might learn through his example (1 Tim. 4:12). Before people will catch a vision for prayer they must see it modeled by the pastor, elders, deacons, and ministry heads. The pastor must place prayer as a priority and the elders should hold him or her accountable for the amount of time he or she spends praying. The elders should be accountable to the congregation for their dedication to prayer.

Step five: Develop opportunities for corporate prayer. Because the church needs to be together to pray, the leadership should develop strategies for giving people this opportunity. People can be brought together for prayer in a number of different ways, and each church needs to develop ways that work best for it. Time can be designated for sharing requests and praying together during the worship service; a church can periodically hold retreats or a twenty-four hour day of prayer, establish prayer chains, special prayer meetings, etc. When groups gather together to discuss the business and programs of the church, they should spend as much time in prayer as they do discussing church business. Prayer should be on the agenda of every meeting.

Step six: Develop strategies for keeping prayer a focus. Not only must the leadership think about how to develop the prayer base of the church, but once it is established, they need to think about how to keep it a vital part of the congregation. Sustaining prayer requires work. It requires that we be intentional in our efforts and planning.

Step seven: Provide opportunities where answers can be shared. Perhaps the single most important way to keep prayer vital and ongoing is seeing God answer our petitions. Often we share requests but we forget to praise God and give thanks when he responds. Every time the community gathers to pray, there can be opportunities given to share how God has been working.

Loving God Through Obedience

Christ sets the standard of loving God when he states, "Whoever has my commands and obeys them, he is the one who loves me" (John 14:21), and again, "If anyone loves me, he will obey my teaching. My Father will love him, and we will come to him and make our home with him. He who does not love me will not obey my teaching. These words you hear are not my own; they belong to the Father who sent me" (John 14:23–24). Teaching people to love God involves teaching them to be obedient to him and live in submission to his expressed will revealed in Scripture. A purpose of the church is to instruct people in the Scriptures so that they live in obedience to God, even if that obedience is costly and demanding. Obedience requires consistency within each live. The spiritual health of the church is not to be measured by just what happens on Sunday but by how the congregation is living throughout the week. Thus, the church needs to examine the totality of the Christian life.

Developing a Life of Obedience

In his book *Balancing Life's Demands*,[2] Grant Howard provides an overview of each individual's responsibilities. These responsibilities provide the framework from which we are to examine our lives in light of God's Word. By doing so, we align our lives with the responsibilities God has given us.

Our obedience is revealed in our attitude and actions toward God. As the people of God we are responsible to respond to God correctly. We are to praise him, approach him with respect, set aside time to worship him, pray and communicate with him, read his Word, share in his sufferings, witness of him, etc. Teaching people to be obedient requires that we know what God expects in our relationship with him.

Our obedience is revealed in our attitudes and actions toward ourselves. Scripture has a great deal to say about how we view ourselves. We are to have a proper assessment of ourselves, we are to remain morally pure, we are to take care of ourselves physically, we are to spend time relaxing and enjoying the life God has given to us. We are to avoid any controlling substance that would distort the Holy Spirit's control of our lives.

Our obedience is revealed in our attitude and actions regarding the church. Fellowship is not an option; it is expected and commanded. In participating in the church we are to be active, utilizing our gifts for the benefit of the whole congregation. We are commanded to pray for one another, to encourage and strengthen one another, and to proclaim Scripture to one another.

Our obedience is revealed in our attitude and actions at work. Scripture has a great deal to say about our attitude toward our jobs. We are to work hard and not be a freeloader. We are to avoid being a workaholic so that our lives do not become unbalanced. We are to treat people under our authority with kindness and integrity while submitting to the authority of those placed over us. In so doing we are manifesting Christ within our work.

Our obedience is revealed in our attitude and actions regarding our government. We are to pray for our leaders, pay our taxes, and support our government. Likewise, we are responsible to obey God and fulfill our responsibilities to him and his Word even if they contradict or violate the laws and policies of the nation.

Our obedience is revealed in our attitude and actions with our family. God has established the family unit as an expression of his love and fidelity to the church. Therefore we are to act differently than what is common in today's culture. Husbands are to set aside their personal ambitions and desires and be servant leaders who train and teach their children through example, words, and discipline. They are to be spiritual leaders who lead their families in a faithful walk with Christ. Wives are to learn submission and not compete with their husbands for dominance. Rather they are to support and encourage his leadership, and assist him as he fulfills his role as the spiritual head of the family. Children are to be taught obedience and respect for their parents.

Our obedience is revealed in our attitude and actions toward our neighbors. We are to cultivate relationships to proclaim the gospel of Christ, but in doing so we are to be sensitive to our neighbors' needs and problems. We are to respect their property and live an exemplary life before them. To those who mistreat us, we respond in love and unconditional compassion.

Developing Character Within the Church

The responsibility of character development rests upon the church and the leadership of the congregation. The church does more than come together to worship; the members gather to encourage one another in the quest for godliness and character (Heb. 10:24–25).

Step one: Preach and teach to the will. The goal of the teaching and preaching of the church is to address the will of the individual. While the gospel is inherently positive and the content of our message uplifting rather than critical, the Christian life is a life in the process of change. To change people we need to challenge their wills and correct their faulty thinking and lifestyles rather than merely enable them to feel good about themselves.

Step two: Evaluate individual lifestyles. While we are not to judge people, the leadership of the church examines the overall lifestyles of the congregation with respect to consistency in Christian obedience. The purpose is not to condemn people but to provide guidance and to determine the content and focus of the messages and teaching material.

Step three: Develop accountability. Permanent change springs from mutual accountability. This accountability is based upon love so that people are not threatened, but encouraged.

Step four: Provide small groups. Small groups provide the opportunity for people to develop close relationships with others in order to share problems, struggles, and temptations and to provide mutual support and encouragement. These groups may be in a Sunday school class, ministry teams, or Bible studies.

Evaluation and Implementation

1. Complete worksheets 9-11 with the board (see appendix A).
2. Identify the areas where the church is the strongest. How can the church utilize this area in its outreach?
3. Identify where the church needs the greatest amount of improvement. Develop a strategy for improvement in this area.

Further Reading

Carroll, Joseph S. *How to Worship Jesus Christ*. Chicago: Moody, 1984.

Martin, Glen, and Dian Ginter. *Power House*. Nashville: Broadman & Holman, 1994.

Maxwell, John. *Partners in Prayer*. Nashville: Nelson, 1996.

Moreland, J. P. *Love Your God with All Your Mind*. Colorado Springs, Colo.: NavPress, 1997.

Segler, Franklin M., and Randall Bradley. *Christian Worship*. Nashville: Broadman & Holman, 1996.

Willimon, William H., and Robert L. Wilson. *Preaching and Worship in the Small Church*. Nashville: Abingdon, 1980.

FIVE

Developing the Character
of the Church: Loving People

*T*he strength of the small church is the relationships that exist within the congregation. But often friendship and social unity can be mistaken for genuine love and biblical fellowship. The call of the church is to be a loving organism that reaches out and includes people of all ages, social and economic backgrounds, ethnic descent, and cultural patterns. While genuine Christianity brings radical shifts in one's character and lifestyle, the church is to accept people regardless of how they formerly lived, forgiving them for their past, and helping them change in the present and for the future. While sinful behavior is never to be accepted, the leadership and congregation should always offer a loving embrace for those who desire to know Christ.

It is this depth of love that is to characterize the church. Without such love, the church not only lacks true unity but it becomes a blight upon the universal body of Christ, for the hallmark of true discipleship is love for each other (John 13:35). A spiritually healthy church is one that loves all people, both within the church and the community, and throughout the world. An unhealthy church no longer shows compassion toward people, but quickly judges them, rejecting those who do not fit into the church's sociological patterns that characterize the congregation's subculture. A truly loving church is unified and cares for its own while it readily loves and accepts those who are "different." Christ, in outlining the type of character that is to mark his people, makes it clear that they are to love their neighbors as themselves (see Matt. 22:39).

The Nature of Love

Becoming a loving church begins with an understanding of the biblical nature of love. This love is far deeper than a love dependent upon feelings and emotions. Rather it is a love that stems from the very soul and character of the individual. It is a love that has unique characteristics.

Biblical love is an expression of the will. The love described in Scripture stems from a person's decision to love rather than from the person's feelings. The most popular term, *agape*, focuses upon action and commitment of the will rather than the superficial emotions that plague popular culture today. This love comes ultimately from the Holy Spirit's empowerment in the life of the individual and congregation. A church that has a loving character is committed to people, to meeting their needs, and to serving people without consideration for how those people act and react in turn.

Biblical love involves sacrifice. Often a small church faces extremely limited resources. As a consequence it focuses all its energies and finances to operating the ministries within the church, providing care for the congregation rather than for those outside the church. This focus stands in contrast to the true nature of love. Biblical love is not measured by our attitudes or even by what we do. The ultimate expression of biblical love is a willingness to sacrifice oneself completely and entirely for the needs of others (John 15:12–13). The apostle Paul established the standard for our love: "And live a life of love, just as Christ loved us and gave himself up for us as a fragrant offering and sacrifice to God" (Eph. 5:2). This same model is presented in 1 John 3:16. Thus, a church that demonstrates Christlikeness is a congregation that is willing to sacrifice their time, energies, and resources to benefit those outside the congregation as well as those within the Christian community. The motivation for this sacrificial love is not any reciprocal benefit an individual might receive but solely to benefit the other person (Rom. 12:9).

Biblical love remains unconditional. Because the small church remains a close-knit group, a tendency exists for it to follow cultural and sociological norms, values, and behaviors established by the community. Those who do not fit these norms are considered outsiders until they adhere to them. The result is that acceptance becomes conditioned upon an individual's behavior rather than on biblical standards. Biblical love, however, remains unconditional. So extensive is this unconditional love to be, even those who are enemies of and oppose the church are to be loved. We are to desire their prosperity, pray for them, and minister to them (Luke 6:27–36). To reject them or to rejoice in their suffering is an affront to the God who calls the church to love all people (Prov. 24:17–18). The leadership must foster an atmosphere within the church where all people, regardless of their present condition, are welcomed and included in the activities of the congregation.

Biblical love maintains a universal outlook. The mandate to love is not merely a call to love those who are near to the church or who might enter through the church doors. It is a call to love all people throughout the world. It is to develop and maintain a worldwide perspective of ministry. The ministry of the apostle Paul was earmarked by his passion to see the whole world in an intimate relationship with Christ. Although he remained in certain areas for considerable time, he always kept his ear tuned to what was happening throughout the whole Roman Empire. When he was in Athens, for instance, he was concerned about those in Thessalonica. So much so that he sent Timothy to strengthen and encourage them (1 Thess. 3:1–5). Even though Paul himself was under intense pressure and persecution, he found joy in the report that things were going well with the Thessalonians (3:6–10). His prayer for them was that God would "make your love increase and overflow for each other and for everyone else, just as ours does for you" (3:12). Since God has a passion and love for the whole world, so also should the church develop a love for all people throughout the world, a love that results in missionary support as well as contributions to social programs conducted in other countries.

Biblical love manifests itself through service. To be the embodiment of Christ's love within the community, the church needs to be servants of the community. Love is manifested not by what we say but how we serve, and by our willingness to set aside our own personal agenda and self-interests and serve others. Paul writes in Galatians 5:13, "You, my brothers, were called to be free. But do not use your freedom to indulge the sinful nature; rather, serve one another in love." This service is to be a continual action on the part of the congregation rather than isolated occasions. When love is present within the church community, people desire to exercise their spiritual gifts for the benefit of others, both within the congregation as well as the community in which they are located. Christ himself set forth this pattern when he set aside his garments and washed the disciples' feet; thus, the call to emulate the person of Christ is a call to serve others (John 13:12–17).

Biblical love is learned. Because love is a decisive act of the will rather than a response to the emotions, it can be learned. Paul writes to the church at Thessalonica, "Now about brotherly love we do not need to write to you, for you yourselves have been taught by God to love each other" (1 Thess. 4:9). Biblical love is not natural or inherent. It comes through the guidance and teaching of the Holy Spirit as he works within our lives to conform us to the image of Christ. The work of the Holy Spirit includes the instruction and teaching of the church as the church teaches people how to serve, react, and demonstrate care for others. This teaching, this caring and service begins as the leadership provides the example for others to follow.

Biblical love is unifying. Conflicts and differences are part of our humanness and a reality that no church can escape. But divisions, bitterness, and disunity are a result of an unloving spirit. While conflicts cannot be avoided, when love is present within the church, unity remains intact as people work through issues, forgive one another, and sacrifice their own agendas for the benefit of others. The mark of a loving church is that people live in unity with one another. In Colossians 2:1–3 we discover that we are to strive for unity that springs not from a denial of differences but from the attitude of love: "I want you to know how much I am struggling for you and for those at Laodicea, and for all who have not met me personally. My purpose is that they may be encouraged in heart and united in love, so that they may have the full riches of complete understanding, in order that they may know the mystery of God, namely, Christ, in whom are hidden all the treasures of wisdom and knowledge." (See also Ps. 133:1–3).

The Importance of Love

For the church, love is more than a cliché. Love forms the backbone that supports all the other activities and values that are to mark the church (Col. 3:14). Without love, all the programs of the church are undermined (1 Cor. 13) and there is no basis, that is, no motivation for people's ministry and service.

Love's Motivation for Evangelism

The motivation for God's redemptive program was his supreme and unblemished love for people. While God's justice demands the penalty for sin, his love impelled him to provide a provision for the forgiveness of sins. This provision was in the form of the substitutionary sacrifice of his Son. While his own glorification is the ultimate end, it was God's love that motivated him to act. Christ appealed to God's love in his conversation with Nicodemus as recorded in John 3:16: "For God so loved the world that he gave his one and only Son, that whoever believes in him shall not perish but have eternal life." The apostle reiterates the theme of God's love in his epistles when he writes, "This is how God showed his love among us: He sent his one and only Son into the world that we might live through him. This is love: not that we loved God, but that he loved us and sent his Son as an atoning sacrifice for our sins" (1 John 4:9–10). Christ did not demand that we change before he loved us, but his love is why he sought change in us through his redemptive work.

The love that God has toward people is to be manifested within the people of God so that they are equally compelled to love others. In the Old Testament law, the people of God were to love the alien for they themselves were once aliens who received the benefit of God's salvation (Deut. 10:19). So also in the New Testament, our evangelistic fervor reveals the depth of our love for people, a love that comes not from humanitarian motivation but from our relationship with Christ. A church shows a lack of genuine neighbor love when members fail to assimilate new people and look at their own needs before reaching out to others. The church is to foster a love for people inside and outside the congregation.

Love's Motivation for Fellowship

The theme of the early church was forgiveness, love, unity, and mutual fellowship with the body of Christ. A perusal of the letters of Paul, John, and Peter reveals these themes within their message. For them fellowship was not just a privilege or even a necessity; love was the inescapable result of the redemptive work of Christ. The idea that a Christian would want to (or even could) live independently of the rest of the community was completely foreign and smacked of a failure to understand and appropriate the love and sanctifying work of Christ. John said it most forcefully when he wrote that the failure to love the brothers was a mark of carnality and of being unregenerate (1 John 3:14). Paul, while perhaps not being as direct, is no less forceful when he reminded the church of Ephesus that "you are no longer foreigners and aliens, but fellow citizens with God's people and members of God's household" (Eph. 2:19). Because the fellowship of the church was the expression of true Christianity, Paul continually prayed that the love and fellowship of the body would not only be evident but would continue to grow and abound (1 Thess. 3:12). One important purpose of the corporate gathering of the church is to exhort and encourage the love and fellowship of the church (Heb. 10:24–25).

Fulfilling the command to love our neighbors involves participating in the fellowship of God's local and universal community. This fellowship includes involvement and participation within the local church as well as the realization that we are part of the universal body of Christ, which crosses local and/or denominational boundaries. A church that has godly character ingrained within it will be a church that enjoys gathering together. Fellowship, then, is more than a byword; it is central to the life of the church. Members will seek fellowship not only with the other members of their local church but they will also recognize the importance of developing godly relationships with other congregations within the local community.

Love's Motivation for Correction

While belonging to a congregation brings comfort and encouragement, it also brings mutual accountability. Each member recognizes that he or she is responsible for the spiritual well-being of the other members. When one member suffers, so intricate is the unity, all members suffer (1 Cor. 12:25–26). Thus, accountability finds expression in the mutual encouragement as well as in the mutual discipline of one another. The writer of Hebrews, in discussing God's discipline, points out that the motivation and basis is not a desire to gain revenge but is because of God's love and desire for us to grow into spiritual maturity (Heb. 12:4–13).

John, writing in the overall context of mutual love, places mutual accountability in the center: "If anyone sees his brother commit a sin that does not lead to death, he should pray and God will give him life" (1 John 5:16a). But we are to go beyond praying for the person; we are to go to the individual and confront him or her regarding his or her sin: "My brothers, if one of you should wander from the truth and someone should bring him back, remember this: Whoever turns a sinner from the error of his way will save him from death and cover over a multitude of sins" (James 5:19–20). Correction must, however, be based upon love and humility, with the recognition of our own vulnerability and propensity toward sin (Gal. 6:1–5). When love is the motivation, not only do we correct the wandering member, we do so in a way that seeks the full restoration and spiritual growth of that individual (Eph. 4:15).

Because the small church is often built around bloodlines and long-term relationships that transcend the church doors, people may be reluctant to correct and discipline a fellow member. While church discipline should always be entered into prayerfully with humility and careful thought, the refusal to discipline an openly rebellious member is harmful to the individuals involved, to the overall health of the congregation, and it manifests a lack of genuine godly love for the individual. Love grieves when a person is out of fellowship with Christ, desiring to see the intimacy with Christ restored.

Love's Motivation for Service

The body of Christ is not a luxury ship where the passengers enjoy the services of a few who are on call to their every whim. Instead the church is a work vessel where all must do their parts if they are to make it to their destination. The motivation for service is not, however, out of necessity but stems from the congregation's mutual love for one another. Christ points to this motivation when he states, "Greater love has no one than this, that he lay down his life for his friends" (John 15:13). Genuine love for one's neighbor leads to sacrificial service. When love is not the motivation, then service becomes a duty to perform. In Galatians 5:13, Paul writes that we are to "serve one another in love." It is this desire for the benefit of others that keeps our service from being corrupted by selfish motives. It enables us to sacrifice our time, energy, and resources even when it is inconvenient, difficult, and costly. This love and service for others issues from our love for Christ and our desire to serve him (John 21:15–19). When a congregation truly loves others, everyone is willing to be involved—not because they want the program to succeed or because they want recognition, but because they desire to participate in the spiritual growth of others.

Expressing Love in Fellowship

Unlike the modern concept of love, biblical love is neither an emotion nor a static feeling; it is a determination of the will that leads to actions. Biblical love is active, striving to support, encourage, and serve the object of the love. Within the small church, this love is expressed through the fellowship enjoyed by the congregation; through the mutual care of one another as each supports and encourages the other; through discipline, by which individuals are lovingly confronted; and through edification where the church exhorts people in spiritual growth.

When we experience the regeneration of the Holy Spirit we are called out of the world and into the community of believers. Our baptismal confession, while a testimony of Christ's death and resurrection as applied to our lives, is also a testimony that we have been joined to the body of Christ (1 Cor. 12:13). As we gather together we experience greater spiritual growth (Prov. 27:17), a more dynamic testimony (John 13:35), and a more potent spiritual power (Matt. 18:19) than we would have if we remained isolated from the rest of the Christian community. When we come together in fellowship we experience the full presence of Christ (Matt. 18:20) and we do what pleases God (Mal. 3:16). This fellowship involves mutual acceptance and a desire to benefit the other individual.

The Foundation for Fellowship

Biblical fellowship is neither psychological nor sociological. Rather it is spiritual. The call to Christ involves inclusion within the spiritual communion of both the local and the universal church.

This spiritual communion includes several dimensions. One dimension is a *personal relationship with Christ.* As people come into the church, they come from a variety of backgrounds, cultural perspectives, ethnic diversity, and sociological differences. Yet all these differences are erased in Christ so that we become one body. Paul writes that "for he himself is our peace, who has made the two one and has destroyed the barrier, the dividing wall of hostility" (Eph. 2:14). Paul challenges the exclusivism of our subcultures and the homogeneity of the church that can put up barriers between the church and newcomers (Gal. 3:28; Col. 3:11). Because of Christ we have unity and fellowship with others, but at the same time we cannot have genuine fellowship with those outside the faith (2 Cor. 6:14).

A second dimension of spiritual communion is a common confession of faith. Fellowship can only happen when we have agreement on the fundamentals of biblical doctrine. Those who teach doctrine contrary to the Scriptures are to be identified and avoided (2 John 10). This is not to say that we must have complete agreement in every detail of theology. Such a standard is not only idealistic but unrealistic as well. Insistence on the correctness of personally held beliefs is the mark of doctrinal pride that fails to consider how our minds are affected by our fallen nature. While the fundamentals of our faith are clearly taught in Scripture, there is much that we still do not fully understand. Nevertheless, we must maintain our integrity to the gospel message and the basic doctrines and beliefs that have been upheld throughout church history.

A third dimension is the common presence of the Holy Spirit. Because each person has the indwelling presence of the Holy Spirit we have a basis for unity and fellowship. When the Spirit indwelt us at conversion, he did so not only to strengthen us in our pilgrimage but to unite us with other believers (1 Cor. 12:13).

A fourth dimension of spiritual communion is self-sacrificing love and concern. The call to fellowship is a challenge to set aside our personal ambitions, interests, needs, and desires and to selflessly seek the benefit and spiritual prosperity of the other members of the Christian community. The standard for this self-sacrificing love is none other than that which Christ established in his substitutionary death on our behalf (Phil. 2:1–11).

Threats to Fellowship

The areas in which the Christian faith is most distinct are our attitudes and actions toward others (John 13:35), for it is one place where the presence of the Holy Spirit is most evident. The demand for mutual submission and self-sacrifice violates the "me-ism" that characterizes secular thinking. It is in our self-serving and self-centered attitude that demands of Christ are neglected.

Consumerism

When a person comes to church, he or she, instead of manifesting the mind of Christ, remains influenced by secular thinking and its innate attitudes toward others and toward the church. The first of these might be called consumerism, a "What's in it for me?" attitude. Because consumerism is the product of our materialistic culture, people often come to church bearing the same attitude they have regarding a department store: "This place is here to serve me;

if they fail to do so, I will take my business somewhere else." The result is that people church-hop whenever "this church doesn't minister to my needs." This contradicts the biblical mandate that we are to come to church to serve rather than be served. Paul challenges the church at Corinth, "But just as you excel in everything—in faith, in speech, in knowledge, in complete earnestness and in your love for us—see that you also excel in this grace of giving" (2 Cor. 8:7). While the focus is upon financial giving, the implications relate to one's whole attitude toward others. This outward-focused attitude is further explained in Philippians 2:4: "Each of you should look not only to your own interests, but also to the interests of others."

Divisiveness

Another dimension of secularism is seen when people are willing to divide the body to get their way. Congregations are often torn apart by people who are unwilling to set aside personal agendas and submit to the wishes of others. In their minds there is only one way to do things (whether that way is based on past traditions or their own opinions), and they will not compromise. Some of the strongest words in Scripture are directed toward those who cause internal conflicts. Anyone who destroys the intrinsic unity and love within the church through dissension is not only to be avoided (Rom. 16:17–18) but is in danger of coming under the direct judgment of God (1 Cor. 3:16–17). Instead, people are to be encouraged to resolve their differences and to be united in Christ (Phil. 4:2).

Individualism

A third dimension of secularism in the church is individualism. People who attend small churches (especially in rural areas) are often fiercely independent and do not want to be in the position of needing help from others. These independent types regard themselves as spiritually self-sufficient people. They deny personal weakness and refuse the input of others when weaknesses are apparent. The New Testament paints a different picture of how the body is to relate. We not only need one another (1 Cor. 12:21–22), but only when the congregation is united in mutual support are people's needs truly met (Acts 4:32–35).

Pretense

The fourth dimension of secularism is pretense in which we put up a front. It is always difficult to be vulnerable. By nature we want to hide our problems, struggles, and weaknesses. Yet genuine fellowship is based upon the openness and honesty that is to characterize the body of Christ (Eph. 4:25). For the congregation to develop the intimate bonds that Christ desires, all need to be open to admitting failures, temptations, and problems. Only then can there be true support and encouragement.

Judgmentalism

A final dimension that secularism brings to the church is judgmentalism. (I will judge others by my standard.) The small church, like groups in the secular world, often develops an external code of conduct that corresponds to the homogeneous nature of the group. The result is that spirituality, like attributes valued in the secular world, is measured by this external standard rather than the inward reality, which results in character development. Conduct is evaluated, not by the standards of Scripture, but by the standards of the particular subculture. Paul warns against such evaluation: "Let us stop passing judgment on one another" (Rom. 14:13). Genuine love looks beyond the differences or even the failures (1 Cor. 13:5–7) and sees the progress that each person is making.

The Responsibilities of Fellowship

To reflect the mind of Christ requires the congregation to embrace the relational demands that Christ places upon his people. The church is not just a gathering of believers for the purpose of worship; it is a community that requires mutual interaction and support. Fellowship, while enjoyable and mutually beneficial, requires intent—and intent is demonstrated in several ways.

Assimilation

Assimilation is the process of including new people into the life and ministry of the church. The problem of excluding new people from the church is not new, but plagued the early church as well. After Paul's conversion on the road to Damascus he encountered difficulty in gaining acceptance by the church. Because of his background, people viewed him with suspicion and fear. Barnabas took the initiative, however, to assimilate him into the church (Acts 9:26–27). Newcomers may find it difficult to be included in a church that is dominated by one family. Even after people have attended for a number of years, they may still be regarded as the newcomers. It is the responsibility of the leadership to set the example by giving new people opportunities to serve within the church. If a new person demonstrates godly maturity, he or she should be given opportunities to serve in leadership positions as well.

Service

Everyone is given a spiritual gift (or gifts) that they are to use within the ministry of the church: "Each one should use whatever gift he has received to serve others, faithfully administering God's grace in its various forms" (1 Peter 4:10). To be a part of a community is to be committed to the exercise of one's spiritual gift for the glory of God and the benefit of others. Service is inherent in our responsibilities as part of the community. The leadership should recruit and motivate people to serve by providing them the support, opportunities, and resources needed (see further discussion in chapter nine).

Mutual submission

Submission is a major theme throughout the New Testament. Wives are commanded to submit to their husbands; children are to submit to their parents; everyone is responsible to submit to Christ and to governmental authorities. The writer of Hebrews places submission as central to the church when he commands the congregation to submit to the church leaders (Heb. 13:17). The apostle Paul takes submission a step further when he commands that we are to "submit to one another out of reverence for Christ" (Eph. 5:21). This mutual submission involves the willingness to place the needs and interests of others above those of ourselves so that we are conciliatory in relationships. Submission stems from our willingness to be the least rather than desiring to be the greatest (Matt. 18:1–4; 20:28). We are ready to follow the plans of others while not demanding adherence to our own suggestions and ideas (Rom. 12:10).

Prayer

As the church gathers together there is to be mutual prayer support for one another. The greatest privilege granted to the church fellowship is the blessing that comes through the joy of interceding on behalf of others. Prayer is to be the mark of the church so that it is known as a house of prayer. Whenever the early church gathered together they exercised the responsibility of corporate prayer (Acts 2:42–47). Prayer expresses the unity of the congregation and the concern that it has for other people.

Transparency

To be bonded in one spirit and one body, church members must be willing to be transparent before one another. People must move beyond self-pride, by which one seeks protection from vulnerability, and develop the trust and honesty that results in accountability, support, and edification. James writes, "Confess your sins to each other and pray for each other so that you may be healed" (James 5:16). This depth of relationships is not easily attained, requiring effort and determination, building upon the trust that comes as people protect and accept one another (1 Cor. 13:7). For this to happen in the church, it must begin with the leadership as they set the standard by being open with the people they serve.

Forgiveness

No relationship is without hurt. Because of our humanness and propensity toward selfishness we do incredibly foolish and insensitive things. Likewise, because no one is yet perfect, others will sin and will intentionally or unintentionally wrong us. While Scripture sets the procedure for dealing with these problems (Matt. 18:15–20), the foundation for restoring the relationship is a forgiving attitude. To maintain unity people must be willing to forgive the misunderstandings and disagreements that inevitably occur.

Care: Loving Others Through Mutual Support

The church is a spiritual hospital where people come, broken and wounded, from the spiritual battle to find healing and encouragement. It is to be a safe place in a spiritually threatening world. Because we live in a fallen world, life in general is not only brutally hard but presents the added pressure of suffering because of our association with Christ. Relationships become strained and broken, stress from the job weighs people down, financial pressures squeeze the family, children rebel, sickness and death strike unexpectedly, emotional struggles choke out joy, temptations overwhelm people, the spiritual conflict with the old nature results in spiritual discouragement. All of these problems plague people who walk through the church doors. They come to church because they desire and desperately need spiritual encouragement to face the daily realities of life. While God ultimately takes the responsibility for meeting the individual's needs—whether they be emotional, spiritual, or physical—he has also chosen to use the church body as a means by which those needs are met. We are commanded to "carry each other's burdens, and in this way you will fulfill the law of Christ" (Gal. 6:2). We are to "be devoted to one another in brotherly love. Honor one another above yourselves. Never be lacking in zeal, but keep your spiritual fervor, serving the Lord. Be joyful in hope, patient in affliction, faithful in prayer. Share with God's people who are in need. Practice hospitality. Bless those who persecute you; bless and do not curse. Rejoice with those who rejoice; mourn with those who mourn. Live in harmony with one another. Do not be proud, but be willing to associate with people of low position. Do not be conceited" (Rom. 12:10–16). We are not to remain isolated, nor are we to come to church only to sit. Rather the gathering of God's people is to be a time when we interact with one anther and become sensitive to one another's needs in order to support each other.

The Foundation for Care

The care of the church springs from the willingness of people to live sacrificially in service to others. People who have a deep-rooted love for others are less concerned about meeting their own needs than they are about meeting the needs of others. In meeting those needs, care is demonstrated in many ways.

Care involves a willingness to sacrifice time. Time is perhaps our most important asset. Time is a nonrenewable resource; once it is lost it can never be retrieved. With work hours increasing and leisure time declining people have less time to spend with family, friends, and church activities. This is coupled with the increase of time demands, resulting in people spending less time with others and more time doing things. Consequently, for the church to minister to one another, people need to set others as a priority and be willing to sacrifice their time to be with others. We are told in Scripture to make the most of every opportunity (Eph. 5:15–16). This means that we are to recognize that our time on this planet is short and that the opportunities to serve God can be easily missed. A congregation that learns to love is a community in which people willingly sacrifice their time to spend with others and minister to their needs.

Care involves a willingness to sacrifice personal comfort. When Paul writes that we are to mourn with those who mourn (Rom. 12:15), he is challenging us to set aside our personal comfort in order to experience the pain and sorrow of others. We are not merely to stand outside their troubles and shout advice, but become so intimately involved with them that we share their sorrows. Loving people demands that we do not remain indifferent toward people and their needs. Ministry is accomplished in the context of hurt. It is when we leave the comforts of our secure lives that we learn the joy and the pain of service. Throughout the writings of the prophets we discover over and over that God required them to suffer in order to convey the message to the people.

Care involves a willingness to sacrifice finances. The church in Jerusalem faced intense persecution at the hands of the Jews and Romans. As a consequence, people were not able to get jobs, they were not able to sell produce, and they were not able to earn money even for food and clothing. Because of their suffering, the other churches scattered throughout Asia Minor were called upon to take up collections in order to provide finances to the Jerusalem Christians (2 Cor. 9:1–15; see also Phil. 4:10–19). The finances that God gives to us are not to be used by us alone. Rather, we are also to use them for the benefit of others, ministering to their needs through the abundance of what God has given us.

Care involves a willingness to sacrifice energy. Ministry requires hard work. There are no powder-puff jobs in the kingdom of God. Ministry often results in our lives being "poured out like a drink offering" (Phil. 2:17; 2 Tim. 4:6). Giving of our energies means that we are willing to use our talents and gifts to benefit others, that we are willing to serve even when we are emotionally, spiritually, and physically tired. In Christ's ministry he was so pressed by the crowds that often he could not even get the food and rest he needed (Mark 6:31–34).

The Nature of Care

In caring for people the church has a responsibility to minister to the whole person. To minister to the spiritual nature of the person to the exclusion of the physical and emotional needs misses the biblical mandate of care and results in broken people becoming disillusioned with the body of Christ.

With the poverty rate in rural areas being equal to that of the inner-city, there are many opportunities for the church to minister to the physical needs of others. The church needs to cultivate compassion toward those who lack physical necessities and are going through financial difficulties. While the church should not support those who refuse to work, they should readily give to those who have legitimate needs (James 2:14–17).

The congregation must care, too, for the emotional needs of people. The sage in Proverbs 17:17 describes a friend as someone who "loves at all times, and a brother is born for adversity." A friend is one who provides emotional support during adversity, bringing love and emotional encouragement (Prov. 17:22). The church is a place where people receive both emotional support and teaching on how to encourage people who are going through emotionally difficult periods, be it depression, grief, stress, or any other crisis.

When people walk through the front doors of the church they do so having spiritual needs, having spent the week failing and falling to the temptations that plague their lives. Since we are not perfect, we still sin. John warns that any who thinks himself to be perfect and without sin is deceived (1 John 1:8). Providing for the spiritual health of the congregation requires an atmosphere in which people can confess their sins without being judged or condemned and can be supported through prayer (James 5:16; 1 John 5:16). Those who are spiritually weak are supported and encouraged by the strong (Rom. 15:1–2). The church is to be a place where people can obtain prayer during times of temptation, biblical instruction when confused, wise counsel when faced with difficult decisions, and loving correction when ensnared.

Giving to people is more than a humanitarian concern. It is a response to Christ, so when we give to people we are giving to Christ (Matt. 25:34–39; Mark 9:41).

Discipline: Loving Others Through Correction

Discipline within the church measures our love for others. Discipline reveals a willingness to do the difficult with the goal of restoring a person into fellowship with Christ and the congregation. No form of correction is pleasant. It is stressful for everyone involved. But true correction springs forth from our love for one another. Without the foundation of love, discipline becomes harsh, judgmental, and critical. Without the foundation of love our actions will be resented rather than received, causing harm rather than bringing healing. The purpose of discipline is not to judge the individual or make the person suffer for his or her wrong, nor is it to avenge a wrong or demand justice. The purpose is to restore the individual into fellowship and to correct individuals who have strayed from the truth and thus threatened their own spiritual well-being.

The Purpose of Discipline

There is nothing more difficult for the church and more trauma-tizing for people than to conduct church discipline. It will break the heart of the pastor and stretch the unity of the church. If properly understood, however, discipline is neither judgmental nor destructive; it is part of God's process of bringing people back into intimate fellowship with him.

Thus, a purpose for discipline is to restore the person into fellowship with God. The person who becomes ensnared in sin has a damaged relationship with Christ. Intimate fellowship with God is broken. The goal, then, is to reestablish divine communion. The church's ultimate motivation is to see people mature in relationship with Christ. In 1 Corinthians 5:1–5, Paul challenges the church to confront an individual in an incestuous relationship. The church was to abandon the person to Satan through excommunication, such action causing the person to repent and forsake his sin. James also points out that "if one of you should wander from the truth and someone should bring him back, remember this: Whoever turns a sinner from the error of his way will save him from death and cover over a multitude of sin" (James 5:19–20).

A further purpose for discipline is to restore the person into fellowship. When a person rebels against God, he or she becomes estranged from the church. Instead of the fellowship being a source of comfort and joy, it becomes a reminder of the person's sin and his or her guilt before God. Christ mentions that when we confront a fellow believer who has wronged us, "if he listens to you, you have won your brother over" (Matt. 18:15). Once the person repents, then the individual is to be restored to complete fellowship lest the rejection causes the person to revert back into sin (2 Cor. 2:7–8).

Another purpose for discipline is to purify the body of Christ. Sin left unchecked influences the behavior of others and can easily cause the whole community to be led astray. When the Israelites wandered in the wilderness during the Exodus, the attitudes and actions of a few affected the whole group. When one or two individuals rebelled against God and his appointed leaders, the whole nation became corrupt, and many followed the rebellion. The church disciplines wayward members so that their negative influence will not affect others (1 Cor. 5:7).

Yet another purpose of discipline is to protect the body of Christ against division. A ploy of Satan is to render ineffective the testimony of God's people by causing divisions and conflicts that weaken community and thwart its testimony. Those who stir up strife and cause division are to be warned and then excommunicated from the fellowship (Titus 3:10).

Discipline, too, warns others of the dangers of sin. When an individual is corrected by the church body, it serves as a warning to all the church members concerning the dangers of sin and the necessity for purity of life. While the goal is restoration, often the person will refuse to respond and continues to reject Christ's authority over his or her life and conduct. By publicly rebuking and excommunicating the person, the seriousness of sin is highlighted and the importance of faithful integrity is maintained. In discipline the whole body of Christ is challenged anew to remain faithful to Christ and to take the presence of sin seriously (1 Tim. 5:20).

The Process of Discipline

In Matthew 18:15–17, Christ outlines a four-fold process of church discipline. This process is designed to protect the reputation both of the church and the individual accused.

The first step is personal confrontation: "If your brother sins against you, go and show him his fault, just between the two of you" (Matt. 18:15). When a person continually practices a specific sin and is not dealing with the problem, then the one who is closest to the individual and first aware of the situation is to go to the offending person and gently confront him or her. The person closest to the offending individual already has a personal affinity with him or her and will be able to go with pure motives, desiring to restore the relationship and seeking the best interests of the offending party. If the offending individual acknowledges the sin, he or she is to be forgiven and restored back into fellowship so that nothing more is said. By keeping it private between two individuals, the reputation of everyone involved is protected and the church avoids gossip.

The Biblical Process of Discipline

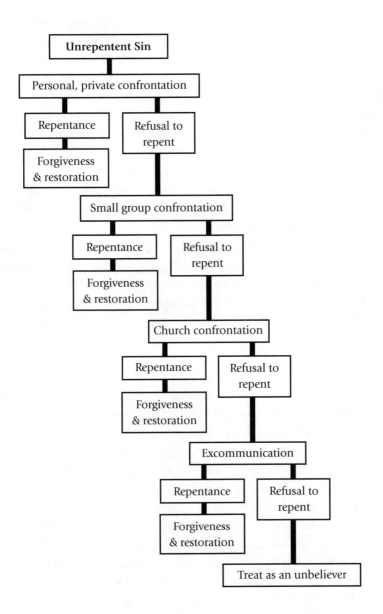

The second step is small group confrontation. The Old Testament law stipulated that before a person could be convicted of a crime there had to be the testimony of at least two witnesses. Christ affirms this: ". . . but if he will not listen, take one or two others along, so that 'every matter may be established by the testimony of two or three witnesses'" (Matt. 18:16). Witnesses protect people from being falsely accused by those who are vindictive and using the discipline process as a personal vendetta against another. These witnesses should be aware of the problem and able to testify in regard to the individual's sinful behavior. They become a witness not only of the offense but also of the attempted reconciliation and response, thus protecting both the offended and the offender. Witnesses should demonstrate wisdom and a willingness to hear both sides of the issue before passing judgment.

The third step in the process of discipline is church confrontation. The church objectively examines the accusations to make sure of their accuracy. Once the examination is complete, the congregation is told the results of their findings, although they should not go into detail regarding the offense. Although the church confronts the sin, they are still to respect and protect the reputation of the offending individual. The intent of church confrontation is not to belittle the offending person in front of his of her peers, but to ascertain whether he or she has refused to deal with the sin. The goal of the public denouncement is to bring about reconciliation by making the offending individual aware of the seriousness of the problem.

The final step is excommunication. If the offending person refuses to repent, even after a public confrontation, then he or she is to be treated "as you would a pagan or a tax collector" (Matt. 18:17). The person is to be regarded as one who is irreligious and disloyal to Christ. With respect to our relationship with the offending individual, we are to relate to him or her as we would to an unbeliever. This means we allow the person to hear the Word of God and attend services, but we refuse fellowship and do not allow the person to participate in the Lord's Table. The offending individual is removed from participation in the ministry and leadership. In treating him or her as an unbeliever, the church can still minister to the person's needs just as the church would minister to those outside the church. If the person repents, he or she is restored to full fellowship and participation in the ministry of the church (2 Cor. 2:5 ff).

Edification: Loving Others Through Exhortation

Scripture employs a number of different terms to describe the process by which we are to strengthen one another in our spiritual lives. We are challenged to edify, build up, exhort, and spur one another on to love and good deeds— phrases that speak of the process by which we become involved in one another's lives so that by mutual involvement we grow and become spiritually mature.

The Nature of Edification

When a person comes to a saving knowledge of Christ and enters the Christian community, he or she is still dominated by secular thinking. Although a person is declared righteous before God (justification), that person is just starting the life-long process of sanctification. Edification is the work the church does in transforming the lives of people and assisting them in the process of growing spirituality. In his discussion concerning the activities of the church, Paul warns, "What then shall we say, brothers? When you come together, everyone has a hymn, or a word of instruction, a revelation, a tongue or an interpretation. All of these must be done for the strengthening of the church" (1 Cor. 14:26).

The Process of Edification

Edification is not an event, nor is it just a program. It is a process that requires the church to continually strive to instruct and train people to live godly lives.

Part of the process of edification is to build accountability. Accountability involves people being responsible for the spiritual well-being of others. In Ezekiel 3:18–22, God challenges the prophet, appointing him as a watchman who is responsible to warn others of sin. If he fails to do so, then he himself will be held accountable and their blood will be upon him. Because our society is marked by individualism that denies mutual accountability, the church needs to instruct and strategize methods for building loving accountability within the congregation, where people ask one another the tough questions and they are open and honest enough to admit the struggles and temptations they are facing.

Another part of the process of edification involves instruction. Because the communication and implementation of Scripture is the foundation for maturity, the church needs to examine how people are being taught and what they are learning. Formal and informal training need to be implemented. People need to be taught not only answers to their life questions but also how to ask the right questions. The focus of the teaching is not upon what people want to hear but what they need to hear.

The process of edification requires, too, mentoring relationships. An often neglected area, especially in small churches, is the development of mentoring relationships. Because people live in close proximity to one another and have close contact, they are taught to respect one another's privacy. While this is good in some respects, it undermines the necessity of being in a mentoring relationship with others. Mentors come alongside others to love them, encourage them in personal growth, and challenge them to catch a vision for what God desires to accomplish through them as they exercise their spiritual gifts. Doing so necessitates the mature believer being willing to enter into a one-on-one relationship with a younger or more immature Christian in order to build a long-term relationship with him or her (Titus 2:1–5).

While the small church excels in developing unity, this unity is often mistaken for a mentoring relationship. To be a mentor, one must be intentional in one's interaction with another, the focus being spiritual rather than merely social.

Establishing a Loving Church

The responsibility of the board is to constantly keep their fingers upon the pulse of love within the church community. Love is to be the hallmark of the Christian community as well as the magnet that attracts people to Christ. Leadership, then, must be intent in overseeing the growth of love within the congregation. Establishing a loving church can be accomplished through several means.

First, *provide opportunities for people to develop relationships.* People need to spend time together to build relationships that move beyond the superficial. Trust provides the cornerstone for mutual accountability, transparent honesty, and loving confrontation. This is not built by gathering for one hour on Sunday to sing hymns and hear the spoken message. It can only come through time, as people learn to accept one another and value each other. To build this trust the church needs to provide opportunities for people to interact with one another informally, to share with one another their joys and sorrows, to help one another through assistance and care, to pray for one another through trials and difficulties. Potlucks, dinners, and other fun events are more than just social events; they are opportunities for people to gain a better understanding of one another in order to open avenues for building trust as members learn to appreciate each other.

A second way to create a loving church is to *strengthen corporate prayer.* People who pray together stay together. Prayer enhances unity, transforms attitudes, encourages mutual concern, builds trust, and moves God. Often conflicts arise in the church not because people disagree (even people in very close relationships disagree) but because people have not learned to trust and care for one another. Corporate prayer binds people and becomes an expression of people's love for one another. When people love one another they pray for one another and when they pray for one another they learn to love one another more deeply. If a church desires to become marked by love and instill love within the congregation, it needs to focus upon prayer.

A third way to build love in the church is to *provide care for people in crisis.* Eliphaz best described the daily realities of life when he lamented, "Yet man is born to trouble as surely as sparks fly upwards" (Job 5:7). No matter who a person is, where that person might live, his or her social status and economic prosperity, that person is not immune to suffering. It strikes unpredictably, showing no favoritism to any, and comes unexpectedly. But while the trials we face are part and parcel to living in a fallen world, they are not arbitrary and purposeless. God allows suffering and trials to work in the lives of individuals, and he allows difficulties in order to build love and unity within the body of Christ (2 Cor. 1:3–5). But loving churches take care of people not only in the congregation; they take care of those in the community as well. That love is manifested in members' verbal responses to and through their actions toward one another and others in the community at large. Members sacrifice their own pleasure and comfort to minister to people in need, whether that be helping them move to a new house, providing meals for people in crisis, or just lending a neighborly hand to someone who needs some assistance. Part of the responsibility of the leadership of the church is to evaluate and implement strategies for organizing people to care for others (Acts 6:1–7).

A fourth way to build a loving church is to *develop accountability and mentoring programs*. There is a vast difference between accountability and judgmentalism. Accountability seeks to hold the person responsible for his or her thoughts, actions, and attitudes in order to encourage and foster spiritual growth within the individual. Judgmentalism desires to condemn the person to lower his or her standing in order to elevate oneself. Accountability focuses upon the issues and needs of others. Judgmentalism focuses only upon one's own issues, desires, and attitudes. Accountability builds upon humility and the awareness of one's own personal vulnerability (Gal. 6:1). Judgmentalism flows from one's arrogance and pious self-righteousness. Accountability is motivated by love; judgmentalism is motivated by selfishness. Church members who genuinely love one another will develop mentoring relationships between people in order to hold one another accountable.

A final way to build love is to *resolve conflicts*. The difference between a loving church and an unloving congregation is not the amount of disagreements and conflicts that arise, but how the congregation responds to them. Congregations marked by the inward quality of love for people resolve conflicts in a way that respects and honors others. Disagreements, resentments, and contentions are dealt with honestly and openly rather than swept under a carpet of denial and fear. Christ challenges the church not to avoid disagreements but to deal with them in a manner that reflects the love of Christ (Matt. 5:21–26). One of the responsibilities of the leadership is to manifest godly attitudes in disagreements—to teach the congregation how to model reconciliation through the leadership's own resolution of problems.

Evaluation and Implementation

1. With the church board complete worksheet 12 (see appendix A).
2. Examine the biblical procedure for church discipline and develop a procedure for how the church will deal with possible disciplinary situations within the church.
3. Develop strategies for how the church will communicate people's needs, and ways they will minister to them in times of crisis. In what ways can the church be more effective in training people and equipping them to help those in crisis? How can the church be more effective in mentoring people within the congregation?
4. How has the church resolved conflicts in the past? What are ways the church can foster better conflict resolution skills within the congregation?

Further Reading

Dobson, Edward G.; Speed B. Leas; and Marshall Shelley. *Mastering Conflict and Controversy*. Portland, Ore.: Multnomah, 1992.

Halverstadt, Hugh F. *Managing Church Conflict*. Atlanta: John Knox, 1991.

Hansen, David. *The Power of Loving Your Church*. Minneapolis: Bethany House, 1998.

Longenecker, Harold L. *Growing Leaders by Design*. Grand Rapids: Kregel, 1995.

McSwain , Larry, and William C. Treadwell, Jr. *Conflict Ministry in the Church*. Nashville: Broadman, 1981.

Sjogren, Steve. *Conspiracy of Kindness*. Ann Arbor, Mich.: Servant, 1993.

Slater, Michael. *Stretcher Bearers*. Ventura, Calif.: Regal, 1985.

White, John, and Ken Blue. *Healing the Wounded: The Costly Love of Church Discipline*. Downers Grove, Ill.: InterVarsity, 1985.

SIX

Developing the Mission of Reaching

*I*n developing the ministry of the church, the leadership needs to understand its mission. A quick perusal of available books on church leadership results in confusion concerning the nature of mission. For some, such as Norman Shawchuck and Roger Heuser, mission is an outgrowth of vision. Concerning the relationship between the vision and the mission of the church, they write, "Out of vision arises a clear and compelling understanding of what the mission of our ministry is to be. Mission is the bridge that connects vision to reality. If vision is God's dream dreamed in us, then mission is the waking dream, embodied in the life of the leaders and the congregation."[1]

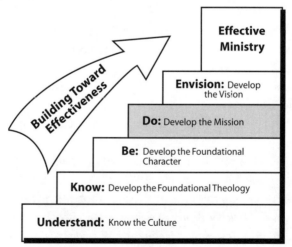

Others see it as the soil from which vision grows. Mission is a general direction and a broad statement of what the church desires to accomplish. Vision itself is specific and distinct to each body. The mission sets the general course, while the vision details how the church will accomplish it. For them, vision "puts feet" on the mission.

Defining Mission in the Church

Because of the confusion regarding the terms *mission* and *vision*, it is important to understand what each term means and how they relate to one another. For the present purpose, *mission* refers to the broad definition of what the universal church is to accomplish. It governs how and what each specific church seeks to realize in its local context. If the foundation of the church is the spirituality and theological basis, then the general framework of the church is the mission. Mission is the biblically established task of the church. It sets the parameters for vision by establishing the biblical goal. Without a clear sense of mission, the vision can easily become aimed on achieving the wrong target. Thus, the mission will have universal application to every church situation, whether the church is in rural Montana or the inner city of Chicago. Mission is the direction toward which the vision seeks to take the church.

The mission of the church encompasses three parts. First, the church is to be a witnessing community. The task of the church is to be a community of believers who seek to proclaim Christ to a spiritually dead world. Second, the church is to be a teaching community where individuals are taught and discipled in the spiritual life. The church is responsible to teach people how to live the faith they proclaim, so that they become people of spiritual impact through developed godliness. Third, the church is to be a ministering community. It is to recruit, motivate, and train people to be involved in the ministry of Christ, serving others through the exercise of its spiritual gifts.

The Witnessing Community

When Christ set forth the mission of the church in Matthew 28:19–20, and then repeated it in Acts 1:7–8, he made it clear that the church is a community obsessed with the task of proclaiming Christ to the world. It is not just a social organization, nor even a spiritual fellowship, but a light to the world (Matt. 5:14–16).

In developing a small church into a witnessing community, one mistake has been to equate evangelism with numerical growth. While stating that the overall purpose of the church is to bring people to Christ, it is then assumed that no matter what the size or location of the church, it will be growing and that all churches will be moving toward becoming a large congregation. The result of equating evangelism with numerical growth is that those outside the small church often view a non-growing church as ineffective, while those inside become discouraged because many of their evangelistic efforts are apparently unproductive. Consequently, the conclusion is drawn that God is not blessing the small church, and only working within the numerically growing or large church. The danger, as Kent and Barbara Hughes point out, is that the church can then become driven by pragmatism that can corrupt the theology of the church.[2]

Nowhere in Scripture is the church called upon to be a numerically growing community nor is it even called upon to "convert" people to Christ. Instead, the apostle Paul points out that the process of conversion is the work of God, and therefore numerical growth within the church is the result of God's achievement (1 Cor. 3:5–9). Even in Acts, when the church experienced significant growth, it was a result of God's sovereignty. The early church, which many have used as the standard for numerical growth, recognized that their remarkable growth was the work of God, not something achieved through their own efforts. Luke writes, "And the Lord added to their number daily those who were being saved" (Acts 2:47).

The mission of the church is not, then, to add numerically to the church. Such is the responsibility of God. Rather it is to be a witnessing community, testifying of the gospel of Christ to the people with whom it comes in contact. From its inception, the church has been given the responsibility to preach the gospel (Matt. 28:19) and to provide answers to people who wonder why Christians have peace and serenity in a chaotic and tormented world (1 Peter 3:15). The church is to faithfully perform this mandated mission regardless of the results achieved. The small church is to constantly affirm its commitment to the Great Commission, to be willing to go anywhere, do anything, and sacrifice everything that God requires for it to achieve that purpose. The call of the church is not necessarily to grow; that may or may not happen. Numerical growth is, however, ultimately outside the control of the church, because growth is governed by the providence of God. The call of the church is to faithfully and effectively communicate the gospel of Christ, inviting others to enter into a personal relationship with Christ. The benchmark of the church remains its faithfulness, not to a tradition, program, or pattern of ministry, but to the obedience of Christ fleshed out in daily life so that obedience becomes a visible testimony of God's redemptive work available to all humanity. David Ray highlights this mission: "God doesn't call the church to grow but to be faithful and effective. A faithful and effective church will pursue fitting and intentional ways of sharing the Good News of the Gospel and inviting others to join their band of disciples."[3] While a number of reasons can be cited to explain why a small church might not experience numerical growth, that does not mean it cannot achieve its God-ordained mission of being a witnessing community.

Proclaiming Biblical Truth

Being a witnessing community involves inviting people to accept Christ as their personal Lord and Savior. But it also includes communicating biblical truth to people so that they gain a greater understanding of the nature and demands of a holy God. To do this, the Christian needs to properly assess someone's level of receptivity to the gospel—that is, whether a person is antagonistic, biblically ignorant, a seeker, an examiner, or a responder. Once we understand a person's spiritual receptivity, we seek to move that person to more receptivity. The antagonist, for example, develops a positive perspective of Christians and is now one who is biblically ignorant. Evangelism is not an event but a process of being used by the Holy Spirit to bring the individual closer to Christ.

The Antagonist

The process may well begin with approaching the *antagonist*. Not everyone is open and receptive to the gospel message. While many are willing to listen, some have such a strong negative reaction to the message of Christ that they are openly hostile to Christianity (for example see Acts 7). They are suspicious of Christians, seeing them as judgmental bigots who unlovingly condemn people. This antagonism stems not only from the perception of Christ, but also as a result of the cultural war that is afflicting society today. Christianity is viewed as a threat to cultural and religious egalitarianism

The Process of Evangelism

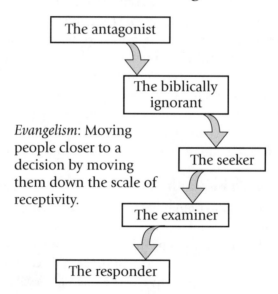

The antagonist

The biblically ignorant

Evangelism: Moving people closer to a decision by moving them down the scale of receptivity.

The seeker

The examiner

The responder

and relativism. This has given rise to a distorted and negative perception of Christianity.

To reach antagonistic individuals for Christ, the Christian first and foremost needs to demonstrate unconditional love and acceptance of that individual. Since evangelism is a process rather than an event, it is crucial that the Christian establishes a relationship with the antagonist so that through the demonstration of love, a bridge is built.

The gospel needs to be communicated through actions rather than words, in which the believer ministers to the social, emotional, and physical needs of that person so that the antagonist develops a positive view of Christianity.

The Biblically Ignorant

As society becomes more secular and continues to move further and further from Christian beliefs as the core of the national religious consciousness, the church will encounter a greater number of individuals who are unfamiliar with the teaching of the Bible. Any

The Process of Evangelism

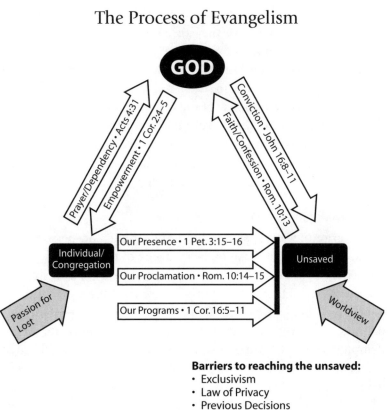

Barriers to reaching the unsaved:
- Exclusivism
- Law of Privacy
- Previous Decisions
- History of Church
- History of Individual
- Discouragement

recognition of Christ will not go beyond the awareness that he was born on Christmas and that he died on Easter. Those who are biblically ignorant will be religiously ecumenical, viewing Christianity as one of many ways to God (see Acts 17:22–34). As with the antagonists, the most important part of the process is cultivating a personal relationship with the biblically ignorant in which love is unconditionally demonstrated. Witnessing to these individuals involves a careful, non-threatening, non-argumentative communication of the gospel and basic tenets of Christianity.

The Seeker

Seekers usually see themselves as "religious." They are familiar with Christian beliefs and want to know more. They see religion as the best way to meet their felt needs. They are aware of the basic elements of the gospel, but they may not yet fully appreciate its implications. The Samaritan woman (John 4) and the rich young ruler (Matt. 19:16–26) were both seekers who were in such a condition.

With seekers, the response of the Christian needs to be ministry and communication. The seeker's desire for felt needs to be met provides an opportunity for the Christian to communicate the distinctive claims and implications of the gospel to that person as the church cares for the needs of the individual.

The Examiner

The examiner understands the implications and personal demands of the gospel. Examiners are aware of their sinful state before a holy God and are looking for spiritual answers to their spiritual problems (see Acts 2:37). With the examiner, witnessing becomes persuasive. Those who understand the full implications of the gospel need to be issued a personal invitation to appropriate the redemptive work of Christ. This can be done individually through personal appeal or by inviting the person to evangelistic events in which the gospel is presented.

The Responder

The responder is ready and willing to embrace the gospel message. When an individual responds to the appeal to accept the redemptive work of Christ, the church is responsible to instruct the person in the foundational truths of Scripture and spiritual disciplines.

Developing the Witnessing Community

The task of witnessing, then, may be described as gentle persuasion relentlessly applied. As explained in the steps above, the process of evangelism involves bringing people to a redemptive knowledge of Christ by moving people closer to Christ. As outlined above, this task is not an event but a process that encompasses human initiative and divine involvement. One evangelizes the antagonist, for example, by helping him or her develop a positive perspective of Christ and the church. Thus, evangelism is not just sharing the gospel message and asking people to make a life-long decision in light of that message. Being a witness for Christ encompasses our whole lives and our continual interactions with every unbeliever with whom we rub shoulders.

And because evangelism is a process, we recognize that while people testify of the gospel, it is God who brings it to fruition in the life of the person. Thus, the focus of the task is not on "converting" individuals; the focus is becoming a witnessing community by communicating the gospel through words and actions.

Nor is evangelism done by "Lone Rangers," who, after converting one soul, ride off into the sunset in search of another. Evangelism is a team sport, involving the individual as well as the congregation. Dann Spader and Gary Mayes point out that "typically an unbeliever needs to have more than five meaningful contacts with a number of Christians before he or she will begin to trust the message of the gospel."[4] Consequently, the evangelism process involves the interplay between the individual Christian and the church community. Developing a witnessing community involves utilizing both of these arms of effective evangelism.

To build a witnessing community, the church must become obsessed with evangelism; otherwise evangelism will remain a task rather than become a mission. Being a witnessing community is not another program—it is central to every ministry of the church. Kevin Ruffcorn emphasizes the importance of integrating evangelism in every aspect of ministry: "Evangelism is woven into the fabric of congregational life. It cannot be separated from the fabric without destroying the material because it is not merely a design imprinted on the surface."[5] Without an evangelistic perspective, every ministry of the church will eventually collapse and become ineffective. The awareness of the mission field around the church remains vital to the overall health and vitality of the congregation. When the church no longer sees the lost around them it stops functioning as a church (John 4:34–38).

Personal Evangelism

The church will only be evangelistic when the people become gripped with their call to the effort. Without each member of the church involved in the process, outreach will only remain on the goal sheet and not in the practice of the congregation.

The Foundation Is Prayer

Personal evangelism is built upon the cornerstone of prayer. Evangelism is a process, but it is a spiritual process, requiring supernatural empowerment. Since evangelizing requires spiritual change, it cannot be accomplished through human means. God has chosen to use prayer as a basis for his involvement within the affairs of humanity. Thus, the first step in motivating people for evangelism involves encouraging them to pray for specific individuals who fall within each person's natural networks.

But prayer needs to be offered not just on behalf of those who are to be reached. Pray also for the one seeking to evangelize. Like the apostle

Personal Evangelism

Pray for opportunity and receptivity.

Build relationships to overcome barriers.

Communicate the gospel with patience and gentleness.

Paul, the believer needs to pray both for opportunities to present the gospel and for boldness to communicate that gospel (Col. 4:3–4). We become engaged on the spiritual battlefield for the souls of people through prayer. We can have all our programs in place, our outreach events planned, our people verbalizing their faith, but it comes to naught if all these dimensions of evangelism are not undergirded with prayer. Prayer prepares the hearer of the gospel message as well as the communicator. Without prayer, there will be no passion for the lost, no power in the testimony, and no presence of God in the message.

The Process Is Relational

Having identified, and begun to pray for, specific individuals within the community, the next step in the evangelism process is building relationships. The apostle Peter, a master of evangelism, writes that we are to "always be prepared to give an answer to everyone who asks you to give the reason for the hope that you have" (1 Peter 3:15). The words *everyone who asks you* implies existing personal relationships in which the non-Christian has seen manifested in daily life the unique hope of the Christian. Developing close relationships remains one of the most productive means of evangelism. After surveying fourteen thousand church members, the Institute of American Church Growth concluded that 75–90 percent came to Christ and the church they attended because of a personal relationship with a friend or relative.[6] Such is especially true regarding the small church, where relationships rather than programs form the backbone of ministry. The strength of the small church is its relational nature. Those who are attracted to the small church are attracted because of the close, intimate fellowship that the small church offers.

Cultivating a witnessing community involves training people how to utilize the personal relationships they have with others in the community. People need to see their friends and neighbors as the mission field they are called to reach. Stressing this importance, Spader and Mayes maintain,

Evangelism happens in the context of interpersonal relationships. It happens when one believer allows God to use him as salt and light within his own sphere of influence. All too frequently evangelistic programming takes people out of their spheres of influence. But personal friends and acquaintances from any arena form the most natural environment in which to begin reaching out. Our friends are our personal mission field.[7]

To become a witnessing community, the church leadership needs to encourage people to develop and utilize the network of friendships as a means of reaching people for Christ. This begins by the leaders becoming committed to spending time with the unsaved and modeling before the people how to develop these networks. What the leader does not model the people will not execute.

First, building relationships involves the willingness to go where the unchurched live. Christ implied this when he prayed that his people would not be taken out of the world but be protected while existing in the world (John 17:15–16). We are sent to go into the world, to penetrate our community with the gospel of Christ. The call to be a witness is not a call to become a monk in a monastery, but to be a migrant worker in the fields of humanity. Being separated to God does not mean that we are segregated from the world. Rather it means that we take a consecrated life and live it before non-Christians, manifesting before their eyes the person of Christ and the hope of his salvation.

Second, forming relationships requires acceptance. Rapport cannot be built when people are viewed as "projects." Love needs to be demonstrated unconditionally. The task of the believer is to introduce people to Christ, not change them for Christ. To do so, we are called upon to love people as individuals and *as sinners*. This does not mean that Christians are to compromise their own conduct. Rather it means that the Christian expects the non-Christian to act like a non-Christian, and the Christian continues to love non-Christians regardless of their actions.

Third, building relational bridges involves being a servant. Friendships are built upon the foundation of service, that is, giving of one's time, energies, talents, and possessions to minister to the emotional, physical, and spiritual needs of others. While love is to be the motivation for the relationship, ministry is to be the expression of the relationship.

The Goal Is Invitation

The third ingredient to effective evangelism is the invitation to accept Christ. In witnessing to people it is important to realize that the proclamation of Christ to the lost is not a one-shot affair. Rather it requires patience and gentle persuasion. Sjogren sets the formula for servant evangelism as deeds of love, words of love, and adequate time.[8] Before the words of the gospel can be disclosed there must be the living demonstration of the gospel through the relationship. Having displayed and proclaimed the gospel, we allow time for the Holy Spirit to bring to fruition the seed that was implanted through our acts and words of love.

Communicating the gospel begins with disclosing the Scriptures to the mind and understanding of the individual. People cannot make a genuine decision of faith unless they clearly comprehend the ramifications of the gospel. The more people have been exposed to the gospel before their decision, the greater the likelihood that their decision will have a lasting effect upon their lives. This multiple exposure of the message can come through direct personal presentation or by inviting the individual to evangelistic events where the gospel message is clearly presented.

Once the person understands the gospel, the ground is prepared for an appeal to the will in anticipation of a response. This too can be done through the direct appeal by an individual or at an evangelistic event sponsored by the church.

Developing Program Evangelism

While the task of the Christian is to be a witness in the community, the responsibility of the church is to develop programs and ministries that are evangelistic in purpose. For this to occur, the church needs to set evangelism as a high priority. Because the small church has limited personnel to perform even the most necessary ministries within the church, evangelistic programs are often neglected. Small churches struggle with maintaining present ministries; therefore people are unenthusiastic about new programs, even ones directed at a goal as critical as evangelism. Developing the priority of evangelism begins not with new programs but with the integration of evangelism into every existing program. Evangelism becomes the purpose of all the programs so that evangelism is completely integrated within the life of the church.

Thus, the first step in developing a witnessing community is to perceive every ministry as a part of the evangelistic efforts of the church. Sunday school becomes, for instance, not just an occasion to teach Bible stories, but a time to bring the gospel to children.

Second, evangelism within the small church needs to be intentional. It does not happen naturally, even within the ministry of the church. For people to experience the redemptive reality of Christ, the gospel needs to be presented. If outreach is not planned, it will not occur. Rarely will the unchurched come to church uninvited, no matter how exciting the service might be. Churches that effectively evangelize their community do so intentionally. They not only train their people regarding the process, they analyze and establish goals for the whole congregation. Ron Crandall's research reveals that "it appears that setting . . . goals, planning to reach them, organizing human energy, and training persons in various skills related to evangelism and outreach are important ingredients in effectively reaching out to others and helping smaller churches grow."[9] Being intentional in evangelism involves establishing strategies for how evangelism will happen.

Program for the Different Stages

Since evangelism is a process by which people gain a greater understanding of their spiritual need, it is important to have different ministries for the different stages. Not every evangelistic event should be directed to the examiner. Not all events should include the direct appeal to accept Christ. For the antagonists such an appeal would only further antagonize the individual. For the ignorant, such an appeal would be confusing. An outreach event for the antagonist is one in which the goal is to present the church and the gospel in a positive light in order to move the individual from being an antagonist to a seeker. Before the reaping, the fruit needs to be ripe. If we attempt to move too quickly in the process then we end up harvesting unripe fruit that only becomes spoiled. In outreach the church needs to help people in the process of ripening, not just in the process of harvesting.

Develop Multiple Methods

Since every individual within the community is different in terms of personality, background, experiences, and spiritual sensitivity, evangelism requires different approaches for different people. Many smaller communities are no longer homogeneous. Within the church and community are farmers as well as business professionals, each responding differently to different ministry opportunities. To be effective, the church needs to understand the difference and tailor outreach to different groups.

Focus upon Community

Often the smaller church exists in areas where there is a strong emphasis upon community. Rural communities pride themselves on their mutual concern and care. Farmers assist other farmers in harvest; people give generously to those going through a crisis; businesses are supported faithfully because they are "local," even though the prices are not competitive. That which builds this sense of community is welcomed, and that which threatens it is fiercely opposed. For the church to be effective in outreach, it must become part of the community, a center for fostering a community spirit within the region. Holding, for instance, a bake sale for a family going through a medical crisis not only reveals Christ to the family, but to the whole community as well.

Fear of anything that might threaten community within a congregation is a hurdle to evangelism. Steve Bierly points out why some small churches oppose evangelism:

The small church has a bad reputation for being "against growth" because it balks at plans coming out of the church-growth movement. But smaller congregations have been unfairly labeled. It's not that they are against growth; it's that they are against changing the characteristics that make them unique. Small congregations aren't opposed to bringing men and women to Christ, but they are opposed to becoming mega-churches. They don't want to be asked to become something they are not.[10]

In creating evangelistic programs, the leadership needs to affirm that it will keep the family relationships and feeling that mark the small church. When outreach further enhances the church's sense of fellowship, it will be readily embraced. One way to achieve a deeper sense of fellowship is to focus upon member's friends and families rather than people they do not know. Strangers are threats to the community, but friends and family will only build the fellowship. Programs that focus upon strangers will be hindered, not because people do not want to evangelize others but because they perceive the program as a threat to a key value within the church.

Programs Must Be Social and Relational

The strength of the small church is its relationships. Close relationships not only bind the church together, they attract others as well. In many small communities, church related activities constitute a major portion of all social interaction within the community. Social and fellowship events can be opportunities for developing the church community and for reaching the unchurched as well.

Distinctives of the small community are its sense of mutual care and the importance of mutual respect and privacy. Ruffcorn describes the importance of privacy:

Along with the neighborliness, a strong respect developed for individual privacy. This distance was necessary to balance the closeness. Certain topics became forbidden in polite conversation. Family matters and marital relationships were never mentioned. A person might become concerned about what was happening in a neighbor's home, but that concern would never be shared unless the neighbor brought up the subject.[11]

To discuss religion is considered to be a violation of this core value. Because of people's close proximity to one another, no one wants to do anything that would embarrass someone. People in small communities do not want to jeopardize relationships that have spanned generations and that form the social framework within the whole community. The church becomes more effective in evangelism when it develops strategies that do not alienate others and strain relationships, but build upon the closeness of the community. By having evangelistic events focused upon social interaction rather than "evangelistic preaching" the gospel can be presented in a clear manner yet in a way that does not violate this value.

Programs Must Have High Quality

There is no substitute for quality in the ministry of the small church. Often, people in the small church are content to do the minimum, for that has served the church well for a number of years. While getting by may be permissible with the church members, those outside the church will find it unattractive. Today people expect quality in every aspect of life, from their shoes to their entertainment. Anything that does not reach their standard of quality is considered insignificant and unworthy of their time and energies. Therefore, in planning evangelistic events, the church needs to make sure that the program maintains a high standard of performance. If the activities of the church manifest shoddy efforts, people will not come. This is not to say that the small church needs to be the best in everything it does, but it means that the small church must strive to do its best with the resources and gifts of people within the church. Mediocrity not only reflects poorly upon the church, it also reflects poorly upon Christ. Everything that the congregation does should manifest their desire to please God (Col. 3:23).

Program for Needs

If privacy is the value marking the small community's relationships, practicality is the value marking its work ethic. The value of anything or anyone within the community is determined by its contribution to the productivity, health, and well-being of the community. It is not enough that people see the church meet together to pray and worship; they want to see what positive impact the group will have on the whole community.

That the church must make a practical contribution to the community applies to the minister. A pastor earns the right to be a part of the community and be heard by the community not by being theologically knowledgeable but by contributing to the community and working alongside people in the community. Before a pastor can win people to Christ, the people must see that he or she is one of them. While sound exegesis and careful study are necessary for the development of the sermon, the pastor gains a hearing when he or she spends time with people, being interested in their lives and adapting himself to their culture. Otherwise the pastor will preach a great message to an empty auditorium.

Thus, both the church and pastor should think of how to meet the needs and contribute to the spiritual and physical well-being of people not only within the congregation but of people within the community as a whole. Meeting needs is especially critical in the rural communities where the community and churches, rather than governmental agencies, are relied upon to provide social support. The Christian life must be demonstrated practically, not just argued and preached theoretically and theologically.

Focus on Faithfulness, Not Results

Evangelism in the small community is difficult, requiring diligent labor to attain fruitfulness. If those involved in the evangelistic efforts of the small church focus only upon results, they will soon become discouraged and unmotivated to witness. Since the results of evangelistic efforts is the responsibility of God, then the focus of the church and individual believer should be upon faithfulness in proclaiming the gospel to a lost world (see Isa. 6:9–13).

Evangelistic Events

Successful events require careful planning. The purpose is to execute an event that is sensitive to the people that the church is trying to reach, is clearly defined in its intent, and is properly organized.

Identify the Target

The methods used to reach people will be determined by the cultural, sociological, spiritual, and religious background of the individuals. In the book of Acts, the apostles often altered their approach to presenting the gospel, depending upon the people they were addressing.

Determine the Purpose

Some events may be pre-evangelistic, that is, they are designed to build relationships with the people in the community. Some may be fashioned to give people a positive understanding of the gospel, while others are devised to bring people to a point of decision. Since people are at different levels in their spiritual sensitivity and perception, the church should plan evangelistic events that are designed for different purposes.

Choose an Event that Meets the Purpose

Decide on the event that is appropriate to the target group and provides a context for accomplishing its purpose. Events not matched with the target group and purpose will be ineffective, bringing further discouragement to the church.

Choose the Location

Not all events can, nor should, be held in the church building. Events may be held in the local school, a park, a community center, or someone's home. Unchurched people are less likely to feel comfortable in a church. Therefore, neutral sites can be more favorable for inviting unchurched people, who are more likely to attend an event in a park than a church.

Outline the Event

Once the event is decided on and the location determined, the next step is to prepare the soil for quality. Preparedness involves identifying who is responsible for what, what will happen, and how it will be planned.

Publicize the Event

The extent of the publicity will be determined by the location, purpose, and target group. Publicity may include personal invitations by congregational members, posters, articles in the local paper, advertising on radio and television, as well as other creative ideas developed by the congregation.

Plan for Follow-up

Even before the event is held, those who are planning it need to consider how they will follow-up those who attend. The nature of follow-up, however, will be different depending on the purpose of the event. Follow-up for pre-evangelistic events may include personal visits or may involve members of the congregation in further developing relationships with those who attend. For anyone who makes a personal decision for Christ, follow-up should always include discipleship.

Evaluate the Event

Did it accomplish the purpose? What was most effective? How could it be more effective in the future? Was there adequate follow-up? Were unsaved present? Was the gospel clearly presented? Were people moved forward in the evangelistic process? Post-event evaluation is crucial for future planning.

Program evangelism should always be the result of planning that works in conjunction with personal witness. Events should never be a case of "outreach or evangelism" but of "outreach and evangelism." Program outreach is the task whereby the church assists people in bringing to fruition their work of personal evangelism.

Whether the church is large or small, evangelism needs to be central to its mission and ministry. For any church to be faithful to its calling, it needs to be faithful in its witness. Evangelism begins when everyone recognizes his or her responsibility to proclaim the gospel of Christ. The church needs to facilitate personal evangelism by providing training on evangelism and by establishing evangelistic programs that minister to the spiritual receptivity of the people.

Evaluation and Implementation

1. Complete worksheet 13 with the board (see appendix A).
2. What is the spiritual receptivity of the community?
3. What are the barriers to evangelism? How can the church overcome these barriers?
4. Develop a training program for evangelism that addresses the following: How do we pray for the unsaved? How do we build relationships with the unsaved? How do we witness to people?
5. What has the church done in the past to reach people with the message of Christ?
6. Develop a list of ten different events that the church could do to minister to the needs of people and reach people for Christ. Identify one or two that the church can begin doing.

Further Reading

Aldrich, Joseph. *Gentle Persuasion*. Portland, Ore.: Multnomah, 1988.
————. *Life-Style Evangelism*. Portland, Ore.: Multnomah, 1981.
Green, Michael. *Evangelism through the Local Church*. Nashville: Nelson, 1992.
Pappas, Anthony. *Mission: The Small Church Reaches Out*. Valley Forge, Pa.: Judson, 1993.
Ruffcorn, Kevin E. *Rural Evangelism*. Minneapolis: Augsburg, 1994.

SEVEN

Developing the Mission of Discipleship

The battle cry of the eighties and nineties in the church has been *relevancy*. At every turn, the cry goes forth, from the development of the church's theology to its worship service. To be successful, the church is told, it needs to understand and cater to the religious market of the age. The marketing researcher, rather than the theologian, has become the guiding light to the church. If the apostle Paul was writing to the contemporary church he might well say, "And God gave some to be apostles, some to be prophets, some to be evangelists, some to be pastors and teachers, and some to be market researchers to prepare God's people for the work of the ministry." For some, marketing is not only a tool to be used but has become central to the overall health and future of the church. In their evaluation of the church they conclude that the greatest problem plaguing the church is the failure to embrace a marketing orientation. While the church may gain a great deal of benefit from effective marketing, the problems of the church cannot be reduced to marketing issues. Doing so denies the spiritual nature of the church. The success of the church is not determined by its marketing strategies but by the spiritual vitality of the congregation.

The Quest for Relevancy

Much, indeed, can and should be learned from books dealing with church marketing. But there is danger in the church becoming so relevant that it becomes irrelevant. If all the church does is address the felt needs of people rather than provide the foundation for spiritual transformation, then the church is providing answers to the wrong questions. The purpose of the church is not only to give people biblical answers, but to teach them to ask the right questions. When the church fails to achieve this, pragmatism rather than clear theological thinking drives the church. The church needs to keep in mind that its ultimate goal is not to teach people how to think rightly about themselves but to think rightly about God. The mission of the church is redemptive not psychological. Michael Horton warns of the dangers of becoming so relevant that we lose touch with our true calling as a redemptive community: "We do need to be relevant. We must be able to demonstrate to our contemporaries that Christianity does not ignore, but in fact faces, the most pressing problems of modern times. But we trivialize our faith when it has to match the evening news."[1]

While we do need to be relevant, we lose the relevance of our faith when market strategies replace spiritual discipleship, when felt needs replace the call to be holy, when public opinion rather than biblical truth determines the expression of our faith. Relevancy must be found in our proclamation of redemptive truth to a spiritually lost and decaying world. As Bill Hull points out, the crisis confronting the church is the problem of the heart. He summarizes,

> The evangelical church has become weak, flabby, and too dependent on artificial means that can only simulate real spiritual power. Churches are too little like training centers to shape up the saints and too much like cardiopulmonary wards at the local hospital. We have proliferated self-indulgent consumer religion, the what-can-the-church-do-for-me syndrome. We are too easily satisfied with conventional success: bodies, bucks, and buildings.[2]

The health of the church is manifested by the manner in which it reflects the character of Christ in its life and witness. People must be taught to ask questions that deal with our response to an infinitely holy and perfect God rather than questions about our own personal happiness, contentment, and self-fulfillment. Only then will the church truly be relevant.

The Making of Disciples

The mission of the church not only involves being a witness of the gospel; it also involves being a disciple-making agency. Christ, in setting forth the Great Commission, places discipleship as the top priority (see Matt. 28:19–20). The verb *make* is a command, thus rendering discipleship the mandate of the church. The aim of the church is not merely to make people feel good about themselves or even about God; it is to make them followers of Christ. By making this the emphasis of the Great Commission, Christ sets this as the center of the ministry of the church. The purpose of the leadership of the church is to train people for ministry and develop their spiritual maturity (Eph. 4:11–12). The healthy church is one that is discipleship driven, one that is not so much concerned about filling the pews as they are about transforming people into the character and image of Christ. For this to happen everything needs to be impelled by that goal.

The process of making disciples is to continue until all nations are reached. In other words, the church is to be involved in the discipleship process until every individual has become an obedient follower of Christ. The leadership of the church and the ministry of the church are to be committed to this assignment "until we all reach unity in the faith and in the knowledge of the Son of God and become mature, attaining to the whole measure of the fullness of Christ" (Eph. 4:13). At no point in its history can the church afford to rest in this work, nor can it afford to become fuzzy regarding its understanding of what disciples are and how they are produced.

Defining Discipleship

The discipleship process begins by understanding what a disciple is. For some, finding someone who is a genuine disciple is like searching for the legendary Bigfoot. They have seen the pictures, followed the tracks, and written many books about the characteristics and eating habits of the elusive creature, but no one has actually captured one. Everyone describes what it is like, but no one is sure it truly exists.

To know if the elusive disciple truly exists, one needs to understand what one is searching for. The term disciple refers to one who is a learner. The Greeks used the word to describe one who was engaged in learning, a pupil who has a relationship with the teacher. Thus it was used of an apprentice to a weaver, a student physician, or a follower of a philosophical school. In the New Testament the verb *to learn* meant more than just acquiring intellectual knowledge; it implied a complete surrendering of one's will and judgment to God (John 6:45; Phil. 4:9; 1 Cor. 4:6). Discipleship, then, is not merely to learn something, but implies the practice as well. To be a disciple involves learning about, following after, and obeying Christ (John 8:31; 15:8); it means recognizing all that is implied and required by one who is joined to Christ (Col. 3:1–4). A disciple is more than one who is a convert to Christ; a disciple pursues after the knowledge of Christ with an uncompromising passion (Phil. 3:7–15). One needs to recognize the cost of commitment, which can only be a total and complete sacrifice of one's will and life to the will and purposes of God (Matt. 10:38; 16:24). In the gospel of Mark, five components of discipleship are listed:

1. being called in the midst of ordinary activity;
2. leaving old sources of identity and becoming members of the new family of Jesus;
3. empowerment for mission and a life doing the things of Jesus;
4. trusting in God even in the face of suffering and death;
5. mutual service and renunciation of all power and prestige.[3]

Disciples are completely committed to thinking and living like Christ in the present world, allowing Christ to mold and transform them altogether, so that they become servants who actively utilize their spiritual gifts to the fullest for the glory of God. Bill Hull summarizes Jesus' teaching on disciples as follows:

A disciple: Is willing to deny self, take up a cross daily, and
follow Him (Luke 9:23–25). Puts Christ before self, family,
and possessions (Luke 14:25–35). Is committed to Christ's
teachings (John 8:31). Is committed to world evangelism
(Matthew 9:36–38). Loves others as Christ loves (John
13:34, 35). Abides in Christ, is obedient, bears fruit, glorifies God, has joy and loves the brethren (John 15:7–17).[4]

These kinds of individuals are, sad to say, all too rare in the contemporary church. Yet these are the people the church must with
all its energy strive to produce. The church needs to lovingly and
gently challenge people to move from a tame faith that merely comforts the soul to a radical faith that consumes and transforms the
soul. Genuine disciples may be elusive, but they can be cultivated.
It is the task of the church to develop men and women into authentic disciples of Christ.

The Nature of Discipleship

Hull defines the process of discipleship as "the intentional training of disciples, with accountability, on the basis of loving relationships."[5] As defined by Hull, the process encompasses four aspects:
it is intentional, it involves training, it requires accountability, and
it is based upon love.

Discipleship is intentional. The disciple-making process does not
happen haphazardly. Rather it requires that the church be intentional
in its purpose and teaching. The teaching ministry of the church, as
it relates to the saved community, is to have as its goal the discipleship of those who attend.

Discipleship involves training. For discipleship to occur within
the church, a prescribed course of study needs to be implemented.
While the goal is not merely to convey content, the process begins
with the teaching of biblical truth, spiritual gifts, and ministry skills.
The very term disciple implies training and teaching. In instructing
the apostles, Christ spent a great deal of time training them in foundational truths. Much of the Gospels are a record of this education
that Christ instilled in the apostles.

Discipleship requires accountability. So crucial is accountability to the disciple-making process that one cannot be a true disciple without becoming accountable to others. This type of accountability should not be judgmental, where outward performance is the focus. Rather, biblical accountability is supportive and challenging, designed to strengthen each individual in his or her personal walk with Christ (see 1 John 5:16; James 5:19–20). Accountability is designed to correct potential weakness, but it is also designed to praise and encourage triumphs and successes.

Discipleship is based upon loving relationships. What distinguishes the church from the classroom is the relationship upon which ministry is built. The greatest strength of the small church is the relational ingredient present in the congregational life. This strength the church needs to utilize in its methodology. While people need to be taught the "how-tos" of the Christian faith, they also need to have a close relationship with others who can model each others' faith and provide loving support for one another. Developing these relationships, however, takes time and commitment. Relationships are developed though long-term interaction, each Christian mutually participating in the lives of other Christians. Gary Kuhne rightly states, "It takes time to build relationships. You will not develop a lasting, meaningful relationship with a new Christian in three follow-up appointments. In your first few meetings you can lay the groundwork for a good relationship and set the basic preconditions for it to occur; but the relationship itself will not develop that soon."[6]

Discipleship cannot take place in a few encounters that cover a few lessons from a book covering spiritual disciplines. It builds on commitment, mutual interaction, trust, and communication. Within the small-church context, opportunities exist to build close relationships with several people. Utilizing these relationships can be essential for discipleship.

Developing Discipleship Within the Church

To be a disciple-making church, the church needs to consider how it will cultivate people to be genuine disciples. Like evangelism, discipleship is not an event; rather, it is a process of spiritual growth as individuals mature in their understanding and awareness of their responsibilities as followers of Christ. As a process, discipleship consists of stages at which each individual stands in his or her spiritual growth. First John 2:12–14 creates an analogy for the various levels of spiritual maturity by referring to the believers as "fathers" and "young men."

The assignment of the church is to train people at each stage and move them to the next step of spiritual commitment. Each level provides the foundation for the next, so it is not a matter of leaving one and moving on to the next, but building one upon the other. This begins by understanding people's maturity and instilling in them the skills and characteristics to be manifested in order to move on to the next level of commitment.

Discipling the Spiritual Infant

An infant is immature in conduct, needing instruction, training, and guidance in the elemental ingredients of the faith. Spiritual infants lack spiritual understanding and perception (1 Cor. 13:11). They are easily influenced by religious fads and false doctrines (Eph.

The Discipleship Process

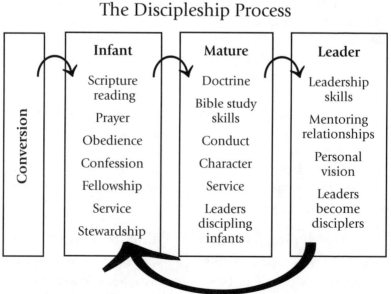

Infant	Mature	Leader
Scripture reading	Doctrine	Leadership skills
Prayer	Bible study skills	Mentoring relationships
Obedience	Conduct	Personal vision
Confession	Character	
Fellowship	Service	Leaders become disciplers
Service	Leaders discipling infants	
Stewardship		

Conversion

4:14). Because of their lack of training and understanding, they need instruction from the mature believer.

Believers may be immature because they are new to the faith and lack knowledge (Eph. 4:13–14) or their spiritual growth has been stunted by a failure to practice what they have learned (1 Cor. 3:1–2; Heb. 5:11-14). In any case, these individuals need the "elemental truths of God's word" (Heb. 5:12). These "elementary truths" are the simplest principles of the Christian faith, the "alphabet" of spiritual and doctrinal teaching. They constitute a basic understanding—the implication of the gospel upon the life of the individual, that is, the basics necessary for the formation of fundamental Christian ethics and morality.

This is not to say that these truths are unimportant and unnecessary for the mature. Peter, in writing to recent converts, exhorts his readers to have an appetite for these things (1 Peter 2:2). This spiritual milk is Scripture, which instructs the believer concerning the person of God and our response to him. A convert needs to be taught the foundations of Christian life, those things that are critical for any growth to occur.

Scripture Reading

Among the foundations of the Christian life is the discipline of Scripture reading. Discipling new converts involves, first, that they have instilled within them the desire and discipline of a consistent and systematic reading of Scripture. The study of the Bible is not mere academic study; it is a spiritual exercise that transforms the character and protects the individual from sin (Ps. 119:9; Heb. 4:12). To become a disciple, one must become a person of the Word—one who has a craving to know the teachings of Scripture and has a passion to live according to it. A steady intake of the Bible is the means by which God communicates his mind and will to the individual in order to cultivate a relationship with him or her. In relationship to the study of Scripture, Richard Foster cites four points.[7]

The first is repetition. Consistent study is important for the development of a Christian mind and character. Persistence and recapitulation are the means by which behavior is changed.

The second is concentration. In reading, one needs to be focused upon the passage, avoiding distractions. Concentrating involves riveting the mind and will upon the text as a person reads.

The third point is comprehension. Without understanding the passage there will be little gained. Having a good study Bible provides insight for dealing with difficult passages and enables the reader to grasp the meaning better.

The fourth point is reflection. Reflection involves giving thought to the meaning and considering how the passage applies to the present situation of the reader. A notebook to write down ideas and applications can be helpful.

Prayer

A second foundation for Christian living is the discipline of prayer. Prayer is the means by which the believer communicates with God and the means by which God forms a relationship with his people and changes their thoughts, motives, and attitudes (Matt. 6:5–15). The primary purpose of prayer is not to ask God to meet our needs (for these he already knows about) but to develop a relationship with God. While Scripture is the primary means by which God speaks to his people, prayer is the means by which God's people communicate to him. Therefore prayer is the focus of the believer (Col. 4:2; 1 Thess. 5:17).

Prayer is both taught and learned (Luke 11:1). Not that one needs to learn how to commune with God, but disciples need to be taught concerning the content and focus of prayer. Learning how to pray comes through practice, the study of the Bible, reading of men and women renowned for prayer, and by praying together with other believers. We learn to pray when we move from the superficial requests of physical and emotional needs, to the in-depth baring of our soul, our passions, our struggles, our dreams before God.

Obedience

A third foundation is the discipline of obedience. The call to be a disciple is a call to obedience, to counting the cost of a life lived in full submission to Christ and Scripture. Too often, people who make a profession of faith experience little or no change in their daily conduct. It is one thing to get people to say a prayer of salvation, but it is a whole different ball game to have people make a lifelong commitment to follow and obey Christ no matter what the cost. While many in America profess to be Christians and acknowledge that Jesus died for them, they never integrate their faith into their daily practice. They are "confessional Christians" but not genuine disciples. Christ warns of the dangers of a confessional faith rather than a transformational belief: "Not everyone who says to me, 'Lord, Lord,' will enter the kingdom of heaven, but only he who does the will of my Father who is in heaven" (Matt. 7:21; see also Luke 9:23–37). While one may debate the issue concerning the acknowledgment of Christ's lordship being necessary for salvation, one cannot argue that completely surrendering one's will to Christ is a prerequisite for becoming a genuine disciple. The church needs to confront people with the requirement of complete commitment to a life of obedience to Christ (see Matt. 8:18–22; 16:24–26; 19:16–22).

Confession

A fourth foundation for the life of a Christian is the discipline of confession. The epistle of 1 John teaches three great truths: First, no one will continue to live a lifestyle of sin if he or she is a genuine child of God (3:6, 9). Second, all children of God will still commit acts of sin (1:8, 10). Third, when we do sin we have an avenue by which those sins may be forgiven, and that is through confession (1:9; 2:1). Confession is more than acknowledging that one has violated God's moral law; it is expressing both the desire to be forgiven as well as the desire to change one's conduct. To confess one's sins is to openly and honestly face sin without attempting to hide, excuse, or justify one's behavior or oneself. It is to accept responsibility for one's actions. Confessing is an ongoing process (literally, keep on confessing), rather than an occasional act.

The habit of confession not only involves the acknowledgment of one's sin before God, but also involves admitting one's sin to fellow believers (James 5:16). In doing so one removes the façade, so that spirituality does not become only external. Concerning this, Foster writes, "The discipline of confession brings an end to pretense. God is calling into being a Church that can openly confess its frail humanity and know the forgiving and empowering graces of Christ. Honesty leads to confession, and confession leads to change."[8]

Fellowship

A fifth foundation is the discipline of fellowship. The Christian life is lived in community not isolation. The greater the spiritual pressures confronted by the believer, the more necessary and important to fellowship with the rest of the church community. For the writer of Hebrews, fellowship is crucial for perseverance: "Let us not give up meeting together, as some are in the habit of doing, but let us encourage one another-and all the more as you see the Day approaching" (Heb. 10:25). The idea that one can worship and commune with God and maintain one's spiritual growth and discipleship apart from the localized church is completely alien to the New Testament concept of the body of Christ. To say that one does not "need" others is disastrous not only to the individual Christian, but to the whole body of Christ as well (1 Cor. 12; see also Ps. 122:1; Acts 16:5; Col. 1:15–18). The process of evangelism is not complete until the individuals are grafted into the body of Christ and involved in a local congregation of believers so that they are growing spiritually in the context of community.

Service

A sixth foundation for Christian living is the discipline of service. Disciples serve Christ by exercising their spiritual gifts and by testifying of Christ to the world. Although the importance of ministry and service becomes more intense later in the discipleship process, the new convert should be taught that all Christians are called to serve others and become a witness. While the extent of one's impact and influence grows as the individual matures, that does not mean that the privilege of laboring for Christ is limited only to the mature.

The discipline of service encompasses two aspects: First it includes the exercise of one's spiritual gift. Such exercise begins by exposing new converts to a variety of ministries in order that they might develop a greater awareness of their own giftedness. Having short-term apprentice programs is one way of giving new Christians an opportunity to see various ministries at work. Apprenticeship is especially helpful in small churches, where it is often difficult for new people to be assimilated into the ministry of the church.

The second aspect of the discipline of service includes witnessing. Having individuals write out their testimony and share it with others is the first step in developing their witnessing skills so that they can effectively serve Christ.

Stewardship

The seventh foundation is the discipline of stewardship. Submission to Christ needs to extend to all aspects of life, including one's pocketbook. Stewardship is more than giving money to the church or ministry; it is the recognition that every possession is a gift from God, belongs to him, and is to be used to the fullest to glorify God. This giving is not to be done out of compulsion but out of a recognition of God's grace—what R. Kent Hughes calls the "grace of giving": "The grace of giving has nothing to do with being well off. It is not dictated by ability. It is a willingness to give. Giving is viewed as a privilege. It is joyously enthusiastic and pleads for the opportunity to give more."[9] It stems from the happy recognition that giving is both a privilege and a response of worship to a God who has not only blessed us with every spiritual blessing but also with the capacity to earn a livelihood (Deut. 8:18). Such enthusiastic giving is what Paul envisions when he writes, "And now, brothers, we want you to know about the grace that God has given the Macedonian churches. Out of the most severe trial, their overflowing joy and their extreme poverty welled up in rich generosity. For I testify that they gave as much as they were able, and even beyond their ability. Entirely on their own, they urgently pleaded with us for the privilege of sharing in this service to the saints" (2 Cor. 8:1–4).

This first stage of discipleship is the process of instilling the necessary disciplines that will govern the individual. Without these habits ingrained within the person and formed into a daily routine, spiritual growth will remain stunted and inconsistent.

Discipling the Mature

The next level of discipleship—developing spiritual consistency—involves the mature believer. Hebrews 5:14 speaks of those who are mature as being ready for solid food. These believers have "trained themselves to distinguish good from evil." In other words, they are grounded spiritually and theologically. Instead of being tossed about by the theological fads, they are steadfast. They are able to adequately teach the Scriptures (2 Tim. 2:15), instruct others to live by biblical truth (Titus 2:1), and provide spiritual training for the immature (Titus 2:5). As mature Christians, they set the example for others to follow in character and conduct (1 Tim. 4:12). Training disciples to become mature thus encompasses three areas: doctrine, biblical interpretation, and Christian character.

Teaching Sound Doctrine

In 2 Timothy 4:2, Paul writes to Timothy that he is to teach people "with great patience and careful instruction." The term "instruction" refers to doctrine and encompasses the doctrinal teaching of Scripture. As pointed out earlier, it is sad and wrong that doctrine has become an unfashionable term in the church today. Nevertheless, the responsibility remains for teaching people sound theology. In the instruction, however, the doctrine needs to be relevant. Formulating a biblical worldview is necessary for becoming a Christian counter-culture in society. The writers of the New Testament saw sound doctrine as being so crucial that the failure to study it was the mark of immaturity (Heb. 5:11–6:3) and even rebellion (2 Tim. 4:3).

With the proliferation of religious views—from Process Theology to New Age Mysticism—the need is great for clear theological understanding that forms the grid for developing a biblically consistent worldview. This training needs to cover the gamut of doctrinal teaching, from theology proper to eschatology. While most

Christians do not need to have the mind equal to the great scholars of the day, they need to have a basic understanding of each of the theological subjects. Part of establishing mature believers is providing fundamental teachings on doctrine.

Enhancing Bible Study Skills

The second area of training for strengthening mature believers is in the area of Bible study skills. Above all else, the disciple is to be a student of the Scriptures. Being a student of Scripture involves gaining a general knowledge of the Bible as well as developing hermeneutical skills. It is most unfortunate that many Christians are thrust into teaching roles without training in this crucial area. The result is questionable exegesis and, often, heretical teachings.

Edward Goodrick, in discussing the various areas (the autographs, transmission, translation, and interpretation) in which pollution might occur in the understanding of Scripture, warns,

> Yet I greatly fear that it is into the final section of the pipe—interpretation—that pollution flows unchecked and in quantities far exceeding what is already there, polluting the very water of life we drink. The amount of this pollution is so great that it renders inconsequential the preceding pollution.[10]

While the evangelical church has defended inerrancy, it has become very slack in its defense of proper interpretation. If people are to be taught the significance of Scripture as the sole authority for life and godliness, they need to be instructed concerning the value of rightly handling the word of truth (1 Tim. 2:15). Goodrick adds,

> The wording of the Bible requires interpretation before it can be applied to the life (mind, heart, and deed) of the believer. Here, our sincerity to aggressively defend the purity at the spring is put to the test. How much concern does one also express over pollution in interpretation? When two or more interpretations are offered for a text, all but the true

one are mistakes; and all mistakes in interpretation are pollutants. We must reaffirm our commitment to a strict adherence to the rules of interpretation.[11]

As in the case of understanding theology, in studying Scripture one does not need a seminary level understanding of biblical hermeneutics. But one should have an understanding of language conventions, culture and history, context, and literary genres. Offering a basic course on Bible study methods should be a part of any serious discipleship curriculum.

Christian Conduct and Character

Besides theological correctness and accurate biblical understanding, Christian maturity involves inward transformation as well. The measure of spiritual maturity is ultimately discovered in the conduct and character of the individual. Paul writes in Ephesians 4:17 that the people of God "must no longer live as the Gentiles do." In other words, Christians are to conduct their lives in a manner that reflects their calling and position in Christ (see Eph. 4:1–16). This character is manifested by "compassion, kindness, humility, gentleness and patience . . ." (Col. 3:12–14). The task of the church is to train people so that they think and act Christianly.

Discipling People to be Servants

At the close of his ministry, shortly before his crucifixion, Christ performed an act that greatly puzzled and even offended the disciples. In John 13:1–17 Christ did the menial task of a servant by washing his disciples' dirty feet. This illustration pointed the disciples to the importance of humility expressed in servitude. Service and discipleship are inseparably linked. Character and conduct relate both to the behavior and motives of the individual, and to the perspective of the person. At the heart of a disciple is the realization that the primary purpose of our earthly existence is to serve Christ through the exercise of our spiritual gifts. Exercising one's spiritual gift(s) includes both the maturation of them as well as the expansion of influence. While the role of the church in recruiting, training, and motivating people to serve is developed in the next chapter, one should not separate service from discipleship as if they were two distinct activities. If an individual is not serving, then that person cannot make any claims to be a disciple of Christ. When people are not involved they eventually leave the church disenchanted. Declining churches have approximately twenty-seven tasks/roles per every hundred adults, whereas growing churches have sixty tasks per hundred adults.[12] Elton Trueblood warns:

> Perhaps the greatest single weakness of the contemporary Christian Church is that millions of supposed members are not really involved at all and, what is worse, do not think it strange that they are not. As soon as we recognize Christ's intention to make His Church a militant company we understand at once that the conventional arrangement cannot suffice. There is no real chance of victory in a campaign if ninety per cent of the soldiers are untrained and uninvolved, but that is exactly where we stand now. Most alleged Christians do not now understand that loyalty to Christ means sharing personally in His ministry, going or staying as the situation requires.[13]

Discipling Within Ministries

While the strength of the small church is the number of people who are actually involved in service—often higher than the sixty tasks per one hundred people—the danger is that the small church can offer a wall of resistance to new individuals desiring to serve. The small church needs to strategize how it will progressively involve and integrate new people into ministry.

The first step in discipling people in service is to involve them in entry-level ministries. These are service areas that present minimal threat, that is, they enable new Christians who lack spiritual maturity and in-depth Bible study to serve within his or her emotional and spiritual comfort zone. Entry-level opportunities should be designed to assist the person in identifying his or her spiritual gift, requiring a short-term commitment. Some possible entry-level jobs might include assistant to a Sunday school teacher, ministries that meet the physical needs of people, or assisting in the upkeep of the facilities.

The second step of the spiritual training process regarding service is providing opportunities in growth ministries that stretch the individual and cause spiritual growth. These opportunities involve moderate risk and commitment, and require a basic understanding of the Scriptures and attainment of spiritual maturity. Growth ministries are designed primarily for the church family, thus protecting the individual from rejection and hostility, and providing a loving, encouraging environment for service. Such duties might include teaching a Sunday school class, being part of the worship team, or leading a Bible study for church members.

The final stage in discipling as it relates to service involves the person in redemptive ministries and the advancement of Christ's kingdom in the world. Redemptive ministries, because they are conducted outside the church walls, carry the highest risk of rejection and spiritual conflict for the individual who serves in this area, and since many of the people on the receiving end of the ministry will not immediately respond to the gospel, the person who serves needs to make a long-term commitment to the ministry. Nevertheless, discipling involves people being challenged to move beyond serving solely the redeemed community. Redemptive ministries place workers on the "front-line" in the active spiritual warfare of bringing the unchurched to Christ. No matter what a worker's spiritual gifts might be, they can be utilized in the redemptive process.

A person with the gift of helps can assist and encourage not only those in the church, but also those in the community. Serving for a redemptive purpose involves utilizing one's spiritual gift in order to build relationships that become opportunities for the communication of the gospel. The mentality of consumerism, however, undermines such ministry, perceiving the ministries and services of the church to be for us rather than for others, for the church attendees rather than for the lost world in which we live. The church can only fulfill the Great Commission (which has been sometimes called the great omission of the church) when it uses all its resources to equip and transform saints and also to reach the lost.

Producing Leaders

The discipleship process is not complete until the person being discipled becomes a leader who influences others. Leadership ranges from those who are key leaders in the community to those who become spiritual leaders within their immediate family. Because of a leader's godly character, he or she has a profound impact on the lives of others.

In Old Testament culture, patriarchs and matriarchs of the family were the influential leaders. David DeWitt describes the patriarch as "a man who has taken on the responsibility for establishing maturity for himself and applying it to his extended family."[14] He adds,

> A patriarch is not an old fuddy-duddy living in the sun someplace, retired, complaining about all the new-fangled ideas, while spending his children's inheritance. A patriarch is on the front lines of life, ever growing, learning, contributing, and challenging the socks off his wife, his children, his grandchildren, and everyone else who knows him.[15]

A patriarch or matriarch never retires from ministry but, as he or she matures, widens his or her influence on others. All too often people, when they are on the verge of becoming true patriarchs and matriarchs, retire from ministry. The driving range becomes the driving force, and the desire to minister for Christ fades.

In the New Testament, the writers refer to the elders. In Titus 2, Paul writes that the older men and women of the church are to expand their influence rather than retire. Instead of letting the younger people do the work, they are to mold and mentor the younger people. Genuine leadership in the church is not found in the establishment of policies and church government, but in the discipleship of others. Leaders are appointed because they have spent time and devoted their lives to disciple and train others. They model and teach people to obey and follow Christ.

The vitality and security of the small church are not to be found, as it is often viewed, in the financial stability or program development of the church. The legitimacy of the small church is not found in its rolls. Rather, the future will be seen in its commitment to establish people as mentors who are not motivated by personal pursuits but are motivated to serve Christ and expand their influence through the growth of other disciples. This commitment is especially critical in the small church where the loss of one leader can greatly affect a number of different ministries.

Developing Mentors

Developing people into mentors involves teaching people to be leaders, assisting them in formulating a personal vision statement, and then instructing them how to build mentoring relationships.

Leaders do more than lead people; they cultivate other leaders. Throughout Scripture leaders not only led the people of God but they also produced future leaders. Moses mentored Joshua; David prepared Solomon; Elijah taught Elisha; Paul instructed Timothy and Titus; and Barnabas encouraged Paul and John Mark.

Developing mentors involves teaching and instructing people how to become effective leaders, and in so doing the effectiveness of the church is multiplied. Mentoring leaders perceive and encourage the leadership skills of others. For the small church to be effective, it needs more than a leader in the pastor, it needs leaders in the pews. The responsibility of the pastor is to multiply pacesetters who will outlast his ministry in the church, people who will transform the church and set direction for the church. For this to happen, there needs to be training, both formal and informal, both corporately and individually, that is designed to teach people how to lead and to become mentors who in turn nurture others into becoming leaders and mentors.

Second, developing mentors involves training leaders in the area of mentoring relationships. Discipleship ultimately is not a program but an affinity between individuals who challenge and impact one another for the cause of Christ. The effectiveness of the teaching in the mentoring process is directly related to the relationship enjoyed between the mentor and the individual being discipled. Mentoring is more than the conveyance of biblical truth concerning life and conduct. It consists of an unconditional loving relationship in which the life of one is imprinted upon the other. The mentor thus needs to commit to the relationship and resolve to spend time with the person being discipled.

Third, developing mentors involves challenging leaders to draft a personal vision statement for his or her personal ministry. Just as the church needs to have a clear vision for ministry (see chapters 10–11), so each individual needs a personal vision. A personal vision is awareness of what God has called and equipped one to accomplish with one's life. Helping people articulate a personal vision enables them to gain a clear perspective of ministry that guides and directs them in the exercise of their spiritual gift. Without such a vision, one's personal ministry becomes a task rather than an awareness of God's involvement in one's life. Having a personal vision distinguishes the occasional volunteer to a social organization from those who give their all to the ministry of Christ on behalf of others.

The task and responsibility of the church is to cultivate disciples. For this to occur, the church and its leadership needs to understand the process of discipleship and clearly articulate what the end product will be. After all is said and done, the most crucial question that the church needs to ask is, "What does one who has been truly discipled look like?" A disciple understands and practices the basic habits of a godly life: prayer, Bible reading, and fellowship. A disciple is biblically grounded, able to understand and communicate accurately the teaching of Scripture. A disciple acknowledges the importance of ministry as a life-long commitment. Lastly, a disciple is committed to ever growing and becoming more influential in the Christian life. One who is truly discipled desires to know and walk with Christ, and desires to imprint his or her life upon others so that they will also know and walk with Christ.

Evaluation and Implementation

1. Complete worksheet 14 (see appendix A). Write out a definition of a disciple.
2. Develop a strategy for discipling people at various levels of their spiritual growth.
3. Who are the patriarchs and matriarchs of the congregation and how are they mentoring others? What program is teaching people to become patriarchs and matriarchs?

Further Reading

DeWitt, David. *The Mature Man*. Santa Ana, Calif.: Vision House, 1994.

Foster, Richard. *Celebration of Discipline*. San Francisco: Harper, 1988.

Hughes, R. Kent. *Disciplines of a Godly Man*. Westchester, Ill.: Crossway, 1991.

Hull, Bill. *The Disciple Making Church*. Old Tappan, N.J.: Revell, 1990.

EIGHT

Developing the Mission of Service

*I*n writing to the church at Ephesus, the apostle Paul set the mandate for all leaders. Their responsibility is not merely to set the course of the church, oversee the budget, and run the programs; they are "to prepare God's people for works of service" (Eph. 4:12). While this reference is frequently quoted as a theme for pastors, it is often overlooked in relationship to the responsibility of the congregation.

The point of the text is that the ongoing ministry of the church requires the involvement of everyone within the congregation. The duty of leaders is to assist, recruit, motivate, and train people to exercise their spiritual gifts "so that the body of Christ may be built up." Involvement in building up the body is to be maintained "until we all reach unity in the faith and in the knowledge of the Son of God and become mature, attaining to the whole measure of the fullness of Christ" (Eph. 4:13). Ministry and maturity are related. People who become involved are more likely to stay in the church and not drop out, and they will mature more rapidly as well. Involvement brings with it the challenge to grow and become more proficient in the application of Scripture.

The church cannot be content merely to point people to ministry; the church needs to be actively involved in the process of including people in the service of Christ. Accomplishing the various ministries of the church is not the function of the professional clergy, but the role of the equipped laity. If the church desires to accomplish the

The Wheel of Ministry

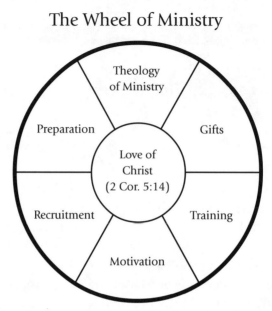

Effective ministry requires six critical spokes to keep the programs staffed. Each spoke forms a basis for properly recruiting and training people in service.

mission that God has given it, then it must with care, strategy, and purpose engage people in the ministry of the congregation.

A Theology of Service

Building ministry requires that the people have an awareness of the nature, character, and activity of God. Strong ministry also demands that members properly understand the biblical theology of service. The theology of service motivates people to be more than pew sitters; it challenges them to be pace setters.

The Priesthood of the Believer

Understanding the theology of service begins with the realization of the priesthood of the believer. First Peter 2:5, 9 speaks of the people of God as a royal priesthood, a term meaning that all believers not only have free access to God but that each member of the body of Christ has a priestly function to perform. No longer is there a priestly cast in which only a few are called into direct service for God. Instead, each individual is now invited to minister before God. Ministering before God involves the performance of the spiritual sacrifice of praise as well as the offering of personal service (Phil. 2:17). Thus, all believers have the privilege of serving God personally. Concerning this privilege John Calvin writes,

> It is a singular honor, that God should not only consecrate us as a temple to himself, in which he dwells and is worshiped, but that he should also make us priests. But Peter mentions this double honor, in order to stimulate us more effectually to serve and worship God. Of the Spiritual sacrifices, the first is the offering of ourselves, of which Paul speaks in Romans xii.1; for we offer nothing, until we offer to him ourselves as sacrifices; which is done by denying ourselves. Then afterwards follow prayers, thanksgiving, alms deeds, and all the duties of religion.[1]

The danger is that Christians can rely solely on paid staff to perform the ministry of the church, and begin to think that they have nothing to offer to the work of God's kingdom. People can easily become pew sitters who no longer see themselves as servants for Christ.

The ministry of the church is not to be performed by a few; it is to be accomplished by the whole body. The task of leadership is to equip and train the church (both spiritual training as well as instruction in skilled areas) so that the whole body accomplishes the ministry (see Eph. 4:11–13). The pastor who has been trained revitalizes and leads the church when he trains others to perform the work of ministry, involving and equipping them to perform the pastoral care of people. The gathering of the church together in fellowship is not solely for the purpose of praise and confession before God. It involves the mutual ministry of each member (Heb. 10:24–25). Refusing to bear one another's burdens is a violation of one's

relationship to the body of Christ, and it is a violation of one's relationship to God. Philip Hughes states,

> The failure of love shows itself, then in selfish individual-
> ism, and specifically here in the habit of some of neglect-
> ing to meet together. Such unconcern for one's fellow
> believer argues unconcern for Christ himself and portends
> the danger of apostasy, concerning which our author is
> about to issue another earnest warning (vv. 26 ff). It is im-
> portant, therefore, that the reality of Christian love should
> be demonstrated in the personal relationships and mutual
> concerns for the Christian community.[2]

Each member is responsible to all other members, and each member has something to contribute to the spiritual well-being of other
members. To neglect one's ministry responsibility damages one's
own personal growth and spiritual health, and it adversely affects
the congregation as well.

Each member, joined with the body of Christ through the bap-
tism of the Holy Spirit (1 Cor. 12:13), is called to strengthen, encourage, and build the rest of the members in spiritual growth. In
1 Thessalonians 5:11, Paul exhorts the Thessalonians to "encourage
one another and build each other up, just as in fact you are doing."
The verbs he uses stress the continual nature of this process. Those
in the Thessalonian church bore a responsibility of strengthening
one another. Paul recognized that his personal ministry accomplishments were achieved by the entire community (see Phil. 1:5; 4:15).
The ministry of the church is the responsibility of every individual
within the body.

The Gifts Given to the Believer

Just as the priesthood of the believer brings responsibility for service, so also the giftedness of the believer brings a divinely ordained
obligation to minister. The obligation to use spiritual gifts is first
and foremost based upon one's theology of God, for it is God who
bestows the gifts.

The Origin of the Spiritual Gifts

In Paul's extended discussion of spiritual gifts in 1 Corinthians 12, he repeatedly stresses that the theological basis of spiritual gifts is the sovereignty of God. No less than six times in this passage Paul makes reference to the source and determiner of spiritual gifts as being God himself (12:6, 8, 11, 18, 24, 28). While in this passage Paul emphasizes the role of God the Father and the Holy Spirit in bestowing spiritual gifts, in 1 Timothy 1:12 Paul states that it was Christ who appointed him to his apostolic ministry (see also Eph. 4:7).

Because it is God who has decided our gifts, we need to honestly assess our giftedness. In Paul's discussion of spiritual gifts in Romans 12:3–8, Paul challenges the believers to "not think of yourself more highly than you ought, but rather think of yourself with sober judgment, in accordance with the measure of faith God has given you." This means that we are neither to over-value nor under-value individual importance and contributions to the body. We are not to regard ourselves as unnecessary to the rest of the body of Christ no matter what our giftedness might be. No one can say that because he or she is not gifted with one of the more visible gifts (i.e., teaching, preaching, etc.) he or she is of no value to the health of the church. Rather the opposite is true. Those who have the "less honorable" gifts (i.e., gifts of helps, faith, etc.) are just as important to the overall health and function of the church (1 Cor. 12:14–20). That all gifts are equally important is because God has arranged the body. To malign one's gift is to malign the character of God. The church would do well to remember that those who do the small, unseen tasks of the church are just as important to God as those who teach and preach.

We need, then, to recognize the value of others to the body (Romans 12). Just as one should not devalue his or her own spiritual gift, so also no one should diminish the role and responsibilities that others have (1 Cor. 12:21–22).

The Universality of Spiritual Gifts

A theology of spiritual gifts reveals that God has given them to every believer. In the discussion of spiritual gifts Paul impresses upon the Corinthian church that the work of the ministry is not conducted by a few; it is conducted by every individual, for everyone is gifted: "Now to each one the manifestation of the Spirit is given for the common good" (1 Cor. 12:7); "All these are the work of one and the same Spirit, and he gives them to each one, just as he determines" (v. 11); "For we were all baptized by one Spirit into one body" (v. 13); "But in fact God has arranged the parts in the body, every one of them, just as he wanted them to be" (v. 18). "Now you are the body of Christ, and each one of you is a part of it" (v. 27).

Serving through involvement, then, is not merely an option. It is essential for the spiritual health of the church and the individual. Since everyone is equipped to serve, all need to be involved in service in some capacity in order to be fully within the will of God. The responsibility of the church is not just to disciple people in the cultivation of inward character; it is also to equip, involve, and lead people in service. The church needs to clearly affirm, instruct, and model an understanding of the biblical teaching regarding every individual's call to ministry.

The Purpose of the Gifts

Spiritual gifts are given with a two-fold purpose. First, the exercise of spiritual gifts should be done so that God is glorified. Humanity was created for the purpose of glorifying God (Isa. 43:7). Thus, every activity we perform we are to do with the intent of glorifying and serving God (Col. 3:23). This includes the exercise of our spiritual gifts (1 Peter 4:11). The glory belongs to God because it is he, not we, who brings to fruition the work we have started (1 Cor. 3:4–15; 2 Cor. 4:7–12). As meager and inept our attempts to minister are, God is capable of using them to accomplish eternally significant results. Thus we have nothing to boast about, nor should we rely upon our own wisdom and strength, but upon God (1 Cor. 2:1–5).

Second, spiritual gifts are given to edify the church (1 Cor. 12:7).

Gifts are not to be used for selfish advantage, nor are they imparted to serve only the one possessing the gift. Instead they are assigned for the community (1 Peter 4:10–11). People are to be challenged to exercise their gifts so that the community is strengthened.

Looking for Priscilla and Aquilla

Priscilla and Aquilla, whose occupation was tent making, were the apostle Paul's close friends. While they were tentmakers by trade, they were ministers at heart. For them, tent making was a vocation, but ministering for Christ was their life. They were two of the many individuals Paul refers to in Romans 16 as being fellow workers in Christ Jesus. Many others mentioned are unknown in the pages of church history except for Paul's brief mention of their labors for Christ. Paul mentions men and women, Jews and Gentiles, aristocrats and commoners. The early church was successful not because of the dedication of twelve men but because of the dedication of the whole church to the gospel of Christ.

What will distinguish the twenty-first-century church in the pages of redemptive history will not be the remarkable ministry of its high profile leaders. If the contemporary church is to have an impact, it will require the involvement of the entire body of Christ in the whole ministry of the church. Nevertheless, many small churches struggle to maintain their ministries because of the unwillingness of people to become involved in church ministry. While many are involved, many others are content merely to sit on the sidelines cheering (or criticizing) those who are out on the playing field. Meanwhile, others are leaving the church because of dissatisfaction and alienation, feeling unwanted and unneeded in the church.

Because the small church has a limited pool to recruit from to fill opportunities, how the church recruits and utilizes its people becomes all the more critical. Involving people requires that the leaders understand five major trends that are significantly impacting the ministry of the church and the availability of people.

The first trend is the decrease of time availability. Time is an endangered commodity in twenty-first-century lifestyle. The mobility of society has resulted in bigger stores and businesses to serve larger geographic areas with cheaper prices. This has caused the closure of many "local shops" and has eaten a chunk from the time availability of people. People today have to travel further and spend more time obtaining services that were once available locally.

With the dawn of the industrial age came the prediction that people would have to spend fewer hours at work, allowing more leisure time. In reality, the opposite has been the case. In the past twenty years, the average amount of time people spend at work has increased nine hours per week, with leisure time declining by as much as one third.[3] The result is that people have less time to give to ministry. Jeffry Brudney reports that "about one-half of adult Americans (47.7 percent) volunteer for an average of 4.2 hours per week, a rate of volunteering that has remained fairly stable for a decade."[4] As a result the church needs to be more efficient with the amount of time that people do offer.

The second trend that affects the availability of church workers is the loss of the homemaker. Today the average median income (adjusted for inflation) of a household is the same as it was in 1970. Today it requires, however, two incomes to maintain the income level. The result is that more and more women are entering the work force. Today more than half of all women are working at jobs outside the home. This has not only had a profound sociological impact, it has greatly influenced the ministry of the church. Women are no longer available to fill many of the demanding responsibilities of the church.[5]

The third trend affecting the availability of people is consumerism. The rise of consumerism as a dominant mentality in American culture that has affected how people approach ministry. No longer do people volunteer solely to aid others. Instead, they often approach service opportunities with the attitude of "What can I gain from doing this?" Satisfaction comes not from the benefit given to others, but the advantage received from the responsibility.

Episodic volunteerism is a fourth trend that affects the church. In a 1989 study of people who were reluctant to volunteer, 79 percent stated that they would be more inclined to volunteer if the time commitment of the jobs was shorter.[6] While people may volunteer to plan or participate in one event, such as vacation Bible school, they are less likely to become involved in any ministry that requires a year-long commitment, such as being a Sunday school teacher. Rather than bemoaning the lack of commitment by people, the church needs to utilize more episodic volunteers to conduct the various ministries. Mark Senter III warns, "Long-term commitments may be a thing of the past. Today, people tend to be project oriented. There is a great desire to be able to get into a job, get it done, and go on to the next thing."[7]

A fifth trend that affects church volunteering is the church's need to become wise stewards. Certainly the church needs to be wise stewards of financial contributions, but it also needs to be wise stewards of the time people give if it is to recruit and involve people in ministry. The church is more likely to run out of volunteer availability than it is financial resources. The viability of the small church is not dependent on its financial resources; it is contingent on its volunteer resources. It can operate on limited finances, but it cannot operate without people. Therefore, how the church recruits, motivates, and trains people for ministry is crucial to effectiveness.

Preparing the Ministry for Service

Enlisting people to serve in the ministry of the church begins not with the appeal to serve but with the preparation of the ministry for volunteers. The success of the early church was not a result of the church's arbitrary appearance on the pages of history. Their exploits were largely due to the preparation God performed before the actual ministry of the church began. The Greek language made universal communication possible; the powerful influence of the Roman government made travel between geographic areas safe; the religious structure of the Jewish synagogues provided a springboard for gaining a hearing. What made the early church successful was not merely the individuals "recruited" by God for the ministry, but the preparation God made before calling them to service.

Preparing the Way: Establish Goals

When God called Moses to become his leader of Israel, he did not send Moses to Egypt with a generic call to "find out the needs and lead the people." Instead, he identified a clear goal and vision for the people and for Moses. He told Moses, "I am sending you to Pharaoh to bring my people, the Israelites out of Egypt" (Exod. 3:10). Before recruiting people to serve, leadership needs to ask, "Why do we need people to perform this ministry?" If the answer is not clearly understood, people will doubt the importance of the responsibility and will be less likely to devote their time and energies to the task. These goals will enable the church to determine what kind of gifted individuals will be needed.

When establishing goals within the small church, however, it is important that the plans enhance and affirm relationships throughout the church. If they are perceived to divide the church, they will be resisted regardless of how beneficial they might be. For example, in small churches, small groups are often met with indifference and even opposition because members see them as cliques dividing the church. Carl Dudley warns,

> **Ministry Preparation Checklist**
>
> Prepare the way by establishing clear goals.
>
> Prepare the person by providing spiritual support.
>
> Prepare the performance by developing clear job descriptions.
>
> Prepare the program by providing sufficient resources.

The affirmation of purpose and clarity of goals should be an aid to the leadership of small congregations. It should support but never inhibit the spontaneous sharing of mundane victories and the quality of caring for people and parish through which God liberates people from the sense of anonymous helplessness in the blur of the mass society.[8]

The goals and programs should be subservient to the simple expression of faith and the depth of human relationships existing within the small church. While goals are important (see chapter eleven), it is also important to keep in mind that the small church desires a simplistic expression of faith, rather than a complex organizational structure.

Preparing the Person: Enlarge Spiritual Support

Becoming involved in a ministry is more than participating in the program and supporting the organizational goals and structure. It is participating in the spiritual program of God. God's spiritual program consists of empowerment, expertise, and engagement.

Give support to spiritual empowerment. In his writing, Paul repeatedly asked for the churches to pray for him, that he might be empowered by God for the ministry to which he was called (Col. 4:2–3; Rom. 15:30–31; Eph. 6:19–20; 1 Thess. 5:25; 2 Thess. 3:1). The apostle recognized that his effectiveness was dependent upon the Spirit's enabling and empowering his life and ministry (1 Cor. 2:1–5). Thus he appealed for people to pray for him.

Preparing the ministry for people to serve entails a commitment to support them in prayer. Since prayer is part of the process of becoming spiritually empowered, the church needs to be devoted to pray for those who serve before they ask them to serve. Establishing an effective prayer base involves the dedication to have prayer partners for everyone serving within the church.

Give support for spiritual expertise. Participation in ministry is not based upon the needs of the program or organization but the gifts of individuals. Increasing spiritual effectiveness includes helping people discover and find ways to express their spiritual gifts. Too often in small churches, because of the limited pool of volunteers, people are recruited to ministries with little or no thought about gifts and qualifications. This does a grave disservice to the individual, and it fails to recognize the sovereign work of God. God always provides the church with gifted individuals to accomplish what he desires the church to achieve (for example, see Exod. 35:30–36:2). If the ministry does not match the gifts of the congregation, it is the program that needs to be adjusted, not the people.

Give support for spiritual engagement. Entering into ministry involves entering into the spiritual conflict between Satan and God (Eph. 6:10–18). Providing support for people consists of praying for them and establishing ways in which they can be spiritually rejuvenated. This includes allowing people to attend conferences in their area of ministry, providing time off for physical, emotional, and spiritual renewal, and giving support for problems and issues confronted in the ministry.

Preparing the Performance

While many small churches chafe at the idea of organizational red tape, clear job descriptions are beneficial. Job descriptions are necessary in helping people understand what they are to accomplish, how they are to execute it, and what skills are required. The job description should include the job title, the purpose of the ministry, the position of the person to whom the volunteer is responsible, the requirements involved in the ministry, the responsibilities and activities involved, the skills and qualifications needed, training provided, and projected areas of the worker's own growth.

In many cases, since the small church has an aversion to formal organization, the job description may need to be verbally communicated to the person rather than written down. In any case, both the leader and the volunteer should have a clear idea of what they are doing, why they are doing it, and how they are going to accomplish it.

Preparing the Program

Before recruiting any individual to a specific ministry the church should have a strategy on how it will provide the financial resources for the program. Since finances remain a significant concern for the small church, it is crucial that the cost of the ministry as well as the source of the funding be identified.

In developing this financial preparation, the church should be creative in its planning. While the general budget may not be able to support the program, having special fundraisers can provide the finances and be an excellent opportunity for outreach. One small church, for example, finances its youth program through pie auctions and dinners. These are planned by the youth, and attract many people outside the church. The dinners include entertainment, which has a clear gospel message, conducted by the youth. Lyle Schaller suggests that "money-raising events, special appeals for specific projects, and a less systematic approach to budgeting are characteristics of smaller congregations."[9]

When seeking to fund the ministries of the small church, remember that people often will not give until they see a specific need and reason to give. While the general budget may always struggle to be maintained, when it comes to special needs, people often rise to the occasion. People in the small church see the budget as organizational skulduggery. Consequently they lack any desire to give. But when the needs become tangible, such as the payment of the mission's fund or the pastor's salary, they dig deep to make up the difference. Funding a program is directly related to the people's perception of relevance and necessity. If they can envision how the program will meet the needs of the people with whom they have a personal relationship (both within the church and the community), they will be motivated to give, and they will give generously and sacrificially. Dudley summarizes:

> When the need is perceived, the small church will stretch to meet it. The small church will stretch to build or remodel their place, the building. The small church will stretch to have the services of a pastor, shared or full time. The small church will stretch to help people in need. But the members will not give blindly to the church budget. Further, they will not accept a goal that they feel is personally unreachable.[10]

Recruiting People to Serve

The single most important principle to remember when enlisting people to serve is that the jobs to be filled are not organizational requirements and personnel slots. Recruitment is involving people in ministry in such a way that they are maximizing their spiritual gifts for the greatest growth and benefit of the kingdom of God. What Nora Silver expresses concerning volunteerism in general can be equally true of the church:

> The future of community organizations, and the independent sector as a whole, depends on the future of our volunteers. Right now that future is at risk. It is not for want of volunteers. It is not for want of good organizations providing good services. It is for want of the capacity of these good organizations to utilize people well.[11]

Recruitment is the process of utilizing people well. Simply understood, the process involves asking people to serve, assisting them in identifying their gifts, then putting them to work in an appropriate ministry.

Asking People to Serve

The first method of recruiting is through a general appeal. This begins with a public announcement of ministry opportunities so that those who are interested might be able to inquire. Conducting church talent surveys is another way to give people an opportunity to express interest. Survey questions should identify interests, hobbies, experiences, time availability, and skills that might be used.

The second method of appealing to people is through targeted recruitment in which specific individuals are contacted for certain responsibilities. When conducting targeted recruitment it is important to avoid using guilt, manipulation, and cajoling as a way of involving people. People who volunteer out of guilt and manipulation will likely perform the task with mediocrity and will not remain committed when the task becomes difficult. The church needs people who have a passion for the ministry and a burden for the people they are called to serve.

Care should be given to the words used. Often people are recruited with the line, "John, we can't find anyone to teach the high school class. Would you teach it?" This cheapens the importance of the ministry, and it belittles the significance of the volunteer's contribution. A better approach would be, "John, the kids in the high school class need to be taught the importance of godliness. Your name came up as someone who would be able to minister to these kids. Would you be willing to teach the class this year?"

Those recruited should always be given the freedom to say no. Just because people say no does not mean that they are unwilling to serve. It may mean that they are not interested in that particular area. It is only when people continually refuse to volunteer in any capacity that they should be confronted.

To discern when to make general appeals and when to ask people specifically, a general principle is that the higher the risk and more skill required, the more likely that a specific appeal is required. Ministries and service opportunities that require no special skill can often be best served by general appeals.

Gift Identification

The obligation of the leadership in the church is to equip and recruit people for the work of ministry (Eph. 4:12). This involves training and encouraging people to serve. It also includes assisting people in the discovery of their spiritual gifts.

The strength of the small church is that the leadership often already has in place the personal relationships necessary to guide them in selecting people for specific ministries. Concerning the importance of this relationship, Mark Senter writes,

> The recognition of gifts also implies personal conversations with people, discussing their inclinations for service, and about people, discussing the emerging manifestations of gifts which may have not been discovered by the Christians who possess them. Perceptive pastors and Christian leaders find that the Holy Spirit provides gifted people to meet every spiritual need which He desires to have met at a given time. The problem of recruitment comes, not because of a lack of

appropriate people, but because we have not activated the resources which God has provided in the local church.[12]

Within the small church, personal interaction often happens on an informal basis, without the need for a formal recruitment and gift assessment. While it may be helpful at times to conduct a gift assessment program, it is even more beneficial to spend time with individuals, guiding them in an understanding of their spiritual gifts.

One group that the church has often overlooked in encouraging and assisting people to get involved is the teenagers within the church. Jeanne Bradner points out that three-fifths of young people between the ages of twelve to seventeen volunteer their time and efforts to various volunteer agencies.[13] When teens become involved in ministry they develop lifelong habits that result in their involvement in Christian missions in their adult years. By being involved they begin to sense the lostness of the world around them and the need to proclaim the gospel of Christ. Recruiting and gift discovery for youth is not only beneficial for the church ministries, it is also necessary for the future ministry of the church.

Ministry Assignment

Once the leader has assisted others in understanding their spiritual gifts, the next step in the recruitment process is directing them to a ministry that matches their individual giftedness. Two avenues are available through which people can serve. The first is for them to become involved in a present ministry of the church. Someone with the gift of helps can assist the children's ministry by baking cookies for special occasions. Those who have the gift of faith can become prayer partners for those who have the gift of teaching.

A second avenue, which is often overlooked in the smaller church, is for the person to develop and create a new ministry within the church. The church needs to remember that it is to be people driven and purpose driven rather than program driven.

Motivating People to Serve

Recruitment without retention results in chaos. To effectively staff programs with effective volunteers the leader must understand what inspires people to serve. It is not enough to merely assume that people will want to remain in service. Motivation is the means by which the leader incites and encourages people to become involved in the ministry of the church and a life of service before God. Motivation is not getting people to do what the leader wants them to do; it is getting people to do what they are called to do for the benefit of others. Lyle Schaller defines motivation as "Enabling the children of God, who comprise the Body of Christ, the church, to become what, by God's grace, they can become, and to do what, by God's grace, they can do."[14]

The key to providing an incentive to volunteer is assuring people that their involvement is part of being spiritually obedient. When we recruit people to ministry and programs without convincing them of the rightness of it, we are not properly motivating them; we are merely manipulating them to achieve our goals. People will only be motivated to serve in areas that they believe are spiritually and biblically right and contribute to the fulfillment of their spiritual responsibilities.

Motivational Factors

Keeping people motivated requires that they obtain satisfaction from their efforts. Because people have different personalities and personal needs, they will be prompted and satisfied differently. Six motivational factors inspire people. While all six may influence the individual's desire to participate, several are predominant in a person's willingness to volunteer.

The first is responsibility and influence. Some volunteers are motivated because of the desire to influence and lead others. The greater the responsibility and influence, the greater is the personal drive of these volunteers. The desire to have influence and authority over others can be positive or negative, depending upon its expression. When the influence is expressed with the desire to benefit the whole congregation and persuade others for their own benefit, that desire for authority is positive. Those who are stimulated by responsibility and influence work best in leadership positions, chairing committees, and public speaking. These people are the movers and shakers of the church who enjoy making policies and serving on policy boards. They like giving advice and offering opinions (even when unsolicited).

The second predominant motivator is challenge and personal growth. Many people enjoy the growth that will occur when confronted with a challenge that exceeds his or her present abilities. People who are inspired by difficulties or personal development are most excited when they are in ministries that stretch and challenge them so that they grow as a result. This growth may come in the areas of skills related to the task or the growth may be spiritual. They enjoy problem solving and do well in starting new ministries or in becoming involved in areas of ministry that they have not previously been involved in.

A third motivator is recognition. While everyone enjoys appreciation, for some it is especially important to be acknowledged for their contributions. Affirmation enables people to see that they are doing their tasks effectively and faithfully. Acknowledgment is more than just public appreciation, it demonstrates belief in the individual and in the individual's abilities. This creates a positive attitude within the church and within people. Proverbs 22:11 wisely counsels, "He who loves a pure heart and whose speech is gracious will have the king for his friend."

Personal notes expressing thanks by the leader and public acknowledgment of a volunteer's contributions encourages people to continue to be involved, knowing that their work is appreciated and vital. Appreciation should be expressed not only for the results, but also for effort and involvement.

A fourth predominant motivator is achievement. Achievers are goal-oriented individuals who tend to be restless and to avoid routine. They are goal setters and desire quality and excellence in their performance. They are not motivated so much by the responsibility but by what the task will accomplish. High achievers need moderate, challenging, and attainable goals, and achievers desire feedback that helps them measure their success.

In motivating achievers, it is important that the leader be able to communicate to them a clear purpose for the ministry and then aid them in performing their tasks with a high degree of excellence. They are the perfectionists who become discouraged if they consider their work second-rate, even if it was effective. Achievers work well in establishing the goals and direction of the church and in aiding the church to achieve those goals.

A fifth motivator is affiliation. People-oriented individuals find satisfaction and motivation in areas where they can enjoy mutual fellowship with others. For them, meetings are not just a time to get things done but a time to be with others. They desire to form alliances and partnerships with individuals or groups. They work best in teams because they can be with someone and they accomplish little when required to work alone. The ministries they enjoy most are those that enable them to be with other people.

A sixth predominant motivator is ownership. Motivation springs from ownership. When people consider the ministry "their ministry" they will have a greater desire to see it succeed. This ownership is derived from participation in the decisions that are made concerning the assignment. Consequently, the leader needs to help people see that the ministry is theirs, not just the leader's. The leader is not a dictator who determines what people are to do, but a coach who helps people achieve what they desire to accomplish.

Training People to Serve

Intrinsic to equipping and involving people in ministry is the need for training. Yet the small church often lacks the resources to train people. Seminars are often too far away, too, and do not correspond to the rural schedule. Therefore, the church needs to give serious consideration as to how it can equip people.

Training is the process of helping people become more knowledgeable, better skilled, and more effective in the ministries that they serve. Skill training is the process of instilling greater expertise and abilities related to specific ministries. Development focuses

> **Training Program Development**
>
> Identify ministry goals.
>
> Identify needs of people:
> - Basic skills
> - Advanced skills
> - Cross training
>
> Choose a training method from available resources:
> - Apprentice mentors
> - Group discussions
> - Other kinds of in-house training
> - Resources for the trainee to read

upon increasing one's competence in a variety of assignments. Education is the instruction in basic concepts and knowledge.

Training programs are needed because people do not immediately possess all the necessary skills to be effective. Spiritual gifts, while divinely bestowed, need to be cultivated. People need training in their particular area to further build the necessary skills to perform the task well.

Few people have the time, energy, and self-motivation to train themselves in particular areas of ministry. Thus, a structured program is needed that encourages learning and ministry formation. As the training addresses issues, the information should be simple and easily assimilated.

The program should address the needs and interests of the volunteers. People learn best when they see the relevancy of the training. The most effective time to instruct people on issues is when they are facing problems that are addressed by the teaching. For example, the best opportunity for instruction in classroom discipline is when it is an area of concern expressed by the Sunday school teacher.

Initiating a program involves four phases. The first is the establishment of the goals. Second is the identification of the needs of the people in relationship to the achievement of those goals. Third, the appropriate method must be identified. Fourth, the process should be evaluated in relationship to effectiveness.

Identify Ministry Goals

Two areas need to be examined before determining training needs. First, what are the corporate goals of the congregation? What does the church desire to achieve in relationship to its ministry? Second, what are the personal goals of the individuals involved in ministry? Since the mission of the church is to equip people to fulfill God's calling in their lives, it is the church's responsibility to assist people in achieving their aspirations in ministry. Too often the church merely looks at its corporate plans and fails to consider how it can help equip people in relationship to their personal aims.

Identify Needs

In what areas do volunteers need to be strengthened? A few basic skills are foundational, regardless of the ministry in which the person is involved. Communication, conflict resolution, problem solving, and strategic planning should be taught to all volunteers, creating a strong foundation in their ministries. Other rudimentary skills might include a survey of the Bible, foundational doctrines, and Bible study methods. By teaching these, people will be more effective in their ministries, and the whole church will be better equipped to work together as a community.

Every ministry within the church should offer occasional training that is designed to help its volunteers become skilled in performing that particular ministry. Those training sessions could also offer instruction that is designed to help volunteers become more effective. A Sunday school teacher, for example, might receive instruction on how to share the gospel with a young child.

Cross training is designed to help people perform a variety of tasks, helping people develop and exercise their spiritual gifts in a variety of ways. Since the small church relies heavily upon people who are willing to do a number of different tasks, cross training is especially needed in the small church. For example, training Sunday school teachers in how to comfort people in a crisis will not only make them more effective as teachers but will open new ministries for them and the church. Cross training can be accomplished by assigning to people different responsibilities, thereby affording them a wide range of experience within the scope of their spiritual gifts.

Develop the Training Method

Once the training need is identified, the next step is to develop a suitable training method. This includes formal as well as informal instruction. Formal instruction is intentional and involves a more academic format. Informal training involves personal one-on-one interaction on a casual basis and is more practical in format. Although both are needed, the best training methods maximize informal structures rather than formal programs.

When considering training, the small church needs to utilize available resources. While small churches often do not have access to training resources outside the church, a number of resources are nonetheless available. Regional seminars and conferences are offered that address different dimensions of ministry. Small churches overcome the financial and logistic problems of sending a group by sending one person who then reports what he or she has learned to the rest of the church. In this way, both the individual and the church benefit. Another means to train people is to contact the various missions and parachurch organizations, which can provide training for the church. Often other pastors or lay leaders from other churches in the area can provide expertise in particular areas of ministry. Packaged seminars in both video and audio tapes as well as CD-ROMs can be used and are more cost effective than sending a group to a seminar.

The small church can also institute apprenticeship programs. Those who lack experience in a particular area can be teamed with more experienced individuals. The veteran gains fresh ideas while the novice benefits from the veteran's experience. While the church may not have an extensive apprenticeship program, one or two individuals can be trained this way. John Maxwell suggests a five-fold process in an apprenticeship program:

1. *Modeling.* The trainer performs the tasks while the trainee watches;

2. *Mentoring.* The trainer continues to perform the task, but the trainee comes alongside and assists;
3. *Monitoring.* The trainee performs the task and the trainer assists and corrects;
4. *Motivating.* The trainer is removed from the task, checking to make sure the trainee knows how to do the task without help and encouraging the trainee as improvement continues; and
5. *Multiplying.* Once the new leader does the job well, it becomes that person's turn to teach others how to do it.[15]

Training can also occur through group discussions. Having a group of people in a related ministry meet together to discuss issues, concerns, problems, and ideas is a way that everyone can benefit and learn from the collective knowledge of the whole. Group discussions are invaluable for addressing any problems that might arise.

Training can be fostered, too, through in-house training. The leader fosters learning by assigning training topics to different people. After they have researched the topic, those people conduct a mini-seminar that covers the material learned. Assigning topics develops "experts" within the congregation and provides for those attending the seminar a sense of involvement in the other's ministry.

Training as well as personal growth can be accomplished through reading programs. The leader should encourage reading by assigning to a group of trainees a book relating to a relevant dimension of ministry. After the group has had the opportunity to read the book, they can meet together to discuss the content and any related material.

The call to belong to a church is a summons to serve within the church. Just as the church has a responsibility to evangelize and disciple people, it also is responsible to actively recruit, motivate, and train people to serve. The more the church involves people in various ministries, the greater will be the spiritual health and effectiveness of the church in accomplishing its theological purpose.

Evaluation and Implementation

1. Complete worksheet 15 with the leadership of the church (see appendix A).
2. With the board, develop a strategy for recruiting and equipping people to serve within the congregation.
3. Identify ways to encourage and reward those who are involved in the ministry of the church.

Further Reading

Brackney, William H. *Christian Volunteerism, Theology and Praxis.* Grand Rapids: Eerdmans, 1997.

Burt, Steve. *Activating Leadership in the Small Church.* Valley Forge, Pa.: Judson, 1988.

Connors, Tracy Daniel. *The Volunteer Management Handbook.* New York: Wiley & Sons, 1995.

Senter, Mark III. *Recruiting Volunteers in the Church.* Wheaton, Ill.: Victor, 1990.

Wilson, Marlene. *How to Mobilize Church Volunteers.* Minneapolis: Augsburg, 1983.

NINE

Developing the Vision of the Church

*C*hurch leaders are daily inundated with a flood of mail advising the pastor that this or that new program is the key to a successful ministry. Depending on the latest book or brochure, the key to success ranges from cell groups to concerts of prayer, from developing higher liturgical services to preaching in jeans and polo shirts. Sorting through this flood of information is like crossing the ocean in a rowboat on a starless night: Not only does the task seem impossible, but there is not even a basic direction in which to head. So it is easy to become lost in the muddled sea. This lack of clear direction is a reason many churches do not survive. These churches

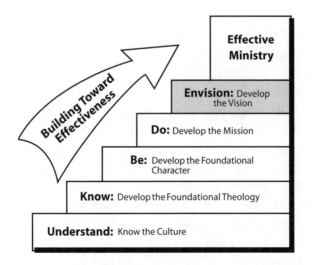

do not lack opportunities, but they fail to see the potential. The greater the secularization of American culture the greater will be the ministry opportunities. The ability to identify these ministry opportunities is the heart of vision.

Understanding Vision

Before a vision can be developed, it must be understood. Without a proper understanding, a church will either pursue wrong objectives or it will be trapped in past traditions, full of activities that fail to make a difference. To understand what vision is, we must become aware of the relationship between the church's vision and the congregation's theology, character, and mission. What we know theologically, what we are in character, and what we do with our mission form the overarching basis for determining vision. Vision determines how we are going to reach, teach, and disciple, so that people are transformed through the knowledge and application of biblical theology.

Vision is the marriage between the biblical purpose and mission of the church and its contextual setting. It is the compelling awareness of the distinct and divinely ordained current and future ministry of the church. The principles of what is envisioned speak to a particular sociological, theological, and cultural setting. Keeping the vision firmly in mind enables the group to accomplish its biblical purpose and mission. This definition encompasses seven key elements.

First, vision is compelling. Vision is more than a mental picture. It is an overriding conviction of what must be. Such a picture motivates people to give themselves to the tasks that demand their time, energies, talents, and resources. Vision is the church's best glimpse of God's passion and will for the community. Gripped by vision, a congregation will devote itself to the task. Vision provides a sense of significance and keeps the group from becoming sidetracked in the mundane. Words, emotions, and actions are joined in the common quest to bring a vision to reality.

Second, vision is distinct. Vision is the unique focus of ministry that is distinct to the individual church. It is "specific, detailed, customized, distinctive and unique to a given church."[1] No two churches have the same vision. Beyond the similarities, two visions will diverge as they reflect the personality of individuals, community culture, the gifts of leaders, and resources.

Third, vision is divinely ordained. Vision determines the will and direction that God has for the church. It is not an organizational exercise, but a spiritual activity, under which the church seeks to conform to the will of God. Barna rightly points out that "the means to success in ministry is to focus upon God and to be committed fully to His vision for your ministry and to what He will do with you and through you in the future. Vision for ministry is a reflection of what God wants to accomplish through you to build His kingdom."[2]

This is not to say that it is a "mystical happening;" rather it is the prayerful desire to accomplish God's will within the church based upon spiritual insight, common sense, and a careful analysis of the circumstances. Because it is the desire of God lived out in the community of the church, vision requires an understanding of God's character and the recognition of the church's dependency upon God for guidance and direction.

Fourth, vision determines ministries. Though future directed, vision is in touch with the present. It describes what the church is to become and how to reach that goal. It determines what the church should be about now. When the church understands its focus, it has a basis upon which to evaluate its present ministries. Thus, the church must constantly be evaluating everything it does through the lens of its vision.

Fifth, vision directs future ministries. The vision of the church serves as a guidepost, directing the congregation where it is to go and what it is to become. Vision is what ties the past, present, and future into one ministry. It directs people to look ahead instead of reliving the past. Because it keeps the focus on the future, it enables the congregation to chart a course through the breakers of change. Without such clarity, change results in conflict as people evaluate change by personal preference alone.

Sixth, vision is based upon the setting. Vision is determined by the sociological, theological, and cultural setting of both the church and the surrounding community. Just as the expression of one's gift is based upon the individual's personality, abilities, talents, and background, so also how the church goes about accomplishing its vision will be determined by the sociological and cultural makeup of the people within the church and community. To know God's will we must know who we are, our abilities and gifts, our values and beliefs, our passions and interests.

Seventh, *vision accomplishes the mission and purpose of the church.* The foundation for the vision is the purpose and mission of the church. The purpose of the church describes what the church is to be. This finds embodiment in the Great Commandment (Matt. 22:37–40), in which Christ summarizes everything that the people of God are to be. That is, the people of God are to be a community that loves God and loves others. The mission of the church describes what the church is to do, which is to reach people for Christ, disciple them so that they are living in obedience to Christ, and to involve them in the ministry of the body of Christ. Vision describes how the church is to go about accomplishing the purpose and mission within its local setting. The vision should always reflect and be consistent with the purpose and mission; otherwise the church can easily become distracted by good but nonessential ideas.

The Biblical Necessity of Vision

While the term vision—as a descriptive word defining a specific focus of the ministry—is new to the church, the idea itself is embodied within Scripture. As has been established, vision is God guiding his people to perform specific tasks within the context of their situation, and in Scripture God continually made clear what he desired his people to accomplish. When God entered the affairs of humanity, he did so to guide them not only in the present but to establish the direction they were to focus upon in the future.

Abrahamic Covenant

In Genesis 12, God revealed to Abraham his covenant. But God did more than just outline how he was going to bless Abraham. The covenant was God's vision for the people of Israel, outlining what

Vision Development: An Overview

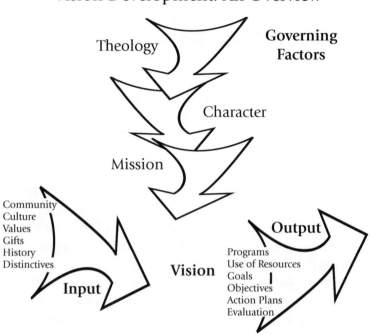

he wanted them to be and do for him. That vision was compelling in that it required them to be completely committed to the covenant. God told Abraham to "leave your country, your people and your father's household and go to the land I will show you" (Gen. 12:1). Such an act demanded complete dedication to the task that God appointed. It was more than just a move across country; it was an acceptance that keeping the promise was, because it was divinely ordained, completely dependent on God. The whole focus of the covenant was not what Abraham or the people of Israel would do, but what God would do through them. Six times in three verses (Gen. 12:1–3) the phrase "I will" is repeated.

The covenant had both present and future implications. Presently, Abraham was to leave his country and go to the land. This required immediate action that transformed what Abraham was presently doing within his life. The future was also outlined in that eventually all people on earth would be blessed through him. Within the covenant, God outlined what Abraham was to be and become, that is, a great nation. This meant that the Israelites were not merely to be a group of individuals connected by a common covenant, but a community who collectively were the people of God. The Abrahamic covenant was God's vision not just for Abraham or even for Israel, but for all humanity. It was the outline of how God was going to accomplish his mission of redemption through the nation of Israel.

Davidic Covenant

Another example of God revealing his vision for his people is the Davidic covenant found in 2 Samuel 7. Like the Abrahamic covenant, it was given primarily to one individual, yet it encompassed all that God desired to accomplish through the nation of Israel. As with the other covenants of Scripture, the Davidic covenant outlined how God was going to accomplish his redemptive purposes through the descendants of David. This covenant distinguished David from Saul, and David's line from all the rest of the Jewish lineage (v. 16).

Nor was the covenant something David had to achieve. God was going to fulfill it through him and his descendants, ultimately culminating in the enthronement of the messianic King (vv. 12–13). Again the focus of the text is upon what God will achieve: "The Lord declares to you that the LORD himself will establish a house for you" (v. 11). Presently David would enjoy peace and prosperity (vv. 9–10). In the future, the kingdom would be established and the throne occupied for all eternity (vv. 12, 16). God's vision for Israel was that they would become a kingdom whose King exerted influence over all the earth, thus bringing redemption to all people.

The Great Commission

While Christ, in Matthew 28, outlines the mission of the church, visionary elements endue the command. The Great Commission not only outlined what the church is to do in the present, but what it is to do in the future. In verse 20 resides both present assurance—"I am with you"—and future direction—"to the very end of the age." God's interest in the process of how the church accomplishes its mission is further highlighted in Acts 1:8. God did not leave the strategy for accomplishing the mission to mere chance. He outlined the process by which the church was to realize the task of going and making disciples of all nations. The church was to become established first in Jerusalem, then branch out to Judea and Samaria, and then to the ends of the earth.

The rest of the book of Acts is a record of how the church set about fulfilling this strategy. Chapters 1–7 deal with the outreach effort in Jerusalem; chapters 8:1–11:18 focus upon the proclamation of the gospel in Judea and Samaria. The remainder of the book describes the gospel penetrating the civilized world at that time.[3]

God did not merely give the redemptive mission to his people; he continually communicated how he was going to accomplish it through his people. In the Old Testament, it was through the unfolding of the promised seed. In the New Testament, it was through the growth of the missionary strategy. In each case God clearly communicated his vision to his people so that they might know both what to do and how to accomplish it.

The same holds true today. At the heart of developing the vision is the church, as the people of God, inquiring of God how they are to go about fulfilling the same universal mission within the context of their setting. The strategies continually change, but the mission remains the same.

God Communicates His Vision to Individuals

God not only communicated his vision to his people as a community, he also gave a vision to specific individuals, communicating what they were to accomplish for him. This vision was unique to the person and tailored to the specific historical situation.

Noah: Preserving a World

In Genesis 6, God gave Noah the vision of building a boat that would house representatives of the entire human and animal world to preserve them through the universal flood that was coming. The call of Noah was to hold the prophetic Word of God in one hand and a hammer in the other. He was to be both preacher and ship builder. Upon his shoulders rested the responsibility of preserving both humanity and the animal kingdom, guaranteeing that they would have a future in the new world that would emerge from the flood.

Joseph: Preserving a Family

The dreams of Joseph were the foundations of a personal vision that guided and upheld Joseph through rejection and adversity. Understanding the faith of Joseph begins with the perception of his personal vision in which he dreamed that he was to rule over his brothers (Gen. 37:5–11). While this resulted in the jealousy of his brothers, for Joseph it was the guiding light that governed his life (45:5, 7–8). But Joseph would eventually gain not merely the prominent position in his family; God placed him in that position to preserve his family. While he may not have fully understood the implications when he first woke from the dreams and imprudently shared them with his brothers, by the end of his life he fully understood God's work within his life (Gen. 50:19–21). God had placed him in the strategic position that he might preserve the family of Jacob lest the promise be destroyed by starvation. While delivering a family, God used Joseph to transform a group of ruffians who despised the favored son (37:20) into a people of God who were willing to sacrifice themselves lest the favored son die (44:33).

Moses: Preserving a People

The vision given to Moses was no less dramatic and no less important. For the promise to be realized, the people had to be delivered from slavery. The slavery of Israel was not only a threat to the promise of a nation, it was a threat to the integrity of God who proclaimed that after some four hundred years the people of Israel would be delivered from the bondage of Egypt (Gen. 15:13). The least likely candidate for the job was Moses. Moses was a failure whose previous attempts had only brought a price on his head. Instead of leading the people into the wilderness, Moses fled to the wilderness like a whipped pup, defeated and humiliated. Yet it was here that God gave Moses the vision of delivering his people (Exod. 3).

Joshua: Establishing a Nation

At the most critical point in the history of Israel, the key leader passed from the scene. Just when the nation was poised to take possession of the land, the leader who brought them there, the leader who had guided them for forty years, died. Human leadership may change, but God's leadership remains constant. Before the time of mourning over Moses had ended, God called a new leader to the task. The vision that God gave Joshua was to both guide the people and to command them in the conquest (Josh. 1:1–11). To accomplish this, Joshua would need unshakable confidence in the presence and empowerment of God (vv. 5, 9). Furthermore, when going against the entrenched forces of Canaan, Joshua would need to be entrenched in the Law of God (vv. 7–8). Having received his vision, Joshua wasted little time in calling the people to action. Joshua's statement in verse 11 is a masterpiece of vision casting. He did not call people to a battle; he called people to the realization of the inheritance that God desired to bestow upon them.

Nehemiah: Building a City

Nehemiah received his vision for ministry in a far less dramatic way. The vision was not received through a spectacular dream, or a burning bush, or an audible voice from heaven. It was born in the quietness of a prayer closet, and the firm conviction that God would fulfill his promise of returning Israel to the land. Yet even without the dramatic conveyance of the vision, Nehemiah was convinced that his vision, which grew from his understanding of prophecy (1:8–9), was given to him by God (2:12). For some, vision may come dramatically; for others, it comes through the understanding of God's Word as it relates to the contemporary situation. Because God promised to bring his people back to the land, Nehemiah had a vision to rebuild the city of Jerusalem. Nehemiah waited to communicate it, however, until the time was appropriate (2:12). Communication involves timing as well as clarity.

Paul: Reaching the Gentiles

When Paul experienced the redemptive grace of God on the road to Damascus, he also received his vision for ministry. God communicated clearly to Paul that he was to be the apostle to the Gentiles (Acts 9:15). The task involved suffering (v. 15), but the vision also sustained Paul when he encountered opposition to his ministry (Acts 13:46–47). Vision was not just a job for Paul, it was a compulsion that no man could oppose. For Paul to forsake his calling would be paramount to disobedience. It was vision that dominated Paul's life and consumed Paul so that he evaluated his life solely by its accomplishment (Acts 20:24). Nor did he allow himself to be sidetracked by other ministries. Although he desired that the Jewish people be reached with the gospel, he did not fall prey to the temptation of forsaking his calling to the Gentiles (Rom. 9:3; 11:13–14; Gal. 2:8–9).

Specific Gifts Serve Specific Purposes

The development of vision for the church is not grounded solely in God's dealings with both the community and the individuals in the Scriptures. It is also grounded in God's equipping people for ministry responsibilities. God has equipped each believer with specific gifts for a specific purpose (1 Cor. 12:7, 11, 28), and, further, he has arranged gifts, believers, and purposes in such a way that each church is able to accomplish what he desires. Paul writes to the church of Corinth that "God has arranged the parts in the body, every one of them, just as he wanted them to be" (1 Cor. 12:18). Spiritual gifts, then, are not arbitrarily given. They are dictated by God's divine plan and purpose for the congregation. So also Peter writes that God gives each member spiritual gifts to be used for the service of others (1 Peter 4:10). An individual's vision for ministry is the understanding of how he or she is to use his or her spiritual gifts for the benefit of others. The church's vision is the discernment of how God has brought gifted individuals together into a community to serve Christ in the larger community. Vision is not an organizational requirement; it is a spiritual requirement, because it encompasses the realization of what God has equipped and called the church to do.

The Necessity of Vision

Without vision, the church becomes lost in confusion and will fail to fulfill its biblical responsibility to God. An examination of Scripture reveals a number of reasons why vision is a prerequisite for the church.

First, vision is necessary to determine the will of God. Paul calls the church to "test and approve what God's will is" (Rom. 12:2). Knowing the will of God is a requirement for genuine spiritual worship. Gaining this understanding comes not from a mystical, esoteric acquisition of divine insight, but is discerned from Scripture and the wise application of it to one's life and ministry as the Holy Spirit gives clarity and insight.

Second, vision is necessary for accomplishing what has eternal value. The church can easily become ensnared by the desire to maintain its structure and organizational activity. Tradition rather than biblical truth can become the guide for the church. The result is that the church can do many different endeavors but accomplish little in eternal value. This is especially acute in the small church where traditions play such an important role. This heritage results in the small church being cautious regarding change. While tradition plays a valuable role in the life of the congregation, it should never become the guide for the church.

Third, vision enables the church to use its talents to the fullest. Christ, in Matthew 25:14–30, tells the story in which a master gives to three servants according to the ability of each. The first two servants use the money to the fullest, doubling the amount. Although the first two servants are given different amounts (the first five talents and the second two talents), and both return with different profits (the first ten talents and the second four talents), both receive the same reward.

The third servant, on the other hand, fails to use his investment wisely. Instead, he hides the money so that there is no return. As a result, the master judges the servant severely for failing to use the money to the best of his ability. This parable is meant to point to the importance of faithfulness in serving the kingdom, measuring faithfulness by use to the fullest of what one is given. The responsibility of the servants of the King is to use what God has given in redemption to the fullest for the glory of God. This includes the spiritual gifts given to the church. Thus, vision is understanding and seeking to faithfully use what God has given to the fullest.

Fourth, vision is necessary to make wise decisions. In Proverbs 24:27 the sage emphasizes the importance of having clear priorities: "Finish your outdoor work and get your fields ready; after that, build your house." Setting priorities involves identifying what is important and what has lesser value. While one may think that building the house is more important, in reality preparing the fields is more urgent for the income from the work provides the means to build the house. Setting priorities and making wise decisions is also based upon evaluating and caring for what one already possesses (see Prov. 27:23–24).

The body of Christ needs to make wise decisions regarding its priorities, programs, and resources. Without a clear vision of ministry, the church will not have a clear basis for making those decisions. Vision enables the church to distinguish between what's good and what's bad for the organization and what is worthwhile to achieve. In light of all the unlimited options and needs confronting the church, without a vision, making decisions becomes a matter of personal preference rather than wise judgment. A church that is driven by the latest fads rather than by God's divine plan will become driven by the agendas of others.

Fifth, vision enables the church to be proactive. Proverbs 21:5 warns, "The plans of the diligent lead to profit as surely as haste leads to poverty." The wise individual learns to be proactive and prepares ahead. The one who comes to ruin is the one who goes forth in haste, being reactive to the situation. Being reactive in planning undermines the fragile morale of the small church. Schaller points out that a reason for "low morale in many congregations is that they tend to follow a problem-based approach to planning. This planning model tends to reinforce gloom, pessimism, despair, and low self-esteem."[4] If the church does not have a solid direction, it will continually be responding to circumstances rather than shaping its future.

Six, vision brings unity. The church is not to be a group of people assembled with divided purposes. When there is no clear agenda, there will be multiple agendas, each member trying to force his or her own on others. The result will be chaos and conflict. Scripture, on the other hand, paints the picture of the church as a unified organism moving in harmony to achieve united purposes. Paul continually writes to the churches to have the same mind. In Paul's final words to the church at Corinth he calls upon them to "aim for perfection, listen to my appeal, be of one mind" (2 Cor. 13:11). When writing to the Philippians he exhorts them to "conduct yourselves in a manner worthy of the gospel of Christ. Then, whether I come and see you or only hear about you in my absence, I will know that you stand firm in one spirit, contending as one man for the faith of the gospel" (Phil. 1:27). He states further that his joy will come when they are "like-minded, having the same love, being one in spirit and purpose" (2:2).

Without vision people become focused upon their own desires and needs rather than the ways they can serve and minister to others. Conflicts, rather than unity, mark the church as people jockey to fulfill their own ambitions (1 Cor. 1:10–17).

Seventh, vision enables the church to avoid burn-out. Morale in the small church is a major problem. David Ray writes that "the dominating and most debilitating problem in a high percentage of small churches is low self-esteem, resulting in low morale."[5] He goes on to warn,

> Low self-esteem is a cancer that kills small churches. It reduces the amount of available money, results in poor building upkeep, repels new members, discourages leaders, erodes organizational effectiveness, changes communication from positive to negative, causes church fights, undermines planning, and limits relationships with those outside. In short, it undermines the ministry and mission of the church. Efforts to enhance personal and church self-esteem and build morale need to top a small church's priority list.[6]

The problem of low morale is not new. It plagued Elijah after his powerful victory at Mount Carmel (1 Kings 18:16–46) and his subsequent ineffectiveness in changing the hearts of Jezebel and the people of Israel (19:1–2, 10). As a result he became discouraged, wanting to die rather than continue his prophetic ministry (19:4). To encourage Elijah God renewed his passion for ministry by calling him back into service (19:15–18). The awareness of what God has called us to do for him is the basis for overcoming discouragement and emotional and spiritual burnout. Without a vision, the enormity of the task, the complexity of the problems, and the vastness of the needs can easily overwhelm the small church.

Developing the Vision

Understanding the biblical foundation for ministry is not enough for an effective ministry. The purpose and mission of the church are universal in their application, governing every church and Christian organization alike. The vision, on the other hand, is seen in context to the specific setting that the church finds itself in. Since the vision of the church relates to its particular setting, the church needs to grasp its geographic, cultural, and sociological setting. Only then can it adequately form a clear vision for how the church is to accomplish its purpose and mission. This understanding involves comprehending the community in which the church ministers, the individuality and distinctives that mark the church, and the organizational idiosyncrasies that characterize small churches. Armed with this information, the church is prepared to formulate a clear vision statement that provides the general direction for the church.

Understanding Our Rome

Understanding the will of God cannot be divorced from the ministry context of the church. The body needs to know its environment. Of all the preachers who have influenced history, none has been more committed to ministering in cultural context than Paul. Nor was there one more committed to upholding the integrity of the gospel than Paul. From the outset of his ministry, his message was centered upon the foundation of the gospel. His one desire was to proclaim the gospel without apology or compromise no matter what the cost. In 1 Corinthians 9:16–18 he mentions that his passion to preach was divinely initiated, and that he had no other reward nor motivation than to merely be a vessel used by God to proclaim the gospel message. For Paul, the faithful proclamation of the gospel was the sole dictate of his life (Acts 20:24–27). Even when this preaching brought him into great disfavor among

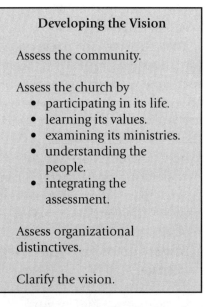

Developing the Vision

Assess the community.

Assess the church by
- participating in its life.
- learning its values.
- examining its ministries.
- understanding the people.
- integrating the assessment.

Assess organizational distinctives.

Clarify the vision.

men, he continued to preach. He gladly went to his death rather than compromise the integrity of the gospel in any way.

Although Paul fervently upheld the absolute authority of Scripture, he recognized that the communication of the gospel had to be culturally sensitive. The proclamation of the gospel was not done in a cultural vacuum, but done in the context of a specific cultural setting. Thus Paul, while not compromising the gospel in any form, was willing to adapt his ministry to the social sensitivity of the people he wanted to reach (1 Cor. 9:19–23). He adapted to the Jewish culture to reach the Jews, he tailored his ministry and message to fit the Gentiles when he ministered to them (see Acts 17:22ff).

The pattern that Paul followed was not new. He was merely following the pattern already established by Christ. Whenever Christ sought to proclaim the message of the kingdom, he began with the needs, hurts, and interests of the people. Rick Warren summarizes the ministry of Christ by saying that "Jesus did three things with crowds: He loved them (Matt. 9:36, et al.), he met their needs (Matt. 15:30; Luke 6:17–18; John 6:2, et al.), and he taught them in interesting and practical ways (Matt. 13:34; Mark 10:1; 12:37, et al.)."[7] Christ was sensitive to the needs of people and he accomplished his God-given mission within the context of ministering to those needs (see Matt. 9:36; 14:4; Mark 1:41; 6:34; 8:2–3).

The task of the church is to start where people are and move them where they need to be. Therefore, if the church desires to effectively communicate the gospel and accomplish its mission within its local setting, the church needs to have a cultural understanding of the community. Like the men of Issachar, who "understood the times and knew what Israel should do" (1 Chron. 12:32), the church needs to understand its times and cultural settings.

Today also, understanding the ministry context of the church includes knowing the culture of the community (for information on assessing cultural context, see chapter two). Culture involves how people formulate their understanding of life. To communicate the message of Christ clearly, the gospel must be presented in the cultural language.

Understanding Our Corinth

Paul, in ministering to the church at Corinth, did not bring a pre-packaged message and program that he pulled from his church ministry file at every stop he made on his missionary journeys. Instead, he sought to understand and evaluate each church on its own and conduct his ministry in a way that fit the specific church. Thus, in writing to the church at Corinth, he wrote to a church that needed bold confrontation and severe discipline. On the other hand, when writing to the Philippians, he wrote words of comfort to a church suffering for the cause of Christ. In his final words to the elders in Ephesus, he reminded them that he preached that which was needed and helpful to the church (Acts 20:20).

Establishing direction and vision involves the understanding of the specific setting within the church. This understanding can be attained through a congregational assessment. The purpose of the congregational assessment is to honestly determine the church's health, strengths, weaknesses, problems, needs, and desires. By inspecting the congregation, the leadership can gain insight into the uniqueness of the church and develop ministries that capitalize on its strengths.

The church assessment process collects data about the makeup of the congregation and involves the people in the process of setting direction. The goal is not merely to talk to people within the congregation, but to talk with them, gaining their ideas, participation, and opinions about the church. In the process of doing so, the church gains the input and valuable insight of a number of people—and the individuals themselves gain a sense of ownership in the ministry of the church. A sense of ownership is crucial to the success of the ministry. Personal involvement is the foundation for the acceptance of change. Without personal involvement and ownership, the people will resist change no matter how positive the change may be. Assessing the congregation involves a multi-step process to gain a thorough understanding of how God has "wired" the church to accomplish his purpose.

Step one: Develop a strategy for participation. Since participation is the key to ownership, the first step is to outline a strategy that will enable people to present their thoughts and opinions about the direction and focus of the church. Leadership can encourage and provide opportunity for participation in several ways. Some of the tools suggested by Lindgren and Shawchuck are "home meetings, statistical and demographic charts, 'town' meetings or public hearings, group discussion in meetings or worship services, every-member canvass, telephone interviews, questionnaires."[8] The goal is to select and develop a method with which people are comfortable and feel "safe" to contribute their ideas and thoughts.

Step two: Assess the key values of the church. The values of the church are the "shared expectations to which people desire or to which they are expected to conform."[9] These may be expressed or unexpressed. They may be biblical or they may be traditional or cultural. Those that are traditional and cultural, if they enhance the ministry of the church, can be accepted and affirmed. If they hinder the ministry of the church, they must be lovingly and carefully changed. Values that are contrary to Scripture need to be confronted and replaced. Those that are biblical, the church needs to uphold and integrate into every aspect of its ministry.

The values of the church will be expressed in the philosophy of ministry that governs the church. While the philosophy of ministry and the values are not necessarily equal, they are related. The type of worship service that the church conducts is more than just a reflection of its worship philosophy; it reflects a value that governs the church.

The first step in examining the values of the church is to listen to the stories that tell the church's history. While stories are humorous anecdotes about people, they also convey the history of the church and the people within the church. They relate what is important to the church and to its members. The stories people share within the small church establish the ministry style of the congregation and define the ministry. Concerning the importance of stories, Alan Wilkens writes,

> My research in organizations suggest that many of the values that are adopted as shared vision, as well as the conventions people learn, are passed on through informal stories . . . . Stories of actual events inside the organization are often more credible than official claims because the person who is telling the story may not be a company official (with obvious pro-company biases) and because the story is concrete, unlike the abstract ideas of vision statements. In addition, stories give people a chance to improve their own implementation of organization-sponsored value.[10]

The importance of stories is especially true in small churches. Those who are unfamiliar with the stories will always be considered newcomers and outsiders—not just because they do not know the stories, but because they do not yet follow the values that undergird them and make them meaningful and important to congregational life. One way to discover the stories is to have people informally describe the past events that mark the church's history.

Second, to assess the values of the church, one should examine the philosophy of ministry that governs the church and then ask, "How does this philosophy reflect key values within the church?"

The different areas that can be examined are the worship and music styles of the church, the type of preaching desired, the authority and leadership base of the church, the budget and financial statement of the church, and the attitude of the people regarding outsiders and newcomers.

Third, as the congregation identifies the values that mark the church, it is important to realize the influence that the community culture has in determining the mores even within the church. For example, the prominence of privacy in small communities often has a higher rank than outreach. Work ethic is more significant than leisure and, at times, even more important than the family. Understanding the cultural setting and the values within the community give insight into the mores within the church.

Another informative source regarding the values held within the church is to identify what is officially and unofficially rewarded, tolerated, and criticized. When the church rewards "Grandma Betty" for her many years of service as a Sunday school teacher, it is recognizing the significance of faithfulness. If the church does not allow newcomers to have leadership positions within the church, even though the newcomer has been attending for ten years, it is expressing the prominence of bloodlines and family ties that are often central to the church. Joe Ellis explains the power of culture in determining people's values within the church:

From the time an individual is born, culture filters into him or her its assumptions about the church. Even before that child is aware of what is happening, the cultural image is well-structured into his or her thinking so that he or she tends to accept and perpetuate what has been heard and observed. The cultural version of religion resembles Christianity in many ways and use [sic] some of the same terminology and forms, but they lack [sic] the essence of biblical Christianity. If congregations are not alert, they can be directed more by cultural images of Christianity than by what the Bible reveals as the intentions of God. The condition has been described as the cultural captivity of the church.[11]

To identify and change the values, the congregational assessment process should not only include identifying key mores within the church, but also identify those that should mark the church. Unless those of the church reflect the biblical standards, the vision will not become a reality in the ministry of the church. Instead of accomplishing its purpose and mission, the church will flounder in spiritual ambiguity, conforming to the cultural mores of the community rather than transforming the ethics of the community through the proclamation of Christ. The key values of the church, which guide the ministry of the church, need to be recognized and thoroughly examined.

Step three: Assess the ministry. The third step in assessing the church is to assess the ministry and programs of the church. This examination involves, first, a comprehensive look at the programs and structures, beginning with an evaluation of past and present activities. What has worked well in the past? What has not worked well and why? Which present programs are effective and which are not? Do the programs not working well need to be dropped or changed? The purpose for evaluating the past and present ministries is to gain insight into what God has previously been accomplishing through the church. Vision is not merely a new idea that is unattached to the past, it is often an outgrowth of the past and present.

Second, identify the strengths and weaknesses of the church. What does the church have going for it? What areas of the church need improving? What problems are being faced by the church?

Third, determine the resources that are available to the church. The resources of the church include areas of time, talents, and finances. In rural farming communities, people have less time during certain seasons of the year to devote to ministry than they do at other periods. Every church has different financial resources available. The financial stability of the church is dependent upon the income of the people. Each church, too, has a different talent base to draw from in developing ministries and a different mosaic of how those gifts fit together. Unless all resources are realistically considered, the church may follow a vision that is unattainable because it does not have the available resources.

Fourth, what are the barriers that the church has to overcome in ministry? Some of these the church may be able to master. Others, the church cannot master and needs to learn how to work within them. No church operates within ideal circumstances. The goal of the church is not to be flawless but to be and do the best it can with the available resources. Every church has some psychological, physical, organizational, spiritual, or image barriers that inhibit its ministry.

Psychological barriers are issues and feelings residing within the church that prohibit people from being active in ministry. Barriers may include, for example, a fear of sharing the gospel and a fear of rejection. People, too, may be emotionally dysfunctional so that they cannot deal with rejection. If a church has suffered a split in the congregation, it has wounds that can sap the energy of the church. Before people can effectively share the gospel, they must be healed emotionally.

Physical barriers exist when the church facilities are not adequate. When the church lacks sufficient seating, parking, or classrooms, physical obstacles exist that will hinder the church from effectively receiving new people. Many church growth experts argue that a characteristic of successful churches is that they have a location that is highly visible and easily accessible. For many small churches, however, relocation is financially prohibitive. Therefore, it needs to consider these barriers when planning.

Organizational barriers include issues that arise because of the organizational structure of the church. This may include programs that demand a great deal of time and energy; programs that are ineffective yet, because of its history, the church is not ready to change or drop the program; programs that lack quality. Perhaps, too, the organizational structure of the church is cumbersome.

Spiritual barriers exist when the spirituality of people obstructs them from reaching out to minister to others. A spirit of judgmentalism and legalism, resulting in a lack of love for others, will destroy unity within the church. Not comprehending the lost condition of people will be a barrier for effective outreach.

A fifth barrier may be the image held (both of the universal and the local church) of the church in the secular community. This is especially meaningful in small towns where a church split in the past can tarnish its image for years.

The purpose for assessing the barriers is not to identify and deal with every problem within the church. Such an attempt would only result in frustration and discouragement. The task is to identify those barriers that are most crucial for the ministry and spiritual health of the church that affect its vision and future ministry.

Step four: Assess the people. Having assessed the ministry, before the church can adequately formulate a clear vision, the people in the congregation need to understand themselves. Just as there is individual giftedness and personality, so also there is corporate giftedness and personality. This corporate identification is based upon the collection of people and their gifts, abilities, personalities, and talents. The purpose of a congregational assessment, then, is not to force people into the vision, but to develop a vision that allows people to express their gifts to the fullest in church ministry. For this to occur, the church needs to have an adequate understanding of the demographics, gifts, and background of the people in the congregation.

Step five: Summarize the assessment. After completing the assessment, the leadership of the church should then summarize the findings to formulate a picture of the present condition of the church. Lindgren and Shawchuck suggest that the summary be no more than ten pages using the following headings: basic strengths of the congregation, basic weaknesses/concerns of the congregation, major issues confronting the community, financial support for the church, major feeling tones in the life of the congregation, changes members would like to see take place.[12] This summary should provide an honest overview of the church so that the vision can be based upon an accurate discernment of the church.

Step six: Integrate the assessment. The final step is to integrate the assessment in the vision development process. Not only does the vision reflect the community surrounding the church, it indicates the makeup and characteristics of the church. Correct vision will always correspond to the individuality of the church. To integrate the assessment, the church should identify three to four of the most crucial ministry needs within the congregation that the church can address.

Understanding Ourselves

In leading the congregation through the process of determining its vision and mission, it is important to understand the organizational distinctives that mark the small church. In the small church there is a high degree of ownership felt by the people for the ministry and future of the church. Unlike the larger church, where the task of vision casting and determining the direction of the church is often given to the pastor or other church leaders, in the small church, such authority should not be assumed and in many cases is not given. Because of this ownership, members will often resist any attempt of the leaders to set the direction of the church without significant input by them in the process. Schaller concludes, "Even in those small-membership churches served by a seminary-trained minister, the pastor usually has less influence in charting the course than is true in the large congregation."[13]

Because the people in small churches often have been members for years, they see the pastor as someone who is temporary, ministering a few years before moving on to another parish. As a result, the authority for setting direction is often not granted to the pastor, but to dominant lay people, often determined by bloodlines. Doran McCarty points out that "power in the small church is accessible to someone, and most often it is not the pastor. Laypersons are the seats of power in the small church in most situations, not the pastor. The pastor has the title but not the power."[14] Most books on vision development wrongly assume that the pastor has the power and authority to set the vision for the church. Within the small church this often is not the case. In setting the direction of the church, it is important that the influential members, and the whole congregation, be a part of the process. The pastor who desires to work effectively in the small church will be more successful by working with, not against or apart from, its contextually rooted, traditional leaders.

Only when the congregation has a sense of ownership in this vision will it become the driving force in the church. The role of the pastor in small churches is not to determine the vision, but to facilitate the process, to lead and guide the people as they develop the focus of the church. When the church realizes the pastor is not going to dictate his will to them but listens to their desires, then the pastor will be given more authority and power within the church.

This is especially true in rural communities where people are self-employed because they want their independence. They enjoy the freedom of being self-employed and self-governed and resist any who attempt to dictate what they should do. Therefore, when they come to church they do not want to be told what to do. While they are willing to be guided, they want the freedom to decide their own future. In formulating the vision for the church, the church leadership needs to be sensitive to this independence. If the leader is perceived to overstep his or her authority, strong resistance will be encountered no matter how significant the vision.

Vision Clarification

Vision clarification is the process of assimilating all the data and information into a succinct statement of direction. To clarify the vision, the first step is to spend time in prayer for clear direction and guidance. There are never shortcuts to spiritual work. To determine the vision and will of God for the church, the leadership and the people must be in submission to God. At the center of a life of submission is a life of prayer. Since the vision is the desire to build the kingdom of God by doing the will of God, it is vital that the church devote itself to pray diligently for God's direction. While God is not playing hide and seek with his will, he does desire that we be dependent upon him and submissive to him in the process.

Once the assessments are completed, and the church has identified the crucial needs both within the community and the church fellowship, then the leadership can write a vision statement that pinpoints the direction toward which the church should be headed. In the formation of the vision, George Barna suggests the following guidelines: First, to effectively communicate the vision, keep it to one paragraph. Second, reduce the vision to a few sentences that have stripped everything away but the essence. Third, keep it simple enough to be remembered but specific enough to provide direction. Fourth, create a vision statement that identifies the people the church is targeting, the purpose and mission of the church, and the distinctiveness of the church.[15]

The statement should provide a clear answer to the question, "How are we as a church going to accomplish our purpose and mission?"

Evaluation and Implementation

1. Complete worksheet 16 in the workbook (see appendix A).
2. Study the passages mentioned in which God reveals his specific will to people and to the nation of Israel. How do these examples help us in understanding how God works through people and how he directs people?
3. Based on the assessment, the board and pastor should develop a clear vision statement. Write a brief description of how the vision statement will help the church accomplish its goal of character transformation and its mission of reaching, teaching, and recruiting people.

Further Reading

Crandall, Ron. *Turn Around Strategies for the Small Church.* Nashville: Abingdon, 1995.

Dudley, Carl S. *Developing Your Small Church's Potential.* Valley Forge, Pa.: Judson, 1988.

Malphurs, Aubrey. *Developing a Vision for Ministry in the 21st Century.* Grand Rapids: Baker, 1992.

———. *Pouring New Wine into Old Wineskins.* Grand Rapids: Baker, 1993.

Warren, Rick. *The Purpose Driven Church.* Grand Rapids: Zondervan, 1995.

TEN

Implementing the Vision of the Church

*N*ehemiah approached Jerusalem with the vision of reestablishing Israel. For this to happen, he needed to rebuild the protective walls of the city. Although he came with the official sanction of the highest ruler in the land, he still faced incredible opposition from within Israel as well as from the groups surrounding them. The building project itself was overwhelming. Yet the biggest hurdle confronting Nehemiah was rallying the people around the task. For some one hundred and forty years they had lived in the ruins of the city as a discouraged, downcast, and beaten people. Through those years, they daily walked by the city, grieving its destruction and seeing no hope for the future. The greatest problem facing Nehemiah was not architectural but psychological and spiritual. Putting a stone in the hands of the people and telling them where to stack it was not enough to rebuild the walls. If the city was to be reestablished, the people needed to understand the vision.

Communication Is the Key to Success

A vision will remain only a dream until it is communicated to and embraced by the people who are involved in the process of fulfilling it. Before the vision can influence and form the ministry of the church, it must be understood and accepted by the congregation. Although the congregation has been involved in the process of developing the vision, it should never be assumed that everyone fully comprehends its full meaning and implication.

Communicating the vision is the foundation for this understanding and acceptance.

In the small church, people desire to know not only what is happening in their particular area of ministry, but what is happening in the whole church as well. It is critical for the leader in the small church to communicate to all levels of the congregation what is going on and why. If people do not understand what is happening, they will become disgruntled and will not actively support the ministry. What Bennis and Nanus say about leadership in general is especially true within the small church:

> Believing in one's dreams is not enough. There are a lot of intoxicating visions and a lot of noble intentions. Many people have rich and deeply textured agendas, but without communication nothing will be realized. Success requires the capacity to relate a compelling image of a desired state of affairs—the kind of image that induces enthusiasm and commitment in others.[1]

Communication binds the church together. First, communication is necessary for unity. For the church to be unified in achieving its goals, everyone needs to comprehend what purpose, mission, and vision are, and they need to grasp how achieving them can enable each person to reach his or her own goals. Understanding the relationship between individual and corporate goals helps nurture positive relationships among those involved in the ministry. When people understand this relationship, they can see the value of the contributions of others, both to the corporate goals and their individual goals. Communication is central to having people accomplish a unified vision, rather than being isolated from one another as they seek fragmented and even conflicting goals.

Second, communication is necessary for commitment. People will commit only to what they clearly understand and see as spiritually profitable. Because people have limited time and financial resources, they commit to that which has importance and value. Paul underscores this desire to "connect" in ministry and not just shadow box

(1 Cor. 9:24–27). It is crucial that people comprehend the results to be achieved and the process.

Third, communication is necessary for motivation. When people understand that the vision has eternal consequences and is the divine will of God, they will begin to see themselves as having the unique privilege of participating in God's over-arching redemptive plan. Motivation stems from both the realization of the ministry responsibility and the realization that ministry is a privilege granted through the all-encompassing grace of God. By communicating the vision clearly, leadership helps people realize that they are fulfilling this responsibility when they support and become involved in the ministries of the church.

Defining Communication

Communicating the vision does not necessarily occur simply by verbalizing the content of the vision. Communication is sharing meaning—not just words. Rush discusses the importance of meaning and understanding:

> Communication can be defined as the process we go through to convey understanding from one person or group to another. Unless understanding occurs, we have not communicated. Therefore, when people complain about poor communication, they are actually complaining about the lack of understanding and not about the lack of conversation, discussions, memos, or correspondence.[2]

For communication to have actually taken place, membership must fully comprehend what the vision of the church is. When people understand the vision, they can grasp why they are being asked to do something. Before they can know how to conduct the ministry, they need to know why it is important.

Successful communication involves, too, people understanding their roles within the vision and how they are to participate in its accomplishment. Without this understanding, the vision remains the church's or the pastor's but not the people's.

Communication also involves people understanding the impact of the vision. When Nehemiah communicated to the people the vision of rebuilding the walls, he stated that "we will no longer be in disgrace" (Neh. 2:17b). In so doing, he outlined for them the impact that the rebuilding of the walls would have. The vision was to rebuild the walls, but the consequences would go beyond just the presence of new walls. It would bring new vitality, hope, and confidence to the people of Israel. Vision has been communicated to people only when they understand the impact that the vision will have upon the church, the community, and the universal work of God. This is especially true regarding the impact the vision will have upon the relationships within the small church. Schaller reveals the contrast between the large and small church:

> In the large congregation, there is a tendency for people to conceptualize reality in terms of functional categories, whether it be in describing the greatest competence of the pastor, in categorizing people, in designing the organizational structure for the congregation, or in evaluating the performance of that congregation. In contrast, in small congregations the members tend to think in terms of interpersonal relationships. The relationships of life, rather than the functions of the church, top the priority list in the small church.[3]

To develop ownership, then, any change or goal must be couched in the context of relationships. The vision needs to relate to the needs of friends, family, and neighbors so people can see how the vision will strengthen these relationships rather than just build the organization.

Thus, effective communication involves certain principles affecting both transmission and reception of information. Between the transmission and the reception, however, distortion can easily occur. To avoid misunderstandings that can derail the vision, the leader needs to think through how the vision is to be conveyed.

Communicate Constructively

First, positive communication is the foundation for acceptance. If the vision is related negatively, people will become defensive and less likely to accept the vision. Positive communication focuses upon what the church has done effectively, what it can do, and what it should do. It will encourage, inspire, and sustain the people and the vision. Negative communication, on the other hand, focuses upon what the church has not done, what it has done wrong, and what it should not do. Negative focus will drain and discourage the church. If there are issues such as past or present sins that need to be confronted, it should be done in the context of God's love and grace and the availability of forgiveness that can result in a renewed blessing upon the church and in the lives of people.

Communicate with Conviction

The second principle is to communicate with conviction. If the leaders do not believe in the vision, neither will the people. Before the vision can grab and direct the ministry of the church, the leadership needs to be convinced that the vision is both possible and essential. The early church was effective in reaching the Gentile world because Peter, Barnabas, and Paul spoke with profound conviction concerning the necessity of proclaiming Christ to the Gentiles (Acts 15:6–12). This certainty stems from the confidence that the vision is God's expressed will for the congregation. This passion is not mere emotion; it is the commitment to fulfilling the vision, a commitment that comes from the conviction that the vision is God's intended purpose for the congregation.

Communicate Clearly

The third principle is to communicate with clarity. Foggy understanding results in haphazard implementation. Clarity is the foundation for clearly defined objectives and plans. When the vision is properly communicated people will have an unclouded picture of the desired result as well as a clearer understanding of the process involved in implementing it. Articulating the vision requires the leadership to explain how it will affect the lives of people involved in the ministry. The vision is not just a corporate vision governing the church; it is an individual vision as well, guiding people in the expression of their spiritual gifts. As discussed in chapter 9, the mission and vision of the church should be reduced to a short paragraph that captures the overarching nature of the mission and vision, and is easily remembered and understood by the people.

Make Communication Contemporary

A fourth principle is to communicate in contemporary terms. In their discussion on communication, Gangel and Canine speak of "presentality" which "tells us communication must be explained in terms of the here and now."[4] In other words, effectiveness is tied to the present experiences and reality of the people involved. While the vision of a church points to the future, small churches tend to be oriented to the present. Thus, the vision should be disclosed so that people understand how their existing ministries will be affected and how their present lives will be influenced. Presentality gets the vision past the "theoretical" and brings it to bear on everyday experience, upon present needs and problems rather than future direction.

Communicate Through Relationship Connections

A fifth principle is to communicate in the context of relationships. Because of limited financial resources, small churches often do not have the mechanical means of communication (such as videos, Internet, newsletters, etc.) that are available to larger churches. As a result small churches are more reliant upon personal communication. Key people have significant influence because of the network of relationships they have within the congregation. Communicating to and through those key people assures that the information will be accepted by the whole church. The "grape-vine," then, is a vital link between leadership and the lay people. Schaller points out,

> The larger the size of the membership and/or the more complex the community setting, the more likely the grapevine will carry more erroneous messages than accurate bits of information. Thus the small, rural church in a sparsely

populated county often can depend on the grapevine, while the large city church must publish a weekly newsletter.[5]

Learning how and when to use this network of relationships can be an effective means of communicating within the church.

Communicate Continually

Sixth, communicate continually. When communicating essential information within the church, one cannot overcommunicate. Often we assume that an announcement on Sunday has sufficiently communicated issues and events and that people will remember what was discussed. Seldom does this happen. The more critical the information the more the leadership needs to communicate it a number of times and in a number of ways. Continually restating the mission, vision, and goals of the church enables new people to understand what the church is about, and constantly reminds everyone of the direction of the church so that ministry is always developing in light of these objectives.

Build Communication upon Heritage

Seventh, communicate in the context of the past. Although the vision directs the church to the future, it must be grounded in the history, heritage, and experience of the church. Dudley and Walrath warn against forming a vision that is unrelated to the past:

> Some congregational leaders urge a vision of the future of the church without first finding ways to interpret their hopes within the history and experience of the church. . . . they do not know the traditions and stories of the congregation, but enter with an agenda for action already prepared to be plugged into the ongoing life of the church. They almost assure failure for their proposals, and, what's worse, they blame it all on the congregation for not seeing it their way.[6]

To avoid this mistake, the goals and direction of the church need to be communicated so that the vision becomes an extension of the heritage of the church rather than a break from the past.

Communicate to the Right People

To whom we communicate is just as important as how we communicate. Effectively enlisting people in the task of fulfilling the vision involves proclaiming the vision to the right people.

Communicate to the Leaders

The burning bush was not the place where Moses first gained the vision of freeing the people of Israel. Some forty years earlier he had the same vision. He failed to achieve the vision because first, he sought to accomplish it in his own strength, and second, he failed to properly communicate it to the people he was called to serve. As a result, when he first attempted to help the people of Israel by taking vengeance on their masters, he was met with ridicule and rejection (Exod. 2:11–14). He did not make the same mistake the second time. Instead, when he came back to Egypt after the wilderness experience, he began by communicating the vision to the leaders of the people (Exod. 4:29–31). So also Nehemiah, when he desired to enlist the people in rebuilding Jerusalem, began by proclaiming the vision to the leadership in Jerusalem (Neh. 2:15–18).

While the process of developing the vision should include the leadership and the whole congregation, it should not be assumed that everyone will fully understand the implications of the vision. Therefore, after it has been developed, the vision should first be communicated to the leadership of the church. Whenever the church leadership meets to discuss the ministry, they should be reminded of the vision and reminded how the various ministries affect the whole ministry of the church.

Communicate to the Power Brokers

Within small churches, position is not nearly as important as tribal recognition. People who are not necessarily in an organizational position of authority nonetheless exert significant influence. Nor is the pastor always the recognized leader in the church. Because small churches are homogeneous, often centered on kinship, certain people, because of their position within the family, are the unofficial power brokers within the church. Therefore, before the church can be enlisted in the accomplishment of the vision, these power brokers within the church need to both understand and endorse the vision. Without their support, the vision will never be realized. The wise pastor remains humble enough to work with these powerbrokers rather than be threatened by them. Communicating to the power brokers can be done individually so that they have opportunity to ask questions and give input crucial to enlisting their ownership.

Communicate to Those Involved

The vision must be communicated to those who are involved in the ministry of the church. Since they will be most affected by any change, they should have input into the vision and changes. They should understand how their ministries will be affected by the vision, goals, and direction of the church before these are carried out. When people do not understand the broad picture, turf battles result as people seek to protect themselves and their ministries from perceived threats.

Communicate to the Congregation

The final step is communicating the vision to the whole congregation. This involves communicating individually with people as well as through various forms of general communication within the church. One means of communication is for the pastor to present a yearly "state of the church message." This sermon can address current needs and goals of the church and can afford an opportunity for the pastor to affirm and recast the vision.

Plan the Vision

Once the vision has been formulated and clearly communicated, the next step is to establish programs and ministries that enable the church to accomplish its mission and vision. But program development is only one element of the planning process. Planning also involves adapting the organizational structure and setting goals for each program.

The planning approach will dictate the outcome, but the most

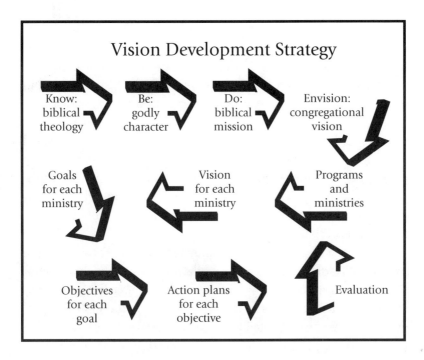

Vision Development Strategy

Know: biblical theology → Be: godly character → Do: biblical mission → Envision: congregational vision → Programs and ministries → Vision for each ministry → Goals for each ministry → Objectives for each goal → Action plans for each objective → Evaluation

important element is not the process itself but the starting premise. Productive planning begins with a "potentialities-based approach."[7] This approach operates from the premise that the church is fully equipped by God to accomplish his ministry in the present and the future. Planning should focus, then, on the strengths and potential rather than the problems or weaknesses.

Develop the Right Programs

Programming defines what needs to be done to achieve the vision and mission. It structures the organization required to accomplish the goals. These programs may be single events or long-term commitments. The danger, however, is that they can become more important than the people involved and the congregation as a whole. Since the small church values relationships above programs, the focus must be upon the relational impact rather than just the organizational impact. The planning process begins by identifying the programs and ministries that can assist the church in realizing the vision.

Step one: Identify the ministry needs. After the relevant assessments have been completed (see chapter 9), the information should be used to identify different ministry opportunities both within the church and the community. While the concerns of programs will ultimately be spiritual, the church can examine the physical and emotional needs of people in order to develop programs that can minister to the redemptive needs. These programs should be related to the general vision of the church. While the programs can be people oriented, they should be vision guided. That is, the ministries developed by the church should enable the church to accomplish the vision and mission. If they do not, the church should carefully rethink its activities.

Once a need is identified, the church should look at the existing programs. Traditional programs, while at times obsolete, often continue to meet important spiritual needs within the congregation and community. Rather than starting new programs, the established programs can often be adjusted to be more effective. Those that are no longer serving productively should be dropped. The purpose for culling certain programs is, according to Lindgren and Shawchuck, "to ensure that no ongoing program area of the church becomes trapped in activities without having any specific goals or clear-cut plans, or that any program is not directly supporting the missional priorities of the congregation."[8]

If the present strategies are incapable of meeting the needs raised, then new ones can be implemented. In doing so, the focus should not be on the program itself but on the need presented.

Step two: Write a purpose and vision statement for the program. Just as the church has a clear statement of purpose and vision, so should each program and ministry. Purpose and vision define why the ministry exists, what it seeks to accomplish, and how it will accomplish it. The statement should communicate the spiritual intention for the ministry, not just the organizational function.

Step three: Recruit a team. Ministry is a team sport. The apostle Paul, in 1 Corinthians 12, outlines the importance of team ministry. There are no "Lone Rangers" in the ministry of Christ. The church is made up of different individuals who are uniquely gifted, working together to achieve common goals. Forming a team enables individuals to accomplish more than they could accomplish in isolation (see Eccles. 4:9–13). Christ, in sending out the twelve disciples, did so by formulating teams consisting of two apostles each. Doing so provided a stronger base of ministry as each could encourage and strengthen the other as each brought different gifts and abilities to the team. The team then is responsible for evaluating the activities, making the decisions, problem solving, and establishing the goals and direction for the program.

This process of selecting the team is foundational for assuring that they work together with clear objectives. In formulating the team, George and Logan suggest five keys to building the leadership team of the church:

1. Focus your time and energy to equip current leaders and develop future leaders.
2. Select and recruit people with leadership potential.
3. Agree on areas for training and development.
4. Recognize the dynamics of an effective training process.
5. Schedule regular appointments for ongoing reporting, encouragement, and accountability.[9]

Once the team has been formed, leaders are responsible to prepare team members to accomplish their responsibilities. There are four necessary requirements for effective teamwork: First, the team has a common goal that they are working to achieve. Second, they cooperate with one another, building trust in the relationship rather than suspicion. Third, they communicate with one another, encouraging and challenging each other. Fourth, they have a commitment to one another and to the project. If the team lacks just one of these four elements, it will suffer and be less effective.

The leaders train people to be effective in ministry and to work together in a team environment. The process of developing this cohesiveness involves four elements. The first is *observation*. When the group is formed, the leadership needs to provide opportunities for members of the group to observe others doing the ministry. This may involve the leader modeling the ministry or it may involve meeting with a ministry team from another church to discuss how they perform their responsibilities. The second step is *participation*. In this, the ministry team takes an active part in the ministry. The third step is *evaluation*. The best time to teach is after the people have served in the ministry rather than before. As they become involved they discover areas where they need training. Evaluating the team results in training that is relevant to the specific needs of the team. The fourth step is *multiplication*. After the team has been taught and been involved in ministry, they then need to identify and train others who can also become part of the team.

Step four: Identify specific goals. After the team has been formed, they should be responsible for determining specific goals and objectives. Allowing the team to decide what they will be enables the team to acquire ownership of the ministry. If the goals are dictated, they will not gain ownership, and the result will be low motivation.

Step five: Determine the resources. Every ministry project needs three critical resources: people, time, and material/finances. The small church, however, is often severely limited in each of these resources. Being effective with a restricted number of people begins by working with, rather than around, the traditional leaders within the church. Attempting to by-pass them will only bring resistance and frustration. Traditional leaders are individuals or families whose authority within the congregation results in considerable influence into the decisions and plans of the group. With the backing of these people, others will be more committed and willing to support any present or future ministry.

The lack of time that people have available requires the church to conserve its leaders. Overworking people will result in burnout; bringing a further shortage of workers. A successful small church, as it struggles to maintain its ministry, focuses upon doing a few things well rather than a variety of ministries haphazardly. The problem is that today's small churches are being pressured to fulfill the multiple service opportunities dictated by the larger church. Walrath warns, "When small congregations try to live according to a large church model, they not only fail to develop their unique potential, they often exhaust their leaders as well."[10] The small church needs to conserve its leaders by focusing upon its unique strengths. Only when new leaders are available should it consider beginning new ministries.

Last, because the small church has limited funds, it needs to have sound accounting procedures. Although the small church trusts the individual responsible for the accounts, it should require the treasurer to provide financial statements and annual audits. To preserve financial resources, if the small church cannot afford a full time pastor, it can allow the pastor to work outside the church to supplement his or her family's income.

Careful planning involves an honest consideration of what resources are required. It includes examining what is available and how the use of these resources will affect other ministries. If necessary, the church may need to either drop a ministry, or wait to establish a new one.

Develop the Organizational Structure

Often organization is viewed negatively within the church, beneficial to the secular world but not applicable to the church. There is the danger that we can see the church only as an organization with its programs, goals, and strategies, and not as a spiritual organism that constitutes the dynamic body of Christ. Nevertheless, organization is necessary to avoid confused priorities, miscommunication, and misunderstandings that result in conflicts. The purpose of the structure is to provide clarity in responsibility and accountability. The church needs to outline who is responsible for what, and to whom they are accountable so that the ministry is done effectively and efficiently. Effective leadership is making sure that the right things get done; management is making sure it is done in the right way. Both are necessary within the church. While each church will have a different organizational structure, it nevertheless should be clearly defined. Structure, however, should always be flexible and fluid.

The Best Goals

Clear, obtainable goals are essential. Without clear goals, the vision will become blurred. Proverbs 21:5 anticipates the importance of planning: "The plans of the diligent lead to profit as surely as haste leads to poverty." Planning is necessary for success, while going off half-cocked only results in disaster. The apostle Paul demonstrated the importance of both short-term (Acts 20:16; 1 Cor. 16:5–7) and long-term planning (Acts 18:21; 19:21; 1 Cor. 16:5–7). A balance is maintained between long and short-range goals because each requires the other. In order to achieve long-term goals, they are to be translated into short-term plans and decisions. On the other hand, short-range goals need to be tied into an overarching long-term plan, otherwise the goals will become disjointed and misguided.

Strategic planning is not organizational trickery, but the attempt to make present decisions based upon the understanding of God's direction for the church in order to organize efforts necessary to carry out God's plan. Strategic planning is necessary to keep the church focused not only on achieving its vision, but also on achieving its mission of reaching, teaching, and recruiting people. Without strategic planning the church becomes a hub of activity going nowhere. Setting goals is a process, developing a "how to" plan for the church that is based upon its mission priorities.

Step One: Define the Mission Goals

While many regard goals as bureaucratic poppycock, they unite the ministry and focus the energy of the people. Without clear goals, the ministry can easily become disorganized, wasting energy. The objectives of each goal define the targets of mission purposes. Well-written goals exhibit any of several characteristics:

Goals should be consistent with the mission. The goals of each program should help the church achieve its ultimate mission and vision. Similarly, the goals should correspond to the intended purpose of the program itself as it contributes to the total mission of the church.

The particular goals of each program should be consistent with the overall ministry environment. Consistency comes through understanding of the context of the church as gleaned through the assessment process (chapter 9). The growth rate of the church, the characteristics of the church constituency, the past effectiveness of the programs, the community characteristics, and the current needs of people are integrated into the process of establishing goals. When the goals are consistent with the environment, people will feel motivated to participate.

Goals should be consistent with the resources. Goals need to be compatible with the time availability of people, the financial resources of the church, the materials and facilities owned by the church, and the skills of the people involved. Goals that are not harmonious with available resources will only result in frustration and discouragement.

Goals should be consistent with the church's organizational structure. If not, the church needs to either reassess the goal or restructure its organization. While it would normally be advisable to change the organizational structure to adapt to the goal, occasionally it may be necessary to reevaluate the goal.

Goals should be achievable. In planning, it is easy to dream dreams that are unrealistic and unattainable. While the goals of the church should require the church to stretch and live by faith, goals should not be so extensive that they become unrealistic. Having a few attainable goals is better than having multiple goals that overwhelm the resources of the congregation. While it may be helpful to write down a number of possible goals, the list should be narrowed down to the best three or four.

Goals should be clear and simple to understand. Clearly defined goals that are simply stated will enable people to understand the purpose of the goal and their role in its attainment. To be comprehended, the goals need to be definable and measurable. This does not mean that the goals should be focused on quantity rather than quality. Perry and Shawchuck point out,

> There is a great danger, however, that as the group writes its goals in measurable terms the goals may become mathematical statements. . . . Some church goals perhaps should be quantitative. But the church is a qualitative institution, and the majority of its goals should be statements of desired qualities, not quantities. They should describe ministries

that capture the hearts and minds of the people, not mathematical problems that send them scrambling for their pocket calculator.[11]

For example, the church may have as its goal to be more evangelistic by reaching the unchurched parents of the children involved in the children's ministry. While this may involve numerical analysis (i.e., visiting the thirty unchurched parents), the focus is upon the quality of outreach.

Goals should be unifying. Because the focus of the small church is upon relationships rather than accomplishments, the goals of the church should seek to unite the church rather than divide the people. Larger congregations have major and minor goals. The multiplicity of goals rallies support from many different groups who have unrelated and diverse goals within the church. The small church, on the other hand, sees goals in the context of unity rather than ministry diversity. The larger churches accept the process, tolerating a diversity of goals. The smaller church tolerates the process only to achieve the goals that serve to unify its ministry.

Step Two: Outline the Objectives

Objectives are the specific activities to be accomplished to achieve the goal. Goals cover work to be done over one and two years; objectives break down the strategy into what needs to be done in the next three to six months. For each goal, the ministry team should determine two to four objectives that outline the necessary activities to be accomplished and the sequence in which they are to occur. If, for example, the goal is to reach all the unchurched parents of the children involved in the children's program, one objective might be to have a parents' night to acquaint them with the ministry. A second might be to establish a visitation program. A third might be to send home literature for the parents to read.

Step Three: Develop Action Plans

Action plans list specific tasks to be done to accomplish the objectives. Action plans address the questions in regard to the church accomplishing its objectives, goals, and plans. Action plans answer the questions:

- What specifically needs to be done?
- Who is responsible for doing it?
- When does it need to be done?
- What resources are required to do it?

The action plan moves the objectives from paper to reality.

Step Four: Monitor Activities to Make Sure They are Effective

Lindgren and Shawchuck suggest the following monitoring questions:

- Where are we in the plan? What steps have been accomplished, and what should we do next?
- Are the steps being done according to the schedule? If not, what adjustments should be made to get the plan back on schedule?
- Are the workers doing their job satisfactorily? Are they in need of resources? Do we need additional workers?[12]

Monitoring makes sure that events and people are moving at the pace needed to accomplish the desired results.

Evaluate to Stay on Track

Good intentions can easily stray into misguided execution. Whether the arrow is ten degrees off or ninety degrees off, it will still fail to hit the bull's-eye. Yearly evaluation is necessary to make sure the arrow of vision is still in line with the bull's-eye of ministry. Evaluation is not criticism or judgmentalism; it is an honest assessment of where the church is, where it needs to be, and whether or not it is going in the right direction. The apostle Paul encourages personal evaluation: "For by the grace given me I say to every one of you: Do not think of yourself more highly than you ought, but rather think of yourself with sober judgment, in accordance with the measure of faith God has given you" (Rom 12:3). Without evaluation, the church can become lost in a forest of idealistic goals, or mired in the muck of inefficiency and self-abasement.

Evaluate the Programs

Evaluation serves two important purposes: it guides work on existing programs, and it gives direction for establishing new ministries. Evaluation begins with current programs and ministries to make sure they are accomplishing the biblical mission of the church.

Step one: Evaluate the goals. Examine goals to determine whether they track with the vision and mission. Annually, the leadership team (i.e., the church board of deacons, session, or consistory and the program directors) should examine the various goals of the different ministries to determine if they are in line with the church's mission and vision. The past goals should be evaluated in terms of their proficiency and accomplishments, while future goals should be evaluated in terms of clarity and whether they can be attained.

Step two: Evaluate the vision. Each year the church should check its relationship to its overall vision. The programs and activities should be assessed, based on what they are accomplishing in relationship to the vision of the church. Are the results achieved consistent with the vision? Are the programs worth the time, effort, and money expended on them? Are the programs and ministries meeting the needs of people?

Step three: Evaluate the programs in relationship to the mission. Since the vision is to serve the mission of the church, the programs should be evaluated in relationship to this mission. Are people being evangelized? Are they being taught biblical truth and discipled in biblical obedience? Are they being recruited and equipped for ministry? How is each program accomplishing this specifically? While some programs and activities are more focused upon one aspect of the mission, each should nevertheless contribute in some way to every aspect of it.

Step four: Evaluate the programs in relationship to the purpose. Ultimately the church is a spiritual organism with the spiritual purpose of transforming people's relationships with God and with others. Every ministry should be accomplishing both. If not, the program is misguided, no matter how effective it might appear to be, and it should be reevaluated and changed.

Evaluate Effectiveness

The church is in the business of transforming people, not developing organizations and programs. The greatest test is not how smoothly the program is operating but the spiritual growth it achieves in the people involved. Everything the church does should be evaluated in terms of the effect that it is having in the lives and conduct of people.

Step one: Evaluate people's spiritual growth. The church needs to examine its effectiveness in instilling biblical and theological knowledge by surveying the spiritual conduct of people. Are people forming a worldview that is consistent with the teachings of Scripture? How much are people being taught in regard to biblical truth and theological understanding? Is prayer becoming more relevant in the lives of people? Are people manifesting obedience to biblical truth?

Step two: Evaluate people's relational unity. While the church will never have unanimity, it should be marked by unity. Assessing spiritual unity of the church requires an examination of relationships within the church. Are people overlooking faults and forgiving hurts? Do people work through differences and disagreements? Are relationships being healed?

Step three: Evaluate people's ministry involvement. Four areas of ministry involvement should be evaluated.[13] People should be evaluated in relationship to their reliability. Ministry requires reliable people who will follow through with their commitments. Throughout Scripture, emphasis is continually placed upon faithfulness as the hallmark of ministry.

Attitudes should be examined. Do people work well with others, or are they critical, dogmatic, and unyielding? Are they always cheerful and do they readily accept responsibilities with a positive attitude?

Examine aptitude. Since the responsibility of the church is to prepare people for the work of the ministry, the church needs to gauge people's ministry aptitude in order to develop training programs that meet people's needs. Do people perform all aspects of their jobs without requiring much assistance, or do they require close supervision with a great deal of assistance?

Last, leaders should examine performance. If people are performing poorly, the leadership needs to detect why. Poor performance may be a result of poor aptitude or reliability. It may be the result of a mismatch. People will become frustrated if they are in ministries not related to their spiritual gifts, or in ministries that exceed their personal abilities.

Evaluation and Implementation

1. Complete worksheet 17 with the board (see appendix A).
2. With the board, develop a strategy for implementing the vision and developing goals, being sensitive to the attitudes and reactions of people regarding the establishment of goals.
3. Develop a strategy for how the church will maintain its focus upon the vision and for achieving the goals that are necessary for the church to accomplish its biblical mission.

Further Reading

Alderson, Wayne T., and Nancy Alderson McDonnel. *Theory R Management*. Nashville: Thomas Nelson, 1994.

Kilinski, Kenneth, and Jerry Wofford. *Organization and Leadership in the Local Church*. Grand Rapids: Zondervan, 1973.

Lindgren, Alvin J., and Norman Shawchuck. *Let My People Go: Empowering Laity for Ministry*. Leith, N.D.: Organization Resources Press, 1988.

————. *Management for Your Church*. Leith, N.D.: Organization Resources Press, 1984.

Powers, Bruce P. *Church Administration Handbook*. Nashville: Broadman & Holman, 1997.

Van Auken, Philip M. *The Well-Managed Ministry*. Wheaton, Ill.: Victor, 1989.

Walrath, Douglas. *Making It Work: Effective Administration in the Small Church*. Valley Forge, Pa.: Judson, 1994.

Ministry Development Worksheets

Worksheet 1: Assessing the Spiritual Climate

1. What do respondents consider to be the greatest need in the area?

2. Where do respondents attend church?

3. For those respondents who do not attend church, why do they think people today do not attend church?

4. What things would respondents look for in a church if they were to attend?

5. What advice could respondents give a church that desires to better serve their community?

Worksheet 2: Assessing the Demographics

1. Median Age:

2. Family Status:

3. Employment and Economic Base:

4. Income Level and Social Status:

5. Educational Level:

6. Nationality and Ethnic Background:

7. Religious Background:

8. Geographic Boundaries:

Worksheet 3: Assessing the Culture

1. Mindset and lifestyle of the community (Circle the words that best describe the perspective of the people.)
   - Active versus sedentary
   - Family versus career focused
   - Individualism versus community
   - Politically conservative versus politically liberal
   - Environmentalists versus land-use proponents
   - Traditional versus progressive
   - Religious versus secular
   - Stable populations versus mobile population.
   - Homogeneous versus multicultural
   - Relationally oriented versus accomplishment oriented
   - Blue collar versus white collar
   - Federalism versus libertarianism
   - Cosmopolitan versus provincial
   - Academic/education versus nonacademic view
   - Futurism versus the here-and-now
   - Hi-tech versus low-tech

2. Cultural centers
   - Where do people congregate?
   - What social events does the community support?

- When people want to "go out" and socialize where do they go?

3. Customs
   - Are there any long established practices that have become an integral part of the community's infrastructure (i.e., style of clothing, mannerisms, habits, etc.)?

4. Community history
   - What is the history of the community? How does it affect the present attitude of people? What stories do the "old-timers" always talk about?

5. Cultural indicators
   - What type of music do people listen to?
   - What type of books and magazines do they read?
   - What type of stories make the local paper?
   - What organizations operate within the community?

Worksheet 4: Assessing the Needs

1. What are the social, emotional, physical, or financial worries of respondents?

2. In what ways can the church minister to these needs?

3. How can the church use these needs to reach people with the gospel of Christ?

Worksheet 5: Personalize Your Target

Write a one page summary that describes the typical person in the community.

Worksheet 6: Integrate the Assessment

1. How are we going to reach this person (see worksheet 5) with the gospel of Christ?

2. What programs would interest and minister to the needs of this person?

3. As these persons join our church, do they carry with them matters that need to be corrected through biblical instruction and discipleship? How are we addressing those matters currently with members?

Worksheet 7: Understanding the Church

1. What are the distinct characteristics that mark your church? How do these affect the ministry of the church?

2. What has been the growth rate of the church over the past ten years? What internal and external factors have affected the growth of the church?

3. What is the organizational type of the church? How does this affect the ministry and programs of the congregation?

4. What trends have had the most impact on the present ministry of the congregation? In what way have they had an influence?

Worksheet 8: Theological Assessment

Write a paragraph summary on how you would evaluate the present knowledge and understanding of the church in relationship to:

1. their ability to properly understand and interpret the Bible.

2. their ability to understand and communicate the overall theme and message of Scripture.

3. their ability to understand and defend the essential elements of the Christian faith.

4. the manner in which they are applying their theological knowledge to their daily conduct, perspective of circumstances, and relationships with others.

Identify the various ministries of the church in which people are being taught the following:

1. Exegetical theology

2. Biblical theology

3. Systematic theology

4. Practical theology

Identify ways in which the church can improve in each of these areas.

Worksheet 9: Worship Assessment

1. List the ways that all people and all age groups are involved in worship. What elements of the service are geared to each age group?

2. To what degree are people's attention drawn to the person of God?

3. Identify ways that the church can improve its worship service.

4. What portions of the worship service provide people the opportunity to praise and adore the person of God?

5. In which portions of the worship service are people given the opportunity to confess their sins?

6. In which portion of the worship service are people given to commune with God?

7. What opportunity do people have to respond to God?

8. What ways does the size of your church affect the worship (both positively and negatively)?

9. With what style of worship are people most comfortable?

10. In what ways can the church be more effective in planning and leading the people in worship?

Worksheet 10: Prayer Assessment

1. Evaluate the prayer base of the church:
   - Are people praying for the people they serve?
   - Are the leaders meeting together in order to pray for the congregation?
   - Are ministry groups praying together for their ministries?
   - Do people pray before decisions are made?
   - Does the pastor have adequate time to pray?
   - Does the pastor have prayer partners who are praying specifically for him or her?
   - Are people open and honest about prayer needs?

2. Do people have a strong sense of dependency upon God and an awareness that nothing can be accomplished except through his strength?

3. What areas of the church ministry need a greater focus upon prayer?

4. When does the congregation have opportunity to pray together?

5. Are people praying for one another?

6. Identify the areas where the church needs to grow in its prayer life.

Worksheet 11: Obedience Assessment

1. Are people living in consistency to God's Word in all aspects of their lives?

2. Are people developing relationships so that they are accountable to one another?

3. How are people being taught to be obedient with respect to their
   • attitude and actions toward God?
   • attitude and actions toward themselves?
   • attitude and actions toward the church?
   • attitude and actions toward their work?
   • attitude and actions regarding the government?
   • attitude and actions regarding the family?
   • attitude and actions regarding their neighbors?

4. Do people have a passion to know and apply God's Word? How can the church further develop this passion?

Worksheet 12: Assessing Love

1. Do people spend time with one another outside the church services? What functions does the church hold throughout the year that enable people to develop relationships with other members of the congregation?

2. Are people being motivated by love to reach their neighbors for Christ? What can the church do to help people develop a more loving attitude toward the lost?

3. How many of the first-time attendees come back for a second visit? How many of those who attend a second time remain in the church? What is the church doing to assimilate new people into the life and ministry of the congregation?

4. Do people in the church naturally provide care for those in a crisis? Are people adequately trained to support others in emotional crisis? Does the church provide physical assistance for those in need?

5. Does the church board have a procedure for disciplining members who rebel? How has the church handled situations in the past where people have been in open sin?

6. Does the church have any mentoring and discipleship programs for new believers, and for young people growing up in the church?

Worksheet 13: Outreach Assessment

1. List the ten most critical needs of people in the community.

2. Identify any current ministries that are addressing those needs, or could address those needs.

3. Identify the five most dominant programs or ministries presently within the church. How are any of these programs reaching unchurched people? What can be done in these programs that would enable them to reach the unsaved community?

4. Identify four evangelistic events the church could do in the coming year.

5. For each event, write out its target, purpose, location, outline, and how it will be publicized.

6. Establish a procedure for follow-up.

Worksheet 14: Discipleship Assessment

1. List each ministry that the church is presently engaged in and identify the primary target that it is focused upon (e.g., the unchurched, the infant, the mature, etc.).

2. Identify the ways that the church is teaching
   • foundational truths to the new Christian.
   • theology and doctrine.
   • Bible study methods.

3. Identify the ministries and areas of service that new people can become involved in. How do these programs assist people in identifying and developing their spiritual gifts?

4. Identify the growth ministries of the church. How are people being prepared for these ministries?

5. Identify the redemptive ministries. How are people being trained for them?

6. How are people being mentored?

Worksheet 15: Service Assessment

1. How does the church provide spiritual support for its workers? Does the church have prayer partners for everyone in ministry?

2. Does the church have a fund in the budget for people to attend training?

3. How are ministry opportunities publicized and communicated?

4. How can the church help people identify their spiritual gifts and match their gifts with ministry opportunities?

5. Does the church have clearly communicated job descriptions?

6. How are people rewarded and recognized for their efforts?

7. What training is being conducted? What training is currently needed?

Worksheet 16: Vision Development

1. Based upon the assessments regarding the community, what ministries does the church have in the present that are serving the unchurched within the community?

2. What programs and ministries have the church done in the past that effectively reached the unchurched?

3. What programs and ministries could the church possibly do that would reach the unsaved (list as many as possible)? Identify one or two that would be the most likely to succeed.

4. Develop a strategy for obtaining feedback from the whole congregation.

5. What are the cultural values that undergird people's attitudes and actions within the community?

6. What are the biblical values that should mark the church?

7. What are the strengths and weaknesses of the church?

8. Within the congregation, what areas of ministry are people strongest in? Weakest in? What ministries are people most interested in?

9. Have the congregation complete the congregational assessment questionnaire. Summarize the results in a half-page.

10. Based upon the past and present ministry of the church, the community and congregational setting, and the strengths and weakness of the church, what does the ministry of the church need to focus on in the coming years?

Worksheet 17: Implementing the Vision

Outline a strategy for communicating the vision to people within the congregation so that they not only understand the vision but want to be involved in its realization.

Outline a strategy for future communication of the vision so that the church keeps focused on accomplishing it.

Evaluate the present ministries and programs of the church, examining how they relate to the attainment of the overall vision.

Based upon the vision, identify the critical needs of the church and community.

With the ministry teams and leaders, write out the specific vision for each ministry.

With the ministry teams write out the goals for each ministry.

Outline the organizational structure of the church, showing who is responsible for what programs.

Using the goals assessment sheet (appendix F), develop goals, objectives, and action plans for each area of ministry.

Model Purpose, Mission, Vision, and Values Statements

Purpose Statement

First Baptist Church exists for the purpose of being a worshiping community that exalts God and a fellowshiping community that loves all people.

Mission Statement

First Baptist Church's mission is to proclaim the gospel of Christ so that people are transformed into faithful disciples of Christ who then influence others for Christ.

Vision Statement

The vision of First Baptist Church is to train, strengthen, and heal families so that the redemptive power of God may be realized in the lives of people who live in the communities of Stevenson, Carson, North Bonneville, and Cascade Locks.

Values Statement

At First Baptist Church we are committed to

In Relationship to God

1. Worship God. As a community of God's people we seek to worship God genuinely and completely by providing a worship service that is contemporary to our cultural setting and sensitive to the various expressions of worship by individuals within the church body and community (Col. 3:16; Eph. 4:19–21).
2. Pray continually for God's guidance and direction. As a community of God's people we recognize that we are absolutely dependent upon God for his grace and power. This dependency is manifested by our desire to have prayer as the basis for every decision and direction affecting the church (1 Thess. 5:17).
3. Uphold the authority of Scripture. As a community of God's people we recognize that the sole and final authority for conduct and faith is the written, revealed Word of God. Our teaching is always biblically based and practical for contemporary life (2 Tim. 3:16).

In Relationship with One Another

1. Be a caring community. As a community of God's people we recognize that we are responsible for the physical, emotional, and spiritual needs of one another, providing mutual care and encouragement (1 Thess. 5:11).
2. The necessity of fellowship. While recognizing the universal body of Christ, we believe that all believers are called to be a part of a local community of believers. Therefore we will encourage all believers to be involved in a local church body (Heb. 10:25).

3. Disciple all believers. As a community of God's people we seek to assist one another in becoming faithful disciples of Christ by helping one another be obedient to the Scriptures and wise stewards of our time, talents, and treasures through mutual love and accountability (Matt. 28:19).

4. Be a family-oriented ministry. As a community of God's people we seek to strengthen the family unit by encouraging, supporting, and healing families (Eph. 5:22–6:4).

5. Involve each follower of Christ in the ministry of the kingdom. As a community of God's people we will encourage and assist each individual in the exercise of his or her spiritual gifts to the fullest for the benefit of the whole community and the glory of God. We recognize that God has equipped each individual differently by blending his or her individual personality, background, and spiritual gifts (1 Cor. 12).

In Relationship to the World

1. Love all people. As a community of God's people we are committed to uphold the dignity, worth, and individuality of each person within the body of Christ and within the world by loving each person unconditionally and sacrificially, seeking to minister to the whole individual, to the individual's physical, emotional, and spiritual needs (John 13:35; 1 John 3:18; James 1:27).

2. Evangelize our community. As a community of God's people we desire to proclaim the salvation of Christ to every individual within the community in which we minister (Acts 1:8).

3. Support missions. As a community of God's people we are involved in and support God's missionary efforts outside our community by providing financial support for others and by being a sending agent for missionaries that come from within our church (Matt. 9:37–38; Rom. 10:14–15).

4. Fellowship with the universal body of Christ. While maintaining our Conservative Baptist distinctives, we will encourage,

and fellowship with, all true disciples of Christ and every Christ-centered, biblically based church regardless of denominational affiliations (1 Cor. 12:13).

Model Congregation Assessment Questionnaire

Instructions: Please take the time to prayerfully and thoughtfully complete the evaluation. The evaluation will take considerable time and thought. The more we prayerfully think through the answers to the questions, the more effective we will be in determining God's direction for our church. Answer each question as honestly as possible. Keep in mind, however, that we are evaluating our ministry, not individuals. Therefore the answers should be sensitive to the people involved and reflect our view of programs and goals rather than our personal judgments of the spirituality and/or qualifications of the people involved. If you cannot attend one of the meetings, please return the evaluation to the pastor as soon as possible. Your input is extremely important for us to gain a thorough understanding of how we can improve our ministry.

1. In your own words, how would you define what a church is?

2. Based on your understanding of what a church is to be, list the ten most important characteristics/values that should mark the church (e.g., love for people, vital worship, caring community, etc.).

3. What do you think should be the goal and focus of our church?

4. List five ministries the church has done in the past that have been the most effective in ministering to the needs of people within the church (i.e., ministries that have helped people of all ages within the church become spiritually mature).

5. List five ministries the church has done in the past that have been the most effective in ministering to the needs of people within the community (i.e., ministries that have helped people outside the church become true believers in Christ).

6. List five areas of ministry the church has traditionally been the weakest in.

7. Of the three aspects of the mission of the church (i.e., reaching, teaching, and involving), which area has the church been the most effective in? In which has it been the least effective?

8. What kind of program does/should the church have for following up first-time attendees?

9. List five barriers our church faces to effective outreach (i.e., things that hinder us from attracting and reaching new people).

10. List five things the church can do to remove these barriers.

11. List five things you think the church could do differently that would better enhance the ministry of the church in accomplishing Mission 3000.

12. List ten of the most important ministries our church needs to be involved in if we are to accomplish our mission in this area.

13. List five ways the church can be more effective in caring for people outside the church.

14. What ministries would you like to see started in the next five years?

15. What is the one ministry you think is the most crucial in order for us to effectively accomplish our mission?

16. Of the four or five houses that are nearest to you, what are (is) the

    a. ages of the adults?
    b. number of children per family?
    c. employment?
    d. hobbies?

17. List the ten most important needs and/or concerns of people in the community (e.g., future of their children, marriage, economics, employment, single parents, loneliness, etc.).

18. Rank the top five needs/concerns in terms of importance to the non-Christian.

19. List five of the needs/concerns of the unchurched the church can possibly address.

20. Ask three unchurched neighbors the following questions:

    a. What do you consider to be the greatest need in the area?
    b. In order for us to better help people in the community, why do you think most people do not attend church today?
    c. If you were to attend church, what would you look for in a church?
    d. What advice can you give us that would help us to be more effective in our community?

21. Where would you place the above unchurched people on the following scale of spiritual understanding?

   a. Aware that God exists
   b. Initial awareness of the gospel (i.e., have a limited knowledge of what Christianity is and Christ as a good moral teacher who points us to God, but fails to realize that Christ is fully God and that Christ died to redeem humanity from the penalty of sin)
   c. Aware of the fundamentals of the gospel (i.e., beginning to understand the reality of Christ and Christ's death, but not fully aware of all the implications of the gospel such as the need for repentance and inward transformation)
   d. Grasp the implications of the gospel (i.e., although they still may not accept the gospel message, or even accept the validity of the message, they do at least understand what the gospel message means)
   e. Positive attitude toward the gospel
   f. Personal problem recognition (that I need Jesus Christ)

22. List five ways the church can be more effective in inviting and including new people in the life, community, and ministry of the church.

Model Vision Development Plan

To develop a ministry plan for the church we will be proceeding, using the following steps:

Step one: Prayer

The most important element of developing goals, direction, and vision for the church is to cultivate an attitude of prayer and dependency upon God. As we go through the process of determining the direction and future ministry of the church we are asking each person to join with us in prayerfully seeking God's direction for our church. We would request that you continue to pray daily for our church through the months ahead as we desire to determine what God has in store for us. The most important contribution that you can make to this process is praying for our church. As you pray for our church, please pray for the following:

1. God's direction and guidance for the church
2. Wisdom for the board and pastor
3. Unity within the church body
4. Mission 3000: That we would present the gospel of Christ to the over 3000 unchurched individuals within our communities so that they may become faithful disciples for Christ who influence others for Christ

Step two: Congregational meetings

Our desire is that everyone would be involved and provide input into the establishment of direction for our church. To enable people to participate, we have scheduled the discussions to be held during the adult Sunday school hour. For those not able to attend, several meetings will be scheduled on alternate days and times. Every person in the church is invited to participate in these round-table discussions and to aid in our evaluation of our present and future ministries. During these feedback sessions we will discuss the following:

1. The purpose for the meetings and the reason why the establishment of direction is important
2. Questions you might have
3. Evaluating our present constitution
4. Evaluating our present organizational structure
5. Evaluating our community in order to gain a better understanding of how we can effectively minister
6. Evaluating our church and ministry so that we can better understand who we are and how we can improve our ministry effectiveness
7. Formulating a possible vision statement

Step three: Development of a proposed vision statement

After the congregation has evaluated the ministry of the church and formulated a possible direction for the church, the board will then consolidate the information received in order to develop a proposed vision statement and directional outline for the church.

Step four: Congregational approval

After the board has synthesized the information they will present at a special meeting the proposed plan to the congregation for discussion and consideration. The meeting will be preceded by a twenty-four hour day of prayer and a concert of prayer for direction and unity within the ministry of the church.

Step five: Implementation

Once the direction and vision have been developed the last stage is implementing the vision by evaluating and restructuring our present organization and ministry programs to facilitate the accomplishment of the vision. An ad hoc steering committee will be formed, consisting of the board, pastor, and committee chairs who will develop specific strategies for implementing and accomplishing the vision.

Model Community Profile

Community: Stevenson, Washington

John (who represents the typical person in Stevenson) is forty-four years old and has lived in Stevenson for approximately ten years. He is married with two children (a son age fourteen and a daughter age seventeen) and works as an electrician at the dam. Although he never obtained a college degree he has developed skills that enable him to earn a middle class income. He owns his own home, which has four bedrooms and which has doubled in value in the last five years. While this has increased his overall financial portfolio it has also caused him immediate financial pressure as his taxes have likewise doubled.

He enjoys his job but is having to spend more and more time at work in order to keep up with the cost of living. His wife also works as a schoolteacher. Family, however, is more important to John than his career and he is not concerned about moving up the corporate ladder. Instead, he is content to be a blue-collar worker.

On the weekends John and his family enjoy the natural resources that abound in the area. In the summer they go camping and spend time fishing for lake trout as well as salmon and steelhead. The children enjoy windsurfing in the summer and snowboarding in the winter. John's son has always been active in sports, playing soccer and in little league when he was younger, and basketball and football in junior high. John's daughter is active in school, playing on the tennis team as well as being involved in a host of other school-related activities. During the summer she swims on the local swim team. On almost every night of the week the family is going to some school or sports-related activity. John's kids are involved in 4-H, so the whole month of August is planned around the county fair.

In regard to religion, John believes in God but is not active in any church. With so many extra-curricular activities, he and his family have little time for any church functions. Consequently, while they would consider themselves religious, they do not attend any church in the area. He regards his faith to be something very private and sees God as one who helps those who help themselves. If he did attend church he would want a church that has effective ministries for his children.

Politically, John is conservative, believing that social programs are a waste of taxpayers' money and that those who are on welfare are merely taking advantage of the system. While he does not belong to any political activist groups, he sympathizes with those who believe that the federal government is being run by a bunch of liberals who want to take away all our personal freedoms. Because he enjoys hunting, John believes firmly in the right to bear arms and is a member of the National Rifle Association.

He enjoys country music and does little reading. What little he does read focuses on issues related to hunting and fishing. He enjoys being close enough to a big city that he can appreciate all the benefits, but is glad that he does not live in it. One of the reasons that he moved to Stevenson was to get away from the city and all the influences that might hurt his children. John does not particularly care for electronic gadgets, but he does have a computer that he uses at home to access the Internet and maintain his records.

Goals Assessment Sheet

Goals	Objectives	Action plans
Goal 1:	**Objective 1:**	**Action Plan 1:**
		Action Plan 2:
	Objective 2:	**Action Plan 1:**
		Action Plan 2:
Goal 2:	**Objective 1:**	**Action Plan 1:**
		Action Plan 2:
	Objective 2:	**Action Plan 1:**
		Action Plan 2:

Notes

Chapter 1

1. Rick Warren, *The Purpose Driven Church* (Grand Rapids: Zondervan, 1995), 190–91.
2. Lyle Schaller, *The Small Membership Church* (Nashville: Abingdon, 1994), 27.

Chapter 2

1. Juliet B. Schor, *The Overworked American* (New York: Basic Books, 1991), 5.
2. Cornelia Flora, et al., *Rural Communities: Legacy and Change* (San Francisco: Westview, 1992), 285.
3. Donald C. Dahman, *Residents of Farms and Rural Areas: 1991* (U.S. Bureau of the Census, 1991), 28.

Chapter 3

1. Donald W. McCullough, *The Trivialization of God* (Colorado Springs: Navpress, 1995), 38.
2. Quoted in J. I. Packer, *Knowing God* (Downers Grove, Ill.: InterVarsity, 1972), 13.
3. Thomas C. Oden, *The Living God* (San Francisco: Harper & Row, 1986), 11.
4. *Trivialization of God*, 71.
5. Carl F. H. Henry, *Twilight of a Great Civilization* (Westchester, Ill.: Crossway, 1988), 142–43.
6. Stephen Charnock, *The Existence and Attributes of God*, 2 Vol. (Grand Rapids: Baker, 1979), 1:23.

7. David Wells, *No Place for Truth* (Grand Rapids: Eerdmans, 1993), 100.

8. Ibid., 101.

Chapter 4

1. Joseph Stowell, *Shepherding the Church into the 21st Century* (Wheaton, Ill.: Victor, 1994), 127–28.

2. J. Grant Howard, *Balancing Life's Demands* (Portland, Ore.: Multnomah, 1983), 56–65.

Chapter 6

1. Roger Heuser and Norman Shawchuck, *Leading the Congregation* (Nashville: Abingdon, 1993), 73.

2. Kent and Barbara Hughes, *Liberating Ministry from the Success Syndrome* (Grand Rapids: Eerdmans, 1988), 29–30.

3. David Ray, *The Big Small Church Book* (Cleveland: Pilgrim, 1992), 157.

4. Dann Spader and Gary Mayes, *Growing a Healthy Church* (Chicago: Moody, 1991), 157.

5. Kevin Ruffcorn, *Rural Evangelism: Catching the Vision* (Minneapolis: Augsburg, 1994), 90.

6. Win Arn and Charles Arn, *The Master's Plan for Making Disciples* (Pasadena, Calif.: Church Growth Press, 1982), 43.

7. *Growing a Healthy Church*, 154.

8. Steve Sjogren, *Conspiracy of Kindness* (Ann Arbor, Mich.: Servant, 1993), 22.

9. Ron Crandall, *Turn Around Strategies for the Small Church* (Nashville: Abingdon, 1995), 94.

10. Steve R. Bierly, *Help for the Small-Church Pastor* (Grand Rapids: Zondervan, 1995), 91–92.

11. *Rural Evangelism*, 13.

Chapter 7

1. Michael Scott Horton, *Made in America* (Grand Rapids: Baker, 1991), 53.

2. Bill Hull, *The Disciple Making Pastor* (Old Tappan, N.J.: Revell, 1988), 12.

3. Fernado F. Segovia, *Discipleship in the New Testament* (Philadelphia: Fortress, 1985), 57.

4. *Disciple Making Pastor*, 57.

5. Bill Hull, *The Disciple Making Church* (Grand Rapids: Chosen, 1990), 32.

6. In Billie Hanks, Jr., and William A. Shell, *Discipleship* (Grand Rapids: Zondervan, 1981), 138.
7. Richard Foster, *Celebration of Discipline* (San Francisco: HarperCollins, 1988), 64–66.
8. Ibid., 157.
9. R. Kent Hughes, *Disciplines of a Godly Man* (Wheaton, Ill.: Crossway, 1991), 177.
10. Edward Goodrick, *Is My Bible the Inspired Word of God?* (Portland, Ore.: Mulnomah, 1988), 85.
11. Ibid., 89.
12. Gary McIntosh and Glenn Martin, *Finding Them, Keeping Them* (Nashville: Broadman, 1991), 87.
13. Quoted in *Disciple Making Pastor*, 19.
14. David DeWitt, *The Mature Man* (Gresham: Vision House, 1994), 13.
15. Ibid., 182.

Chapter 8

1. John Calvin, *Calvin's Commentaries* (Grand Rapids: Baker, 1984), 22:65.
2. Philip Hughes, *A Commentary on the Epistle to the Hebrews* (Grand Rapids: Eerdmans, 1977), 415.
3. Juliet B. Schor, *The Overworked American* (New York: Basic Books, 1991), 1, 5.
4. Tracy Daniel Conner, ed., *The Volunteer Management Handbook* (New York: John Wiley, 1995), 37.
5. Mark Senter, *Recruiting Volunteers in the Church* (Wheaton, Ill.: Victor, 1990), 21.
6. *Volunteer Management Handbook*, 188.
7. *Recruiting Volunteers*, 23.
8. Carl S. Dudley, *Making the Small Church Effective* (Nashville: Abingdon, 1978), 136–37.
9. Lyle Schaller, *The Small Church is Different* (Nashville: Abingdon, 1982), 66.
10. *Making the Small Church Effective*, 118.
11. *Volunteer Management Handbook*, 129.
12. *Recruiting Volunteers*, 33.
13. *Volunteer Management Handbook*, 63.
14. Lyle Schaller and Charles A. Tidwell, *Creative Church Administration* (Nashville: Abingdon, 1975), 67.
15. John Maxwell, *Developing the Leaders Around You* (Nashville: Thomas Nelson, 1995), 99–101.

Chapter 9

1. George Barna, *The Power of Vision* (Ventura, Calif.: Regal, 1992), 39.
2. Ibid., 30.
3. F. F. Bruce, *The Epistle to the Hebrews* (Grand Rapids: Eerdmans, 1983), 39.
4. Lyle Schaller, *The Small Church is Different* (Nashville: Abingdon, 1982), 59.
5. David Ray, *The Big Small Church Book* (Cleveland: Pilgrim, 1992), 141.
6. Ibid., 141–42.
7. Rick Warren, *The Purpose Driven Church* (Grand Rapids: Zondervan, 1995), 208.
8. Alvin J. Lindgren and Norman Shawchuck, *Management for Your Church* (Leith, N.D.: Organization Resources Press, 1984), 74.
9. Robert Blake and Jane Srygley Mouton, *Consultation* (Reading: Addison-Wesley, 1989), 82.
10. Quoted in Harold J. Westing, *Create and Celebrate Your Church's Uniqueness* (Grand Rapids: Kregel, 1993), 31.
11. Quoted in Aubrey Malphurs, *Developing a Vision for Ministry in the 21st Century* (Grand Rapids: Baker, 1992), 37.
12. Alvin Lindgren and Norman Shawchuck, *Let My People Go* (Leith, N.D.: Organization Resources Press, 1988), 76.
13. *Small Church is Different*, 28.
14. Doran McCarty, *Leading the Small Church* (Nashville: Broadman, 1991), 55.
15. *Power of Vision*, 137ff.

Chapter 10

1. Warren Bennis and Burt Nanus, *Leaders* (New York: Harper & Row, 1986), 33.
2. Myron Rush, *Management: A Biblical Approach* (Wheaton, Ill.: Victor, 1987), 115.
3. Lyle Schaller, *The Small Church is Different* (Nashville: Abingdon, 1982), 31–32.
4. Kenneth O. Gangel and Samuel L. Canine, *Communication and Conflict Management* (Nashville: Broadman, 1992), 15.
5. *Small Church is Different*, 30.
6. Carl Dudley and Douglas Alan Walrath, *Developing Your Small Church's Potential* (Valley Forge, Pa.: Judson, 1988), 84.
7. Lyle Schaller, *Effective Church Planning* (Nashville: Abingdon, 1979), 101ff.

8. Alvin Lindgren and Norman Shawchuck, *Let My People Go* (Leith, N.D.: Organization Resources Press, 1988), 91.
9. Carl George and Robert Logan, *Leading and Managing Your Church* (Grand Rapids: Revell, 1987), 106–12.
10. Douglas Walrath, *Making It Work: Effective Administration in the Small Church* (Valley Forge, Pa.: Judson, 1994), 72.
11. Lloyd Perry and Norman Shawchuck, *Revitalizing the 20th Century Church* (Chicago: Moody, 1982), 32.
12. *Let My People Go*, 87.
13. Patricia H. Virga, ed., *The NMA Handbook for Managers* (Englewood Cliffs, N.J.: Prentice Hall, 1987), 164–65.